Economic Empowerment and Sustainable Development

ECONOMIC EMPOWERMENT AND SUSTAINABLE DEVELOPMENT

Edited by:

Sushila Sinha

SOCIETY Publishing

www.societypublishing.com

Economic Empowerment and Sustainable Development

Sushila Sinha

Society Publishing
224 Shoreacres Road
Burlington, ON L7L 2H2
Canada
www.societypublishing.com
Email: orders@arclereducation.com

ISBN: 978-1-77469-482-4 (Hardcover)

ABOUT THE EDITOR

Dr. Sushila has received the Ph.D degree in Agriculture Economics from Banaras Hindu University, Varanasi in year 2011. She is currently working as Assistant Professor, Agricultural Economics, in College of Agriculture and research station, Marra (Patan), Indira Gandhi Krishi Vishwavidyalaya Raipur, India. Her teaching and research interests are in the area of Rural development, Micro finance, Agribusiness management. She has guided 06 M.Sc students and published numbers of research papers in national and international journals.

TABLE OF CONTENTS

LIST OF FIGURES

LIST OF ABBREVIATIONS

AAEA	American Agricultural Economics Association
AEA	American Economic Association
AGI	adolescent girls initiative
AI	artificial intelligence
AIDS	acquired immune deficiency syndrome
BOD	biological oxygen demand
CACP	Commission at Agricultural Costs and Costs
CE	circular economy
CGE	computational general equilibrium
CO_2	carbon dioxide
COVID	coronavirus disease
CSR	corporate social responsibility
CVM	contingent valuation method
DAC	deferred acquisition cost
DALY	disability-adjusted life years
DFID	Department for International Development
DHS	demographic and health survey
EE	environmental education
EFR	ecological fiscal reform
EIA	environmental impact assessment
EKC	environmental Kuznets curve
EPA	Environmental Protection Agency
ESD	Education for Sustainable Development
ETR	ecological tax reform
GBV	gender-based violence
GDP	gross domestic product
GE	green economy
GG	green growth

GG-GE-SD Model	Green Growth–Green Economy–Sustainable development model
GGND	global green new deal
GMM	generalized methods of moments
GNP	gross national product
GWP	gross world product
HDI	human development index
HIV	human immunodeficiency virus
HLPF	high-level political forum
IPCC	intergovernmental panel on climate change
IUCN	international union for conservation of nature
M&E	monitoring and evaluation
MDGs	millennium development goals
MFE	Ministry of Finance of Ecuador
ML	machine learning
MSD	managed sustainable development
MSPs	minimum support prices
NCS	national conservation strategies
NCS	neoclassical synthesis
NEAMP	National Environmental Management Action Plans
NEPA	National Environmental Policy Act
NGO	Non-Government Organization
NSSDS	National Strategies for Sustainable Development
O_2	oxygen
ODA	official development assistance
OECD	Organization for Economic Co-Operation and Development
PCRA	Protection of Civil Rights Act
PPP	purchasing power parity
PV	photovoltaic
R&D	research and development
SDGs	sustainable development goals
SDMS	sustainable development management system
SEA	strategic environment assessment
UN	United Nations

UNCED	UN Conference on Environment and Development
UNDP	United Nations Development Program
UNEP	United Nations Environment Policy
USDA	United States Department of Agriculture
WCED	World Commission on Environment and Development
WEAI	Women's Empowerment in Agriculture Index
WORTH	Women Overcoming Recidivism Through Hard
WTO	World Trade Organization
WWF	World Wide Fund for Nature

GLOSSARY

A

Assimilation – the process whereby individuals or groups of differing ethnic heritage are absorbed into the dominant culture of a society.

Axiom – A statement or proposition which is regarded as being established, accepted, or self-evidently true.

B

Biocapacity – The biocapacity or biological capacity of an ecosystem is an estimate of its production of certain biological materials such as natural resources, and its absorption and filtering of other materials such as carbon dioxide from the atmosphere.

Biodiversity – the variety of plant and animal life in the world or in a particular habitat, a high level of which is usually considered to be important and desirable.

Biomass – It is a plant-based material used as fuel to produce heat or electricity.

C

Capitalism – An economic and political system in which a country's trade and industry are controlled by private owners for profit, rather than by the state.

Circular Economy – A circular economy entails markets that give incentives to reusing products, rather than scrapping them and then extracting new resources. In such an economy, all forms of waste, such as clothes, scrap metal and obsolete electronics, are returned to the economy or used more efficiently.

Climate change – long-term shifts in temperatures and weather patterns.

Commerce – Commerce is the exchange of goods and services, especially on a large scale.

Consumer Goods – Consumer goods are products bought for consumption by the average consumer. Alternatively called final goods, consumer goods are the end result of production and manufacturing and are what a consumer will see stocked on the store shelf. Clothing, food, and jewelry are all examples of consumer goods.

Critics – A person who judges the merits of literary or artistic works, especially one who does so professionally.

D

Deforestation – Deforestation or forest clearance is the removal of a forest or stand of trees from land that is then converted to non-forest use. Deforestation can involve conversion of forest land to farms, ranches, or urban use. The most concentrated deforestation occurs in tropical rainforests.

Discrimination – The unjust or prejudicial treatment of different categories of people, especially on the grounds of race, age, sex, or disability.

E

Ecological footprint – the impact of a person or community on the environment, expressed as the amount of land required to sustain their use of natural resources.

Ecology – the branch of biology that deals with the relations of organisms to one another and to their physical surroundings.

Economics – Economics is the study of scarcity and its implications for the use of resources, production of goods and services, growth of production and welfare over time, and a great variety of other complex issues of vital concern to society.

Ecosystem – An ecosystem consists of all the organisms and the physical environment with which they interact.

Ecosystem – An ecosystem is a geographic area where plants, animals, and other organisms, as well as weather and landscape, work together to form a bubble of life. Ecosystems contain biotic or living, parts, as well as abiotic factors, or nonliving parts. Biotic factors include plants, animals, and other organisms.

Engendering Development – Planning for eliminating all forms of violence against women and girls in the public and private spheres.

Environmental degradation – a process through which the natural environment is compromised in some way, reducing biological diversity and the general health of the environment.

Epistemological – Relating to the theory of knowledge, especially with regard to its methods, validity, and scope, and the distinction between justified belief and opinion.

Epistemology – Epistemology, or the theory of knowledge, is the branch of philosophy concerned with knowledge. Epistemologists study the nature, origin, and scope of knowledge, epistemic justification, the rationality of belief, and various related issues.

Evaluation – The making of a judgement about the amount, number, or value of something; assessment.

G

Gender norms – Gender norms are ideas about how women and men should be and act.

Gender prejudice – It is discrimination, prejudice, or stereotyping based on gender, and is most often expressed toward women and girls.

Global economy – the economies of the world's individual countries considered together as a single economic system.

Green Economy – A green economy is an economy that aims at reducing environmental risks and ecological scarcities, and that aims for sustainable development without degrading the environment. It is closely related with ecological economics, but has a more politically applied focus.

H

Harvesting – Harvesting includes marking the trees to be removed (in selective cutting), feling, and processing (conversion) of trees, and transportation of the wood from the felling site, or stump area, to a roadside storage site or a central processing yard (landing) in the forest.

Hydrological cycle – a biogeochemical cycle that describes the continuous movement of water on, above, and below the surface of the Earth.

I

Intertemporal – Describing any relationship between past, present, and future events or conditions.

L

Liberalization -the practice of making laws, systems, or opinions less severe, usually in the sense of eliminating certain government regulations or restrictions.

Life expectancy – Life expectancy is a statistical measure of the average time an organism is expected to live, based on the year of its birth, its current age, and other demographic factors like sex.

M

Marginalism – Marginalism is the economic principle that economic decisions are made and economic behavior occurs in terms of incremental units, rather than categorically. The key focus of marginalism is that asking how much, more or less, of an activity (production, consumption, buying, selling, etc.)

Microeconomics – Microeconomics is a branch of mainstream economics that studies the behavior of individuals and firms in making decisions regarding the allocation of scarce resources and the interactions among these individuals and firms.

O

Ontology – Ontology is the branch of philosophy that studies concepts such as existence, being, becoming, and reality. It includes the questions of how entities are grouped into basic categories and which of these entities exist on the most fundamental level.

P

Poverty – Poverty is the state of having few material possessions or little income.

Q

Quadruple Helix Model – The Quadruple Helix Model of innovation recognizes four major actors in the innovation system: science, policy, industry, and society. In keeping with this model, more, and more governments are prioritizing greater public involvement in innovation processes.

R

Renewable Energy – Renewable energy is energy that is collected from renewable resources that are naturally replenished on a human timescale. It includes sources such as sunlight, wind, rain, tides, waves, and geothermal heat. Although most renewable energy sources are sustainable, some are not.

Renewable Resource – a natural resource which will replenish to replace the portion depleted by usage and consumption, either through natural reproduction or other recurring processes in a finite amount of time in a human time scale.

S

Social Indifference Curve – A social indifference curve consists of distributions of welfare of members of a group that the policy maker views as achieving the same social welfare.

Social ramification – Social ramification refers to the consequences of actions in a social setting, toward a particular culture or a change in a person's social status.

Social trust – Social trust is a belief in the honesty, integrity, and reliability of others – a faith in people.

Subsidy – A direct or indirect payment, economic concession, or privilege granted by a government to private firms, households, or other governmental units in order to promote a public objective.

Subsistence Farming – The practice of growing crops and raising livestock sufficient only for one's own use, without any surplus for trade.

Sustainability – Avoidance of the depletion of natural resources in order to maintain an ecological balance.

Sustainable Development – Sustainable development is an organizing principle for meeting human development goals while also sustaining the ability of natural systems to provide the natural resources and ecosystem services on which the economy and society depend.

U

Unemployment – is people above a specified age not being in paid employment or self-employment but currently available for work during the reference period.

PREFACE

This book introduces the readers to economic empowerment. This book sheds light on sustainable development, economic empowerment models, economic growth and environmental degradation, the role of agricultural economics, neoclassical economics, and green economy and sustainable development.

The first chapter introduces the readers to economic empowerment. This chapter will also emphasize on the concept of empowerment and economic development, women's economic empowerment in general and in India, why it matters and how it lays a potential pathway for women to gain control over sexual and reproductive health.

The second chapter takes the readers through an overview of sustainable development. This chapter will provide highlights on objectives, normative approaches, education, the role of technological change and sub groups of sustainable development. The chapter also explains relationships among environment, economy, and society, strategies, global trends, challenges, and system approaches for sustainability.

Then, the third chapter explains the economic empowerment models. This chapter also sheds light on methodological answers to decision making, methodological criteria, candidate models for sustainable development and model implications of intergenerational considerations. This chapter also explains economic-ecological integration, transformation, change processes and primary as well as secondary applications of sustainable development.

The fourth chapter takes the readers to policies and practices of sustainable development. This chapter introduces the de-coupling environmental pressures from economic growth and key challenges, social dimensions, frameworks, policies, strategies, and planning of sustainable development. This chapter also sheds light on national policies and campaigns, environmental policies and strategies of governments.

The fifth chapter introduces the readers to economic growth and environmental degradation. This chapter explains the causes, factors, extends, effects, and solutions of Environmental Degradation. The chapter also addresses basic environmental Kuznets curve (EKC), its causes, criticisms, and empirical models of environment and growth.

The sixth chapter throws light on the role of agricultural economics for sustainable development. This chapter contains the characteristics, importance, nature, role, and scope of agricultural economics for sustainable development. This chapter also sheds light on the brief history, contribution, current issues in agricultural economics and discusses about agricultural economic policy and development.

The seventh chapter takes the readers through the concept of neoclassical economics and sustainable development. The readers are then told about neoclassical growth models, Solow model, capital-growth model and the ecological economics critique of neoclassical economics.

In the last chapter of this book sheds light on green economy and sustainable development. This chapter also mentions the importance, principles, and macroeconomic dimension of green economy (GE). The chapter also discusses green growth, GE-GG models, policies, and measures for promoting a green economy and sustainable development and stimulation of green economy transition.

This book has been designed to suit the knowledge and pursuit of the researcher and scholars and to empower them with various aspects of economic empowerment on which the modern world is based, so that they are updated with the information. I hope that the readers find the book explanatory and insightful and that this book is referred by the scholars across various fields.

CHAPTER 1

INTRODUCTION TO ECONOMIC EMPOWERMENT

CONTENTS

Economic empowerment is the capacity of women and men to participate in, contribute to and benefit from growth processes in ways that recognize the value of their contributions, respect their dignity and make it possible to negotiate a fairer distribution of the benefits of growth.

1.1. THE CONCEPT OF EMPOWERMENT

The idea of empowerment is now frequently used to define the states and social processes of individuals and groups in a variety of fields. It is defined roughly as power (control over one's own life and resources) and agency (capability to originate and direct actions for given purposes).

According to Wikipedia, the term derives from community psychology and refers to "measures designed to increase the degree of autonomy and self-determination in people and communities in order to enable them to represent their interests in a responsible and self-determined manner, acting on their own authority."

According to this viewpoint, empowerment is both a collaborative process and an outcome. It is a set of characteristics acquired as part of the transition to adulthood, according to the literature on individual psychology and human development (Zimmerman and Cleary, 2006).

In the management literature, empowerment is a strategy for influencing employee behavior—it involves providing people with resources, information, and decision-making authority so they can make decisions that increase corporate performance; in other words, a particularly successful delegation.

1.2. EMPOWERMENT AND ECONOMIC DEVELOPMENT

Amartya Sen's work formally introduced empowerment into the field of development economics. Sen (1999) emphasized in his important work, Development as Freedom, that genuine development must broaden people's options—their liberties.

In other words, development is more than simply an increase in goods and income; it is also an increase in what a person can and cannot achieve. Sen defined development as a process that improved people's capacities—their flexibility to function given their unique choices—going beyond the more simplistic conceptions of human and social capital.

Sen also emphasized the variability of individuals' abilities to respond to development policy, and so suggested that impoverished people, in particular, need to be active in development policy, in order to feel empowered, they have a vested interest in the result. This need empowerment (Figure 1.1).

Figure 1.1. A snapshot from women empowerment forum.

Source: Image by flickr.com.

The rise of behavioral economics, which seeks to combine psychological and microeconomic principles of human behavior with markets in order to generate better policy, has pushed the concept of empowerment into the mainstream of economic development thought.

Banerjee and Duflo (2012) demonstrated how an aspirational deficit (a lack of hope) among the poor is a barrier to poverty alleviation through a series of experiments and observations. Low ambitions result in a low agency, which results in a lack of investment, which keeps individuals impoverished.

In other words, impoverished people's conduct reflects their personal emotional experiences of lack of control over their surroundings—crop loss due to unexpected weather, early and unexpected death due to sickness, or the social ostracism and economic suffering that result from breaking India's stringent caste and gender standards.

The consequence of their research is that in order to be successful in boosting the incomes of the poor, development policies and programs must create agency. Other economists began to put this theory to the test in their own experimental studies. In an article on the economics of hope, Lybbert and Wydick (2016) examine this research.

They mention a variety of examples where low expectations result in negative economic consequences, such as a failure to invest in education. Kosec et al., (2014) summarize the findings of several research initiatives that show that long-term goals are essential for reducing rural poverty.

They observe that desires interact with restrictions so that if an individual has not experienced the capacity to alter their wellbeing (or seen others do so), they are less likely to do so. They will not consider alternatives. According to this viewpoint, there may be another explanation for the frequently observed link between high inequality and low economic development.

If the difference between my current situation and what I consider a reasonable level of living is large, and this gap has been for a long time and no one I know has been able to bridge it, I may be easily discouraged from making sacrifices now for my future. Similarly, as the fundamental economic dynamic shifts, I may become blind to prospective possibilities.

Initially, psychologists focused on "hope" as an individual idea.

Garcia and Sison (2012) extended this to incorporate social and communal aspects. Hopefulness may be a community trait, and it can be strengthened in individuals by common ideas or experiences.

For example, if a community values social relationships and social relationships increase positive emotions, then the community experience can create a sense of hopefulness about the future, as well as a sense that individuals can cope with life's difficulties through the community, and thus it is worthwhile to invest in the future.

Individual members' goals and choices of activities and routes will be influenced by a society that favors one sort of economic activity over another (or does not value economic activity) (Figure 1.2).

Figure 1.2. Women empowerment logo.

Source: Image by maxpixel.com.

Kosec et al., (2014) believe that the community experience is important because they discovered that households living in a community that experienced exceptionally heavy flooding during an extreme monsoon season in Pakistan in 2010 experienced a drop in aspirations among the poorest 60% who were the most reliant on rain-fed agriculture (those least able to help each other cope with the disaster).

South Asia's caste system is another example of communal beliefs and norms that stifle economic growth in lower caste regions by impeding the development of ambitions (World Bank, 2014). Behavioral economists working in development began to investigate the extent to which norms—informal standards that governors facilitate conduct—influence economic decisions.

One of the most hotly debated development standards the literature is abundant with policy analysis and evaluation studies on ways to address these obstacles to girls' education.

World Bank (2014) provides a number of other examples of how social norms may prevent people from adopting sanitation innovations, seeking health care or following health care provider recommendations, using contraception, or punishing corruption - all of which are examples of where development investments have not paid off as expected.

Existing employees do not want their employers to require that they meet greater objectives than they do now, therefore they ensure that new employees believe that the additional money from a larger volume of individual production is not worth it. Non-behavioral economists frequently overlook the fact that breaking norms has implications for the individual, their family, and/or their social network (if not they would not be norms).

This economic research on capacities, hope, informal behavioral rules, and economic consequences is strongly related to the empowerment notions outlined above. A person who is empowered has a good outlook on the future, can envision possibilities and paths to transform their lives, and has the confidence to follow those options and pathways.

The literature on how a gendered set of limitations impacts women's mental processes and behaviors is congruent with research indicating that chronic exclusion leads to a loss of power and agency. And the idea that hope (positive aspirations) is a communal feature is compatible with the gender and economics literature's emphasis on women's need for collective action and social support to progress in their empowerment process.

If impoverished people need to be empowered in order to escape poverty traps, cope with unfavorable shocks, and take advantage of possibilities brought about by advancements such as more education or new technology, then both men and women must be empowered. Disempowering laws, norms, and habits stifle progress.

One reason for the research finding a discrepancy between women's and men's agricultural output is power asymmetry in the family between men and women. If societal conventions and practices restrict women's and girls' mobility, breaking those norms have social ramifications for the family, girls will not seek education, and parents will not encourage their daughters to make this investment (Figure 1.3).

Figure 1.3. Symposium on women rights and empowerment in Afghanistan in 2014.

Source: Image by flickr.com.

If women do not have a say in local or national development choices, they will not be invested in the outcome and may not endeavor to make policies or programs effective.

They will not take the collective action required to advocate and protect their interests, as well as change their society. Their suggestions will be ignored, putting project design and implementation at risk.

National development goals such as living longer or being free of hunger will not be attained. Recognizing these connections, women's empowerment has been included in national, regional, international, and transnational development objectives, such as the recently approved Sustainable Development Goals (SDGs).

1.1.1. Women Empowerment and Economic Development

The problem of "missing women" exemplifies the continuance of gender inequity. Amartya Sen created the phrase in a now-classic essay in the New York Review of Books (Sen, 1990) to describe the reality that the proportion of women is lower than what would be expected if girls and women in the developing world were born and died at the same rate as boys and men in Sub-Saharan Africa.

Every year, it is believed that 6 million women go missing (World Bank, 2011) of them, 23% are never born, 10% are absent throughout childhood, 21% are missing during reproductive years, and 38% are after the age of 60 as Stark excess mortality does not convey the reality that women in poor nations are treated differently than their brothers throughout their lives, even from birth, and trail behind males in many sectors.

For every lost woman, many more women are denied an education, a career, or political power that they would have had if they had been males.

In a number of areas, both the relative deprivation of women and the extent to which advances have occurred over the previous twenty years are visible. In terms of educational access, girls enrolled in secondary school at a rate of 34% in low and middle-income countries in 2010, while boys enrolled at a rate of 41%.

Twenty years ago, the percentages were 22% and 30%, respectively. Meanwhile, elementary school enrolment for both boys and girls is practically universal. Women are less likely to work, earn less than males for comparable employment, and are more likely to live in poverty even when they do work.

Women spend about twice as much time as men do on housekeeping, nearly five times as much time on child care, and around half as much time on market jobs (Berniell and Sánchez-Páramo, 2011). In terms of political representation, women made up just 19.4% of members of parliament's lower and upper chambers in July 2011 (Inter-parliamentary Union, 2011).

In terms of legal rights, several nations still deny women the ability to own land, manage property, conduct business, or even travel without the approval of their spouse. In 21 of the 63 nations investigated by Htun and Weldon (2011), men, and women have uneven inheritance rights.

In one way, growth may play a significant role in reducing gender disparity; in the other, as Sen has persuasively demonstrated, persistent discrimination against women can stymie progress. In other words, empowerment can hasten progress. Policymakers and social scientists have often focused on one of these two links.

Those who focus on the first have suggested that as poverty decreases, gender equality increases. Policymakers should consequently concentrate on providing the circumstances for economic development and prosperity while attempting to preserve a fair playing field for both genders, but without implementing special initiatives aimed at improving women's situations.

Many, on the other hand, highlight the second linkage, which goes from empowerment to growth. For example, UN Secretary-General Kofi Annan has argued that achieving gender equality is a "prerequisite" for achieving the other Millennium Development Goals (MDGs), such as eliminating poverty, reducing infant mortality, achieving universal education, and closing the gender gap in education by 2015. (United Nations, 2005).

The World Bank (2001) calls for policies to address gender imbalances in "rights, resources, and voice" in its report, "Engendering Development," and recommends that institutional structures be overhauled to promote equality, as well as specific measures, such as girls' scholarships and quotas for women in parliament, be implemented.

According to the research, these policies are warranted not just because they promote fairness, but also because they are required to speed growth. Surprisingly, the 2012 World Development Report (World Bank, 2011) takes a much more nuanced approach.

While it highlights the "economic case" for women's empowerment, it mostly assumes that gender equality is a desirable objective in and of itself, and that policies should try to accomplish that goal.

1.1.2. Can Economic Development Cause Women's Empowerment?

Gender inequality is frequently worse among the poor, both within and across nations. While the gender gap in primary and secondary gross enrolment has narrowed rapidly between 1991 and 2009 globally, it remains larger in poor countries (7% points for primary enrolment, 13% points for secondary enrolment) than in middle-income countries (3% points for primary enrolment, 2% points for secondary enrolment) and rich countries (0% points for primary, 1% point for secondary) (Figure 1.4).

Figure 1.4. UNIDO global platform for the promotion of women's economic development.

Source: Image by flickr.com.

Within countries, gender disparities persist in poorer and more isolated populations (World Bank, 2011). Between 1971 and 1995, women's labor-force participation increased by 15% in East Asia and Latin America, a pace greater than that of males, and the gender wage gap has also shrunk.

Women's life expectancy in poor nations has grown by 20–25 years over the last 50 years (World Bank, 2011), whereas male life expectancy has not improved as much. Is it true that when countries grow, women's empowerment would automatically follow, negating the necessity for explicit measures aimed at improving women's conditions?

Is it enough to combat poverty and provide the conditions for economic progress in developing countries? According to recent studies, economic growth may have a significant beneficial influence on gender equality by eliminating poverty and boosting opportunity.

1.3. WOMEN'S ECONOMIC EMPOWERMENT AND DEVELOPMENT

Given the numerous links between empowerment and development processes, it is not unexpected that the subject of women's economic empowerment has become increasingly prominent in the development microeconomics literature. Initially, proposals centered on giving girls with education and women the ability to obtain earned money.

Both factors were regarded as critical to increasing household earnings and alleviating poverty. Over time, the term has come to refer to women's power and agency in all economic domains and market-related interactions—earning income, spending or saving income, purchasing, owning, and selling assets, holding or inheriting wealth, starting, and operating a business, obtaining a bank account or credit, and participating in or leading a union or other form of economic collective action.

Pereznieto and Taylor's wide definition of economic empowerment (Based on Golla et al., 2011) encompasses four major characteristics. Some definitions of economic empowerment, like the wider idea of empowerment, incorporate legal and structural restraints that impact the outcomes of women's economic actions (e.g., laws regulating whether a woman can open a bank account in her own name).

SIDA emphasizes the eradication of "structural imbalances in the labor market" in its definition, which encompasses both laws and norms and conventions such as socioeconomic disparities (Kabeer, 2012).

The economic literature's emphasis on women's labor market results as empowerment outcomes stems primarily from a fundamental assumption in microeconomics: if individuals have money, they can attain better wellbeing and wield economic power (including both powers to and power over discussed above).

The empowering effect of group microfinance for women justified its extension as a vital development instrument (Garikipati, 2008). While Sen's work in 1999, as well as the work of radical and feminist economists dating back to the late 1970s, criticized this simple approach, it pervaded mainstream gender economics, particularly in the development realm.

In the United Nations report "Progress of the World's Women" published in 2000, it was argued that assisting women in generating income will increase their ability to "generate choices, exercise bargaining power, and develop a sense of self-worth, a belief in one's ability to secure desired changes" (Elson and Keklik, 2000 cited in Brody et al, 2015).

Buvini and Furst-Nichols openly explain in their 2014 assessment, "Promoting Economic Empowerment: What Works?" that they are only examining women's productivity and wages as "proxies for the more complicated idea of empowerment" (Buvini and Furst-Nichols, 2014).

The World Bank specifically linked women's income-earning prospects with women's voice and agency in economic issues in the 2016 edition of its flagship report, World Development Indicators. Finally, Pereznieto and Taylor (2014) define economic empowerment as a process that leads to women having more influence over other aspects of their lives.

This brings up two points: (i) causation from economic outcomes to other outcomes is incorporated in the idea once more; and (ii) "power over other parts of their life" cannot be assessed or inferred just from labor market outcomes or expenditure decisions.

However, the evidence for this connection is actually rather poor. As Duflo (2012) observes in her overview of the research on economic growth and empowerment, poverty is undeniably disempowering, as is individual lack of access to resources.

And, while Duflo discovers substantial evidence that increased income-earning opportunities for women motivate parents to send their girls to school, Duflo also discovers that such opportunities may not always lead to broader empowerment as reflected in women's social status, the value of daughters relative to sons, political participation, or the enforcement of laws giving women equal rights.

Kabeer (2013) correlates women's education, labor force participation, and types of employment with values, perceptions, and attitudes, role in household decision-making, quality of relations within and beyond the family, participation in local and national-level politics, and collective action to protest injustice or claim rights in three countries.

She discovers that secondary education and formal wage employment (nearly always in the public sector because private enterprises were less likely to recruit educated women) correspond most strongly with empowerment indicators in three nations. However, the issue of selectivity severely restricts the conclusions that can be derived from this study.

In other words, were the women already empowered, as a result of which they were able to obtain an education and a formal sector pay job?

Is empowerment more closely tied to class (richer households can afford to send their children to secondary school) than to gender? Nonfarm self-employment had slightly weaker connections, but the issue of selectivity remains.

Blattman finds no link in experimental analysis between a highly effective program to assist women in post-conflict Uganda in starting a self-employment trading business and improvements in women's self-reported empowerment, as measured by women's status in society, self-reported physical or emotional abuse by their partner, or self-reported independence (Blattman et al., 2016).

Banerjee et al., (2015) discovered no effect of a program that increased impoverished women's wages, assets, and family consumption in six countries on broader economic empowerment using self-reported involvement in household decision-making on spending as a measurement of financial empowerment (the graduation projects).

They do discover empirical proof that the training boosted women's self-esteem, whereby the participants associated with the beneficial outcomes. This provides evidence for a relationship between a good mentality—hope, self-esteem, and so on—and better economic outcomes.

Moreover, a relationship between inputs (increased economic resources) and economic outcomes has been discovered when projects specifically target more complex, psychological aspects of women's economic empowerment (i.e., agency) as a specific outcome (intermediate or final) and make efforts to measure change as a result of their women's economic project interventions.

Evaluators discovered that a component aimed to boost the women's self-efficacy and self-confidence created better sales compared to a control group that did not get this component as part of their training in a project to teach Kenyan women to market energy-efficient cookstoves (Shankar, Onyura, and Alderman, 2015).

Women overcoming recidivism through hard (WORTH) key projects in Nepal targeted both women's agency and savings/business operations objectives, and success on both was evaluated. A quasi-experimental study revealed gains in self-reported self-confidence, civic involvement, and intra-household decision-making power, as well as a drop in reported gender-based abuse and improvements in economic results (Mayoux, 2008).

Researchers in India discovered that rural women who participated in the Mahila Samakhya program, which integrated adult education and vocational training with support groups and life skills training, reported more mobility and civic involvement, as well as higher labor force participation (Kandpal, Baylis, and Arends-Kuenning, 2012).

Participants in numerous World Bank-sponsored adolescent girls initiative (AGI) programs had similar outcomes (World Bank, 2015). Except for the Kenyan cookstoves, none of these studies assessed whether the program's attitude and agency features were required for the other economic benefits obtained.

Only the WORTH study in Nepal included community perceptions regarding women's conduct in its measurements (which also changed). This project also includes elements intended to support this conclusion. An important and unsolved topic in the impact evaluation literature is: what are the many forms of empowerment, and how do they relate to other results (economic, reproductive health, or other)?

1.4. UNDERSTANDING AND MEASURING WOMEN'S ECONOMIC EMPOWERMENT

Economic empowerment of women is increasingly recognized as critical to achieving both women's rights and larger development goals such as economic growth, poverty reduction, health, education, and welfare. In the last five years, a diverse spectrum of groups has been dedicated to the objective of economic empowerment for women.

These organizations understand that economically empowering women is a win-win situation that benefits not only women but society as a whole. It supports women's rights and wellbeing while simultaneously lowering family poverty, promoting economic development and production, and enhancing efficiency.

1.4.1. Defining Women's Economic Empowerment

When a woman has the potential to thrive and grow economically, as well as the power to decide and act on economic decisions, she is economically empowered. Organizations must address the underlying issues that contribute to women's economic empowerment, including individual and community resources, norms, and institutions.

Resources are the building elements that women can use to achieve economic success or to exert power and agency. Individual or community resources are available. Norms and Institutions are the "rules of the game" or the organizational and social structures that control activities and mediate relationships between individuals and their social and economic surroundings.

Economic empowerment may be approached through projects that either increase the resources accessible to women or change norms and institutions. Projects may also seek to advance women economically or to increase women's power and agency.

A microcredit program for women, for example, aims largely to promote women's economic growth through resources. A literacy or life skills program, on the other hand, primarily develops women's own resources in order to increase their power and agency. While both programs aim to enhance women's economic empowerment, they do it in different ways.

Furthermore, economic empowerment may be handled at several levels. Projects may, for example, function at the person, home, or organizational level, as well as at the community or social network level. In various situations, the specific indicators of progress toward women's economic empowerment may differ. They may even evolve over time as countries or areas grow.

There is no single program that can address all of the elements that influence women's economic empowerment. Rather, if economic empowerment is viewed as a multilayered, multifaceted pie, programs should "choose their slice."

That is, they should set their sights on areas where they can have the greatest impact given their resources, timeframe, and local environment, even while taking into consideration what other groups are doing. Regardless of the fact that the majority of applicants for most programs concentrate on a single piece of the pie, it is vital to contextualize their efforts within a broader framework of economic empowerment.

1.4.2. Measuring Women's Economic Empowerment

Projects approach economic empowerment in many ways. Indicators that are appropriate for one location or program may not be appropriate for another. There is no common collection of indicators that is appropriate for any project, industry, or setting.

While gauging women's economic empowerment entails taking into account measures of both economic development and women's power and agency, many programs fail to accomplish improvement in both areas. This means that particular projects may measure one component more than another or may not measure both components.

In designing monitoring and evaluation (M&E) plans, the framework underlines the significance of not relying just on effect indicators. It is also critical to emphasize the measurement of process, output, and outcome indicators, such as the percentage of women who participated in the project and which women participated.

Basic process outputs and outcomes should be measured in all initiatives. These indicators can give preliminary assessments of whether a project is on track and engaging women as planned. They are frequently easier to quantify than signs of deep or prolonged influence. Not all indicators can or should be assessed at the most rigorous level.

In project and program assessments, researchers have utilized a range of measures of empowerment, particularly economic empowerment, although, as previously stated, impact on or control over family spending is by far the most prevalent.

For example, three recent systematic reviews of types of development projects found that this was the most common measure of empowerment used in these project evaluations: Brody et al., (2015) on women's SHGs and empowerment; Banerjee et al., (2015) on graduation projects for extremely poor women; and Upadhyay et al., (2014) on fertility and empowerment.

In fact, just a few different metrics were employed or gathered. Other metrics, however, have been utilized in certain research. The particular measures differ across evaluations. This might be due to the context-specific theory of the change that the project designers have detected and dealt with in order to achieve the intended project results.

The anticipated final effect may not have been empowering; however, empowerment may have been considered an intermediary goal in some situations. However, in some situations, it appears that assessing empowering changes was an afterthought, and this was not included in a theory of change.

This might be due to the fact that impact assessment designs often do not focus on the impacts of various project components, therefore they are not seeking to discover which components affect empowerment, but rather if it was a final consequence. Another confusing element is that empowerment measurements are frequently pooled into an index, making comparisons difficult.

Some writers employ the "relative deprivations" technique used by Alkire et al., (2013) and Garikipati (2008) to create an index, assigning a score to each category and then aggregating the aspects into a simple index. While this strategy provides a clean variable to be used in multivariate statistical analysis, it does not aid in determining which dimensions are important for a certain result.

Furthermore, Peterman et al., (2015) demonstrate, predictably, that how women are scored on empowerment is significantly reliant on how the index is built. Furthermore, Hanmer and Klugman (2016) discovered relatively poor correlations across demographic and health survey (DHS) indicators on attitudes and actions that indicate aspects of empowerment, indicating how an index of these factors may be problematic.

Is it possible to standardize measurement across countries? For some years, DHS surveys in low-income countries throughout the world have utilized a standardized set of questions to assess women's decision-making authority in the family as well as women's and men's opinions regarding the acceptability of gender-based violence (GBV).

These factors are currently often employed in empowerment research. Are they dependable across borders? According to Donald et al., (2016), the degree of connection between husbands' (male partners') and wives' replies on making decision power is less than ideal and differs significantly among nations.

When partners were asked individually who makes significant purchases, 1/3 of the women said the male did it alone, while 1/3 of the men said it was a mutual decision. The significance of this argument concerning women's economic empowerment in the home is unclear, but it is evident that the wives did not always feel consulted.

Field and Glennerster's ongoing research have demonstrated that the more detailed the questions concerning specific scenarios (e.g., buying medicine vs. a broad question about health-related spending decisions), the higher women's self-reported engagement in expenditure decisions).

One-way researchers have sought to standardize subjectively or self-reported responses across nations, especially in areas where the variable has a meaning unique to the setting, culture, and tradition, by using vignettes, or brief descriptions of various sorts of individuals and their situations.

Respondents are asked to choose the description that best describes their circumstances. Donald et al., (2016) demonstrated that the vignette survey offered a more consistent measure of agency than the standard self-perception survey without vignettes in a Women's Empowerment in Agriculture Index (WEAI) index test in Uganda. This was especially crucial in determining how rural social norms and practices influence women's decisions and actions.

As previously noted, broad definitions of empowering results encompass both attitudes (self-perception; perspectives on institutions that control gendered behavior) and acts (action taken). Separating the two dimensions is one method for standardizing indices and making results easier to comprehend. Another option is to standardize the dimensions.

This is the technique taken by the WEAI index, for example; nevertheless, its usefulness outside of agriculture is restricted. The economic, social, political, and psychological empowerment categorization offered by Brody et al., (2015) may be a helpful subdivision.

For example, a respondent's self-reported opinions about her ambitions, confidence, and perspectives on the limits put on her might be used to gauge the attitude dimension of economic empowerment. The behavioral component might be examined using regularly used variables that measure money generating decisions as well as ones that evaluate expenditure decision making, aided by vignettes if this shows useful in future experiments.

It may be beneficial to identify even finer sub-elements to aid with uniformity. For example, within the realm of economic empowerment, views regarding paths to labor market results would be distinguished from savings confidence and financial abilities.

In this manner, researchers might define the subdimension of empowerment they hope to improve ex-ante in the project in their theory of transformation and/or pre-analysis study plan. They might then create a subdimension-specific metric for each setting. While this technique would still be susceptible to the flaws mentioned by Peterman et al., (2015), it would be less ad hoc than the present practice and would allow for an easier comparison of outcomes across nations.

Another advantage would be the ability to identify which aspects of empowerment a specific intervention influences, determine which aspects appear to be necessary for desired final outcomes, and identify affiliation between dimensions, and, if possible, identify which subdimensions are necessary for which final outcomes.

Upadhyay et al., (2014), for example, conducted a comprehensive evaluation of the relationships between women's empowerment and fertility-related outcomes. Of the 60 studies examined, 37 utilized women's negotiating power over spending (as evaluated by the DHS) as a proxy for empowerment.

That would be the only empowering measure that was even marginally standardized across studies, which they ascribe to DHS surveys' strong role, particularly in the study of reproductive health factors. They conclude by urging greater study into operationalizing women's empowerment.

In other words, if studies examined empowerment across several dimensions and included both attitudinal and behavioral measures. They might have been able to determine which aspects of empowerment were most important for reproductive health outcomes.

Social scientists appear to gain from collaboration when designing measures of empowerment aspects. Psychologists, for example, have established a variety of standard measures to evaluate attitudes, including the "Big Five" personality characteristics linked to academic and economic success.

While these scales must be tailored to the circumstances, there is general agreement on the five aspects (and ten sub-elements). If economists could agree on five dimensions of economic empowerment attitudes and behaviors, it would make it easier to compare results across studies and build a body of evidence on which aspects of empowering (economic or otherwise) matter for which common person and household economic outcomes.

1.5. WHY WOMEN'S ECONOMIC EMPOWERMENT MATTERS

Economic empowerment refers to women's and men's ability to engage in, contribute to, and profit from economic processes in ways that appreciate the importance of their efforts, respect their dignity and allow them to negotiate a more equitable division of the advantages of growth.

Economic empowerment improves women's access to productive opportunities and opportunities such as jobs, financial services, real estate and other productive resources, skill development, and market knowledge. Economic engagement and empowerment of women are critical to advancing women's rights and allowing women to have control over their life and have influence in society (Figure 1.5).

Figure 1.5. IWD-2016 for gender equality meet in India.

Sources: Image by flickr.com.

It is all about establishing just and equal communities. Women frequently endure discrimination and persistent gender inequities, with some women facing several forms of discrimination and exclusion due to characteristics such as ethnicity or race.

Women's economic empowerment is required for long-term development, pro-poor growth, and attainment of the MDGs. Gender equality and empowered women are multipliers of development initiatives.

Gender equality investments produce the best returns of any development investment. Women often devote a greater percentage of their incomes in their families and communities than males. A research in Brazil found that when the mother regulated home income, the chance of a child's survival improved by 20%.

Increasing women's economic participation is part of the answer to the financial and economic crises, and it is vital for economic resilience and prosperity. At the same time, we must keep in mind that women are facing the brunt of the expenses of recovery from the crisis, with job losses, bad working conditions, and increased precariousness.

1.6. ECONOMIC EMPOWERMENT OF WOMEN IN INDIA

India will be the most populous country in the world by 2050. The country's economy and progress are entirely dependent on women's empowerment. The atmosphere that provides women with independence and freedom is the sole option for progress. However, empowerment is still a work in progress. Economic empowerment is critical for all women.

In today's world, the majority of women are economically, physically, and morally dependent. Despite rising rates of literacy and awareness among women, they require economic empowerment. They must make their own autonomous choices. Women's employability can only lead to economic emancipation.

Women in India should indeed be allowed to spend their own income for their own benefit. In many Indian households, the whole earnings of the females are taken from them. Husband or family members are dominant.

There are vast social cleavages throughout India, and gender discrimination is prominent in sectors such as health, schooling, and literacy. There are numerous national and international Non-Government Organizations (NGOs) and civil society players trying to improve women's rights, but the fraction of those focusing solely on women is low (Figure 1.16).

Figure 1.6. Educating women in rural parts of India by UN women members.

Source: Image by flickr.com.

The policy space available to a company working for women's empowerment is fairly limited; nonetheless, research and activism on women's rights and work is increasing, as are various government programs to improve women's empowerment.

Empowerment is a transformation process that provides people more choice and freedom and action. Economic empowerment for women depends on the availability of resources as well as whether women have had the skills to exploit them. Furthermore, it is dependent on women's access to and control over economic advantages.

In reality, women encounter challenges when they translate resources into smart choices. Among the most significant barriers to women's economic empowerment is society's reliance on unpaid labor by women, whether at home or in the market (in the agricultural sector, for example).

As a result, women experience higher time poverty, limiting their capacity to engage in paid and formal labor. Many of the hurdles to women's economic empowerment will require a structural change to be removed and overcome, to aggressively promote gender equality and women's rights inside social institutions.

Women's economic empowerment faces new hurdles in war and post-conflict settings. This is due to the low importance of gender-related development objectives in the rebuilding political agenda, as well as the weak implementation capabilities of various players (e.g., government, civil society).

However, there is typically a greater understanding of the chances for women's economic empowerment during and after conflict, including the opportunity to overturn discriminatory gender conventions from the past. Furthermore, women's economic empowerment has the ability to contribute to a company's strategic goals and new economic opportunities for women, expanding on their new economic responsibilities learned during the war.

Women's economic empowerment is one of the most important aspects leading to gender equality. Given that women constitute the majority of economically disadvantaged groups, a special emphasis on women is required. Gendered power structures and societal conventions confine both men and women to positions that limit their productivity and capacity to make choices to improve their circumstances.

Despite its increasing economy (7.3% GDP in 2014–15), chronic poverty, corruption, clientelism, and inequality continue to damage India's social and economic ethos. Women continue to be marginalized in social, economic, and political realms, demonstrating an insufficient focus on inclusive growth and uneven gender relations.

In terms of gender equality, India ranks 127th out of 187 nations with a value of 0.536, on the inequality index Women's economic position will improve when they gain employment. According to the data, India is ranked 120th out of 131 countries.

Despite having a graduation level of 42%, females do not enter the labor force for a variety of reasons, including safety, physical surroundings, and undue concern for the female from their families. Only rural women in the unorganized sector have a high proportion. Women make up less than 20% of the workforce in service and industry.

Gender prejudices persist within the family as a result of patriarchal culture and tradition, affecting women's lives in both the public and private spheres. Caste barriers exacerbate discrimination against women, particularly those from lower castes such as Scheduled Caste and Dalit women.

Recognizing Dalit women's historical disadvantage and vulnerability, the government has passed many laws, including the Protection of Civil Rights Act (PCRA) and the Scheduled Castes and Scheduled Tribes (Prevention of Atrocities) Act, which aim to bring Dalits on a level with other caste groups.

The funding allocation for the Department of Women and Child Development has just been significantly increased. Women's economic empowerment is primarily based on their involvement in decision-making processes, including the generation and distribution of income, investments, and spending at all levels.

The goal of all attempts to empower women is to assist them in exercising their rights in decision-making at all levels, both within and beyond the home, and to enable them to make decisions for themselves and be considered equal members of society Efforts are being made to increase women's earning ability and ensure that they have access to and control over the whole family or community's assets.

Economic empowerment is assessed by a gain in the value of assets, income, savings, loan amount, and family income. Women's economic empowerment is a focus in Swedish development assistance in order to promote gender equality and women's rights.

To eliminate poverty, a greater emphasis on gender equality and women's economic empowerment is required. According to the World Bank, tackling gender inequities through women's economic empowerment is "smart economics." They claim that greater gender equality boosts productivity, improves future development outcomes, and makes institutions more representative.

Women make up 40% of the worldwide labor force, 43% of the agricultural labor force, and more than half of all university students. Productivity will increase when their knowledge, skills, and abilities are put to work completely. According to the World Bank, increased female control over household finances can improve nations' economic prospects by shifting spending habits in ways that benefit children.

Indeed, gains in women's education and health have been related to improved results for their children in nations ranging from Brazil to Nepal to Pakistan to Senegal. The World Bank's third message is that empowering women as economic, political, and social actors may influence policy decisions and promote more representative decision-making.

Gendered power structures and societal conventions confine both men and women to positions that limit their productivity as well as their capacity to make choices to improve their circumstances. Gender equality helps both men and women, but because women face more economic marginalization, this study concentrates on women's economic empowerment.

This is not to say that we should ignore the need of empowering certain groups of impoverished males or the importance of empowering women for addressing males in their relationships with women (e.g., spouses enabling women to generate financially, dads promoting daughters' secondary schooling, etc.), which is frequently a critical component for effective outcomes.

1.7. ECONOMIC EMPOWERMENT: A POTENTIAL PATHWAY FOR WOMEN AND GIRLS TO GAIN CONTROL OVER THEIR SEXUAL AND REPRODUCTIVE HEALTH

Economic empowerment is the ability to decide and act on financial resource control and distribution decisions (Golla et al., 2011). Women's financial power is associated with increased usage of preventive health services by children and women (Lagarde et al., 2009; Ahmed et al., 2010), including contemporary contraceptive techniques (Ahmed et al., 2010; Do and Kurimoto, 2012). Thus, interventions aimed at increasing women's and girls' economic power may improve reproductive health behaviors, including long-term use of modern contraception (see Figure 1.7), especially when combined with investments that directly address reproductive health, family planning, and/or gender norms.

Figure 1.7. A forum discussing on women empowerment and sexual and reproductive health.

Source: Image by flickr.com.

The barriers depicted in Figure 1.7 in the illustrated theory of change are those that Economic empowerment programs are expected to directly address these issues. Although the theory of change is arranged in a linear fashion, the mechanisms of action are more likely to be bi-directional and complicated.

These potential links inspire the family planning community to look for ways and opportunities to speed the transition toward more economic equality between men and women by expanding women's control and authority over financial resources. Although our present toolbox of treatments is limited, the global community has learnt a great deal by executing these sorts of initiatives over the previous three decades.

1.7.1. What Is the Impact?

This synthesis comprised initiatives targeted at improving economic empowerment as well as a research component that examined critical family planning outcomes.

Although some of these programs did not explicitly seek to promote contraceptive usage, they were included in the synthesis if they examined other important family planning outcomes such as reductions in unwanted pregnancy, fertility, marriage delay, birth spacing, or breastfeeding. The majority of the studies did not contain comprehensive implementation data, such as intervention duration and substance.

1.7.2. Vocational Training

Programs in Bangladesh, the Dominican Republic, Malawi, and Uganda investigated the impact of vocational training on family planning outcomes such as contraception usage, adolescent pregnancy, and marriage age (Population Council, 2016; Bandiera et al., 2012; Ibarraran et al., 2012; Cho et al., 2015; Rotheram-Borus et al., 2012).

All of these programs were aimed at young people aged 10 to 24, with the goal of providing them with the skills they needed to enter the workforce. Two projects in Bangladesh and Uganda focused solely on teenage females (Population Council, 2016; Bandiera et al., 2012), while others included both boys and girls (Ibarraran et al., 2012; Cho et al., 2015; Rotheram-Borus et al., 2012).

The exercise intensity varies. In Bangladesh, females got 44 hours of life skills training in addition to 100 hours of schooling, gender rights awareness, or both., and/or livelihoods training over 18 months, whereas the Dominican Republic program included 225 hours of training (Population Council, 2016).

The sample sizes in the five investigations ranged from 100 to 10,000. Only two programs incorporated health components: one focused on raising information (e.g., about Human Immunodeficiency Virus (HIV) and pregnancy) and lowering hazardous behaviors, including sex without condoms and coerced sex (Bandiera et al., 2012), and the other on HIV prevention (Rotheram-Borus et al., 2012).

Three of the five studies collected data on condom use. The two Ugandan initiatives that incorporated a health component recorded an increase in condom usage as well as other beneficial outcomes (Bandiera et al., 2012; Rotheram-Borus et al., 2012). The Malawi program discovered no substantial effects on condom use (Cho et al., 2015) (Figure 1.8).

Figure 1.8. Girls getting vocational training in Indonesia.

Source: Image by flickr.com.

A professional training program in the Dominican Republic achieved a 5%-point decrease in the pregnancy rate among 16–19-year-old individuals the authors ascribed the difference to the program's favorable influence on young people's future expectations (Ibarraran et al., 2012).

The Bangladesh scheme attempted to raise the marriage age. Females were 23% less likely to get married as youngsters in areas where girls got livelihood training in entrepreneurship, mobile phone repair, photography, and basic first aid than in control groups.

Girls in intervention arms focused on education or gender rights awareness were 31% less likely to marry as youngsters than girls in control neighborhoods (Population Council, 2016).

1.7.2.1. Microfinance

Two randomized controlled studies of multi-component programs that incorporated microfinance as well as other activities such as reproductive health education and life skills revealed no influence on condom or other contraceptive usage (Dunbar et al., 2014; Desai and Tarozzi, 2011).

Contraceptive use was the same at 24 months post-intervention in Zimbabwe between female orphans ages 16–19 who were randomized to take part in combined microcredit, HIV education, life skills education, and social support program and those in the comparison group who received only HIV education and life skills.

The intervention group's within-group changes in condom usage (from baseline to end line) were statistically significant (odds ratio [OR]=1.79, confidence interval [CI]=1.23 to 2.62) but not the comparison group's (OR=1.29, CI=0.86 to 1.95) (Dunbar et al., 2014).

Communities in Ethiopia were randomly assigned to either a microcredit program, a reproductive health program, both programs, or no program. In models that controlled for demographic and family variables, differences in contraceptive usage by women in each community group were not statistically significant.

Randomized reviews of village savings and loan schemes in Ghana, Malawi, and Uganda revealed little influence on beneficiary consumption of health services. Two recent research found that microfinance had a favorable influence on contraceptive use.

In rural Uttar Pradesh, India, researchers examined the impact of incorporating family planning information and referrals into a microfinance program. The study found a 5-point rise in contemporary contraceptive usage and a 24-point increase in periodic abstinence among microfinance program participants after the intervention.

In Nigeria, researchers discovered a substantial difference in contemporary contraceptive use between women living in areas with access to microfinance and those living in comparable groups (30% vs. 21%, respectively). Both studies highlight a number of critical methodological concerns.

In the Nigeria research, for example, there were several significant changes between the intervention and control samples, and the intervention comprised improvements in service delivery and Demand generating activities that the control sites did not have.

1.7.2.2. Cash Transfers

As detailed in the Educating Girls HIP Brief, conditional, and unconditional financial transfers promote girls' access to, retention in, and advancement in school. Identifying the proper beneficiaries—the groups most in need and grade levels with the highest dropout rates—is crucial to the efficacy of these programs.

Some argue that cash-incentive benefit schemes may have the unintended impact of rising birth rates. The World Bank stated that there is little or no evidence of higher fertility rates as a result of social safety net transfers, and the transfers do not appear to alter the ability of the woman to choose whether or not to use contraception (World Bank, 2014). Conditional cash transfers frequently incorporate anti-fertility elements such as the inability to add more children to the beneficiary list and awareness sessions.

These findings are consistent with findings from evaluations of a large-scale conditional cash transfer program in Mexico: three of the four evaluations found no effect on fertility or conception rate (Darney et al., 2013; Feldman et al., 2009; Stecklov et al., 2007), whereas one found minor effect on contraceptive use among young adult women but not between many youths (Lamadrid-Figueroa et al., 2008).

The youth was not expected to attend promotional lectures, although young adult women were. In India, a conditional cash transfer program encouraging facility delivery led to an increase in postpartum contraception usage among participants (OR= 1.31). 2013 (Zavier and Santhyas).

An unconditional cash transfer program for female orphans aged 15–24 in Kenya reduced pregnancy even after adjusting for schooling, but not early marriage (Handa et al., 2015). According to beneficiary interviews, the girls spent the money on food, health care, and clothes. Beneficiaries may have resorted to transactional sex to get these products in the absence of monetary transfer.

1.7.3. Multi-Component Economic Empowerment Plus Health Activities

Some initiatives combine different methods to economic empowerment alongside health education and promotion programs. We discovered three studies that looked at how these combination programs affected family planning results.

Savings and credit (microfinance), professional, and/or business skills, and reproductive health education were all part of the programs. Married adolescents in Ethiopia reported higher contraceptive usage in all four study arms of economic empowerment and reproductive health program:

- Those who received only economic empowerment information and guidance (9 percentage point increase);
- Those who received only sexual and reproductive health education (27 percentage point increase);
- Those who did receive only economic empowerment information and guidance (9 percentage point increase);
- The fourth group is the control group (no intervention) (5 percentage point increase).

Although the differences between the intervention and control groups were statistically significant, the sexual and reproductive health content may have been the most important factor in increasing contraceptive usage among married teenage females.

The evaluation ascribed the rise in contraceptive usage to improved contraception attitudes among spouses of enrolled females (Edmeades and Hayes, 2014).

The evaluation attributed the increase in contraceptive use to the improvement in the attitudes about contraception among husbands of enrolled girls (Edmeades and Hayes, 2014).

Unmarried adolescents exposed to microfinance, vocational training, sexual, and reproductive health education, and mentoring intervention in Kenya were slightly more likely to use condoms than non-participants (52.1% vs 44.3%, respectively), but the difference was not statistically significant (Erulkar and Chong, 2005).

Another Ethiopian initiative aimed to delay marriage for teenage girls by offering access to literacy, numeracy, and livelihood skills, as well as cash support for school and a goat for the girl and her family if her parents did not arrange for her to marry. The initiative also collaborated with community leaders to address child marriage norms.

An end line comparison of participants and non-participants revealed that, when compared to their counterparts in comparison communities, 10–14 year olds in the intervention community were less likely to be married, 15–19 year olds in the intervention community were more likely to be married, and girls in the intervention community were more likely to use condoms (Erulkar and Muthengi, 2009).

1.7.4. Economic Empowerment and Gender-Based Violence

Experts express worry that women's empowerment initiatives, particularly economic empowerment programs, may increase intimate partner violence if males react badly when their household responsibilities are first challenged.

Two literature evaluations seek to characterize the link between women's empowerment initiatives, including economic empowerment programs that directly target GBV and those that do not, and the risk of domestic violence (Heise, 2011; Mejia et al., 2014) (Figure 1.9).

Figure 1.9. Economic development can bring an end to gender-based violence.

Source: Image by flickr.com.

Mejia and colleagues (2014) found 19 economic empowerment programs, 15 of which targeted gender norms and/or gender-based violence directly. Eight of the 15 gender-related programs reported a GBV outcome (i.e., attitudes toward or experience with GBV): Three of the eight participants reported a decrease in GBV experience, five reported no change in experience, and none reported an increase in GBV experience.

Whether or whether economic empowerment initiatives directly address GBV, rigorous evaluations of program participants' experiences with GBV should be conducted.

1.8. CONCLUSION

Women's empowerment is now widely accepted as an objective having social, moral, political, and economic benefits. Yet economic empowerment is much more. lower women's wages relative to men's). occupational/ sectoral segregation or lack of access to credit); or inequality of market outcomes (e.g., Most countries measure a lack of empowerment for women through either inequality of market participation (e.g., It includes not only what women do, but what women aspire to do. It is also about the economic capabilities and behaviors of women and girls within households, communities, and societies, and it is shaped by the institutions which govern these. Enshrined in the recently adopted Sustainable Development Goals, (SDGs), most nations of the world have committed publicly to taking steps to advance this agenda through changes in discriminatory laws and by supporting changes in behavior, including those which affect economic opportunities and outcomes.

REFERENCES

1. Anne, M. G., Anju, M., Priya, N., & Rekha, M., (2011). *Understanding and Measuring Women's Economic Empowerment*. [e-Book] International Center for Research on Women (ICRW. Available at: https://www.icrw.org/wp-content/uploads/2016/10/Understanding-measuring-womens-economic-empowerment.pdf (accessed on 21 June 2022).
2. Duflo, E., (2012). Women empowerment and economic development. *Journal of Economic Literature, 50*(4), 1051–1079. [online] Available at: https://economics.mit.edu/files/7417 (accessed on 21 June 2022).
3. Kimberly, A., Joan, K., Shefa, S., Reena, S., & Shawn, M., (2011). *Economic Empowerment a Pathway for Women's Wellness Care-HIPs.* [online] HIPs. Available at: https://www.fphighimpactpractices.org/briefs/economic-empowerment/ (accessed on 21 June 2022).
4. Louise Fox and Carolina Romero, (2017). *Concepts and Measurement of Women's Economic Empowerment*. [e-Book] Social Protection and Labor Global Practice Group. Available at: https://documents1.worldbank.org/curated/en/436011496234827185/pdf/WPS8079.pdf (accessed on 21 June 2022).
5. OECD, (2011). *Women's Economic Empowerment.* [e-Book] OECD. Available at: https://www.oecd.org/dac/gender-development/47561694.pdf (accessed on 21 June 2022).
6. Thanikaivel, M., & Priya, K., (2018). Economic empowerment of women in India. *International Journal of Technical Research & Science, 3*(VII). [online] Available at: https://www.researchgate.net/publication/329521756_ECONOMIC_EMPOWERMENT_OF_WOMEN_IN_INDIA (accessed on 21 June 2022).

CHAPTER 2

SUSTAINABLE DEVELOPMENT: AN OVERVIEW

CONTENTS

2.1. INTRODUCTION

Sustainable development is a key topic today worldwide. It is both a means of comprehending the world and a strategy of resolving global issues. This book will introduce you to this intriguing and important subject of thinking and action.

Our congested planet serves as our starting point. There are currently 7.2 billion people on the earth, which is about nine times the 800 million estimated to have existed in 1750, at the dawn of the industrial revolution. The global population continues to grow fast, adding 75–80 million people each year. Soon, there will be 8 billion people by the 2020s, and maybe 9 billion by the early 2040s.

These billions of individuals are searching for a place in the global economy. The impoverished are trying to obtain food, potable water, health care, and shelter in order to survive. Those living just over the poverty line hope for more prosperity and a better future for their children.

High-income group are hopeful that technological advancements will provide them and their families with even greater levels of happiness. It appears that the super-rich is also competing for a spot on the world's richest individuals list.

In summary, 7.2 billion people want the economy to develop. They do so in a global economy that is becoming increasingly interconnected through commerce, finance, technology, production flows, migration, and social networks. The current size of the global economy the predicted annual production of $90 trillion (known as the Gross World Product, or GWP) is unparalleled.

According to rough figures, the GWP is at least 100 times more than it was in 1750. In reality, such a comparison is meaningless because the majority of the international economy now comprises things and services that did not even exist 250 years ago.

What we do know is that the global economy is enormous, fast increasing (by 3–4% per year on an average), and very uneven in terms of wealth distribution within and across nations. Ours is a world of incredible prosperity and severe poverty, with billions of people enjoying longevity and excellent health that past generations could not have imagined.

The global economy is not just incredibly unfair, but also remarkably dangerous to the earth. Humanity, like all other creatures, is dependent on nature for food and water, resources for sustenance, and protection from dangerous environmental hazards such as disease outbreaks or natural disasters.

Yet, as a species that relies on nature's goodness, or what scientists term "environmental services," we are failing to maintain the physical foundation of our basic life. The massive global economy is causing a massive environmental disaster, one that threatens our wellbeing as well as the existence of thousands of other species, if not our own.

We will discover that environmental challenges are emerging on several fronts. Humans are altering the Earth's temperature, fresh water supply, ocean chemistry, and the habitats of other species. These consequences are now so significant that the Earth is suffering clear changes in the functioning of essential systems on which life depends, such as the water, nitrogen, and carbon cycles.

We don't know the exact scale, timing, or ramifications of these changes, but we really do know that they are exceedingly hazardous and unprecedented in the 10,000 years of human civilization. As a result, we arrive at sustainable development.

Sustainable development, as an intellectual endeavor, attempts to make sense of the interplay of three complex systems: the global economy, global society, and the Earth's physical environment. How does a 7.2-billion-person economy with a $90 trillion Gross World Output evolve over time?

What factors contribute to economic growth? Why is poverty so persistent? What happens when markets, technology, money, and social networks suddenly link billions of people? How does a global society with such income, wealth, and power disparity function?

Can the impoverished avoid their doom? Can human trust and sympathy overcome class and power divisions? And what happens when the global economy collides with the physical environment? Is there one means of reversing direction, a means of combining economic expansion with environmental sustainability?

Sustainable Development is also a normative worldview, recommending a set of goals to which the world should aim. In this normative (or ethical) view, sustainable development envisions a society where economic success is prevalent, severe poverty is eradicated, social trust is fostered via community-building measures, and the environment is preserved from human-caused deterioration.

It is important to note that sustainable development advocates for a comprehensive framework in which society strives for economic, social, and environmental goals. The following abbreviation is sometimes used: sustainable development necessitates socially inclusive and ecologically sustainable economic growth.

To attain the economic, social, and environmental goals, a fourth goal must also be met: effective governance. Governments must perform a wide range of essential duties in order for society to thrive. Of all, this is only a small portion of what people throughout the world expect from their governments. In reality, all too frequently, they receive the opposite: corruption, conflict, and a lack of public services.

Among these core government functions is the provision of social services such as healthcare and education, the provision of infrastructures such as roads, ports, and power, the protection of individuals from crime and violence, the promotion of basic science and new technologies, and the implementation of environmental regulations.

In today's world, good governance cannot just relate to governments. Multinational corporations are frequently the most powerful actors on the global stage. Our wellbeing is dependent on these large corporations following the law, protecting the environment, and assisting the communities in which they operate, particularly in overcoming extreme poverty.

However, as with governments, the reality is frequently the inverse. Multinational corporations are frequently agents of public corruption, paying authorities to bend rules or tax policies in their advantage, as well as engaging in tax fraud, money laundering, and irresponsible environmental harm.

Thus, the normative side of sustainable development anticipates four fundamental pillars of a healthy society: economic success, social inclusion and cohesion, environmental sustainability, and effective governance of important social actors such as governments and corporations.

The idea of sustainable development is heavily debated, with various sectors of the economy assigning different understandings to it. This idea has evolved as a result of a series of multilateral conferences that began in 1972, with the United Nations Conference on the Human Environment in Stockholm.

Typically, the word sustainable development refers to methods that are seen to be more ecologically friendly than others. The Brundtland Commission definition, established in 1987 by the World Commission on Environment and Development (WCED), is the most commonly acknowledged.

While the current notion of sustainable development is mostly based on the Brundtland Report of 1987, it is also influenced by previous concepts about sustainable forest management and twentieth-century environmental concerns. As the notion evolved, its emphasis turned to economic development, social development, and environmental conservation for future generations.

"The term sustainability should be considered as humanity's objective goal of human-ecosystem balance, while sustainable development' refers to the holistic approach and temporal processes that take us to the end point of sustainability," it has been recommended. "Modern economies are attempting to combine ambitious economic expansion with commitments to preserve natural resources and ecosystems, as the two are commonly perceived to be incompatible."

Instead of making climate change and other environmental pledges, Turning and leveraging economic development measures into commercial opportunities would do better. Managed Sustainable Development (MSD) refers to the economic development brought about by such organized concepts and practices in an economy.

2.1.1. Need for Sustainable Development

We have witnessed over the last two or three decades that the health of the ecosystem has suffered for the sake of economic expansion. As a result, the environment has suffered from effects such as decreased air quality and climate change caused by greenhouse gases.

All of these causes contributed to the need for sustainable development, as if left unchecked, they might cause lasting environmental damage.

2.2. OBJECTIVES OF SUSTAINABLE DEVELOPMENT

2.2.1. Economic Growth

Building a robust, competitive economy by ensuring that enough land of the appropriate type is accessible in the right places and at the right time to enable growth and innovation, and detecting and coordinating development needs.

2.2.2. Environmental Protection

Making a significant contribution to the protection and enhancement of our natural and developed environments, while also assisting in the improvement of biodiversity, the wise use of natural resources, the reduction of waste and pollution, and the adaptation to and reduction of global warming, including a global shift to a low-carbon economy.

2.2.3. Social Inclusion

Helping strong, lively, and fit and active people by providing the housing needed to meet the needs of current and future generations; and by fostering skills are important with available local services that reflect the needs of the community and support its health, social, and cultural wellbeing.

2.3. SUSTAINABLE DEVELOPMENT AS A NORMATIVE APPROACH

Sustainable development is a method of looking at the world as a complex interplay of economic, social, environmental, and political systems. However, it is also a normative or ethical worldview, a method to describe the goals of a well-functioning society, one that provides wellbeing for its inhabitants today and in future generations (Figure 2.1).

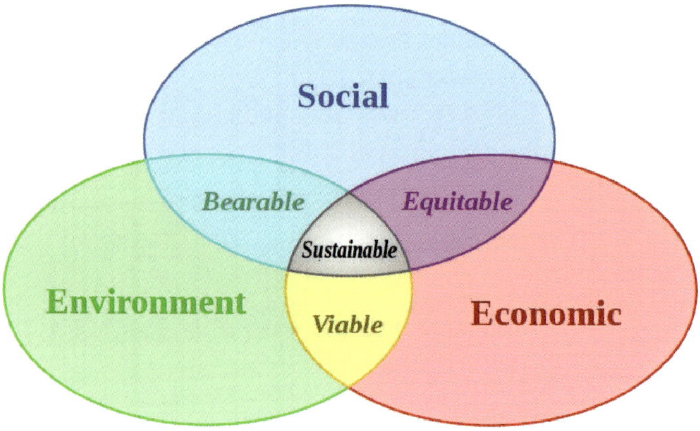

Figure 2.1. Sustainable development.

Source: Image by flickr.com.

In that normative sense, the essential purpose of sustainable development is that it encourages us to have a comprehensive picture of what a decent society should be. Many individuals believe that a good society is a wealthy society where rising earnings are the ultimate goal of economic and political activity. However, such a perspective is plainly too restricted.

Assume a civilization is prosperous on average whereas one guy was extremely wealthy while the rest were quite impoverished Most people would not consider that a particularly appealing society, one that leads to happiness to its citizens.

Becoming a better steward of the natural surroundings is the third facet of a decent society. We will lose immensely if we disrupt the physical systems of freshwater and biodiversity if we destroy the seas and the big rainforests. We will face tremendous consequences if we stay on a path that profoundly affects the Earth's climate.

As a result, from a normative standpoint, protection of the environment appears to be just and compelling if we care, which we should, about the very well of our children, their young kids, and future generations. Many, though not all, of us are concerned about just how our government operates. Widespread corruption, criminality, dishonest politicians, unequal government services, severe discrimination, insider dealing, and other factors contribute to a great degree of dissatisfaction.

People all throughout the world are happy and feel safer when they can trust their government. Unfortunately, many people throughout the world do not trust their government to be truthful, fair, and secure. From a normative standpoint, decent society is one that is not just economically wealthy (with a high per-capita income), but also socially inclusive, ecologically sustainable, and well-governed.

That is my working description of sustainable development's normative aims. The essential challenge is how to apply our understanding of the linkages of the economy, society, environment, and governance to consider how to create successful, inclusive, sustainable, and well-governed societies. We can see that there are several effective strategies to accomplish sustainable growth as a set of common goals for the globe.

2.4. EDUCATION FOR SUSTAINABLE DEVELOPMENT

Education for Sustainable Development (ESD) is described as education that promotes changes in knowledge, skills, values, and attitudes in order to create a more sustainable and equitable society. ESD aspires to empower and equip current and future generations to satisfy the requirements of the economy, society, and the environment through a balanced and integrated approach to the economic, social, and environmental components of sustainable development.

The notion of ESD arose from the necessity for education to address the world's rising and changing environmental issues. To do this, education must evolve to offer learners with the information, skills, values, and attitudes necessary to contribute to sustainable development. Simultaneously, education must be prioritized in all agendas, programs, and actions promoting sustainable development (Figure 2.2).

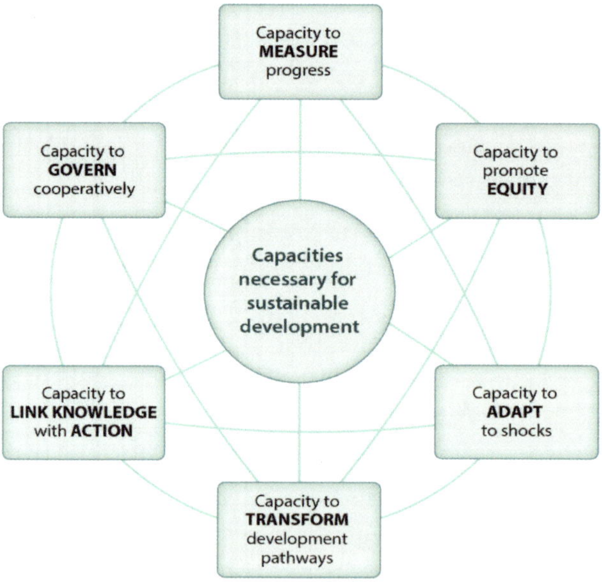

Figure 2.2. Capacities for sustainable development.

Source: Image by commons.wikimedia.com.

Sustainability must be included. within education, and education should be incorporated into long-term development ESD encourages the incorporation of these key sustainability concerns in local and global settings into the curriculum in order to enable students to comprehend and adapt to a changing world. ESD strives to provide learning outcomes that include critical and systematic thinking, collaborative decision-making, and accepting responsibility for current and future generations.

Because traditional single-directional information distribution is insufficient to encourage learners to behave as responsible citizens, ESD necessitates redesigning the learning environment, both physical and virtual. To implant the ideology of sustainable development, the learning environment must adapt and use a whole-institution strategy.

Building the ability of educators and providing policy assistance at the international, regional, national, and local levels aids in driving progress. Alterations in educational institutions When engaged youth and local communities connect with educational institutions, they become crucial actors in furthering sustainable development.

2.5. THE ROLE OF TECHNOLOGICAL CHANGE IN SUSTAINABLE DEVELOPMENT

The Shanghai Maglev is an amazing piece of technology that transports people at speeds of more than 200 miles per hour to and from Shanghai and its international airport. It is the result of a collaboration between engineering firms in Europe and China, and it has been in operation for the past decade. It exemplifies how modern technologies may aid in the achievement of sustainable development.

Unlike previous generations of trains, the Maglev is electrically powered rather than coal or petroleum. If the electricity that powers the Maglev is eventually generated from a clean primary energy source (rather than the coal that currently dominates China), electric-powered intercity transport can contribute to the answer to human-caused climate change (Figure 2.3).

Figure 2.3. Technological development in sustainable development.

Source: Image by flickr.com.

Three components of technology will be highlighted throughout our study of sustainable development. For starters, technical progress is the primary engine of long-term global economic growth. Since 1750, the world economy has grown rapidly as a result of 250 years of technological advances, beginning with the steam engine and steam-powered transportation, progressing to the combustion engine, electrification, industrial chemistry, scientific agronomy, aviation, nuclear power, and today's information and communications technologies.

Without these advancements, the global economy and population would have plateaued decades or centuries ago. Second, even when the direct consequences of technical developments are extremely favorable, they frequently have detrimental side effects. Coal combustion is both the symbol of the industrial revolution and the bane of our environmental predicament.

Through the advent of the steam engine, coal may be said to have enabled modern civilization. Nonetheless, coal is currently employed on such a large scale that it threatens civilization itself. In 2010, humans emitted around 14 billion tons of CO_2 through coal combustion, accounting for over half of the world's total CO_2 emissions from fossil fuels.

Unless coal is phased out quickly or combined with other technology (such as carbon capture and sequestration, which will be described later), the harm to the earth and world economy will be catastrophic.

Third, technological progress is, to some part, guided by humans. Sometimes technological progress is presented as a massive lottery, decided by the good fortune of individual innovators and scientists. Alternatively, technical progress is frequently referred to as simply following the market.

In order to maximize earnings, businesses engage in research and development (R&D). We end up with studies on commercial issues, not necessarily ones of critical concern to the poor or the environment. However, there is another aspect of technology evolution that may be directed toward human aims.

2.6. SUB-GROUPS OF SUSTAINABLE DEVELOPMENT

Scheme of Sustainable Development: At the Confluence of Three Constituent Parts (2006)

The environment, the economy, and society are the three sectors, dimensions, areas, or pillars of sustainable development. Rene Passet, an economist, created the three-sphere paradigm in 1979. It has also been referred to as "economic, environmental, and social," as well as "ecology, economy, and equality."

Some authors have expanded this to include a fourth pillar of culture, institutions, or governance, or alternatively reconfigured it as four domains of the social: ecology, economics, politics, and culture; thus reintroducing economics into the social and treating ecology as the intersection of the social and the natural.

2.7. RELATIONSHIP BETWEEN ECOLOGICAL FOOTPRINT AND HUMAN DEVELOPMENT INDEX (HDI)

Human settlements' ecological stability is part of the link between humans and their natural, social, and architectural contexts. This, sometimes known as human ecology, broadens the scope of sustainable development to include the area of human health.

Fundamental human needs, such as the availability and quality of air, water, food, and shelter, are also ecological foundations for sustainable development; trying to address public health hazards through investment opportunities in ecological systems can be a powerful and transformative force for sustainable development that, in this sense, extends to all species.

Environmental sustainability is concerned with the natural environment and how it survives and continues to be diverse and productive. Because natural resources are drawn from the environment, the status of the air, water, and climate is particularly important (Figure 2.4).

Figure 2.4. Sustainable development.

Source: Image by commons.wikimedia.com.

The Intergovernmental Panel on Climate Change (IPCC) Fifth Assessment Report summarizes current scientific, technological, and socioeconomic information regarding climate change, as well as strategies for adaptation and mitigation. Environmental sustainability necessitates that society creates activities that suit human needs while also conserving the planet's life support systems.

This includes, for example, using water responsibly, employing renewable energy, and utilizing sustainable material supply (e.g., extracting wood from forests at a pace that sustains biomass and biodiversity). When natural capital (the whole of nature's resources) is depleted faster than it can be replaced, the situation becomes unsustainable.

Sustainability implies that human activity only consumes natural resources at a rate that allows them to be restored naturally. The idea of sustainable development is inherently linked to the concept of carrying capacity. In theory, the long-term outcome of environmental deterioration is the inability to maintain human existence.

On a global scale, such deterioration should result in a rise in the human mortality rate until the population falls below what the deteriorated ecosystem can maintain. If the deterioration continues over a certain degree or critical threshold, mankind will face extinction.

2.8. RELATIONSHIPS AMONG THE ENVIRONMENT, ECONOMY, AND SOCIETY

The notion of sustainability is certain to continue to shape future conversations about developmental science. According to Porter and van der Linde, the optimum options are considered to be those that fulfill societal demands while also being ecologically and economically sustainable, economically, and socially fair, and socially and environmentally tolerable.

The above system consists of three interrelated sustainability spheres or sectors that define the links between the environmental, economic, and social aspects of SD. Almost everything man does or proposes to do on Earth has an impact on the environment, economy, or society, as well as the human race's continuing survival and wellbeing.

Similarly, as Wanamaker (argues, the spheres are a collection of interconnected ideas that should serve as the foundation for human decisions and behaviors in the pursuit of SD. Yang (2019) endorses the concept, stating that the graphic essentially demonstrates how appropriate decisions on sustainable resource management would result in sustainable growth for a sustainable society. Decisions on land use, surface water management, agricultural methods, building design and construction, energy management, education, equal opportunities, and law-making and enforcement are examples of these.

The reasoning is that if the concepts constituted in the three spheres of sustainable development are well implemented in the real situations, everyone wins even though mineral wealth is retained, the environment is protected, the economy thrives and is resilient, and social life is improved because there is peace and respect for human rights present a dramatic illustration of the links between economic, social, and environmental sustainability, stating that the three domains must be linked for long-term viability.

2.9. GLOBAL ACCEPTANCE OF THE CONCEPT OF SUSTAINABLE DEVELOPMENT

Many politicians see sustainable development as a goal that professionals from other disciplines, such as scientists and social scientists, should assist them to attain by incorporating environmental concerns into everyday thinking, decision-making, and accountability processes.

According to Mutangadura, nearly all southern African governments have formed sustainable development authorities in charge of coordinating sustainable development efforts and supporting effective environmental management. However, because the majority of these entities' legislative frameworks are based on environmental legislation, their activity is skewed toward the environmental sector.

By enacting laws and regulations, the South African government has incorporated the notion of sustainable development into its policies. South Africa's constitution is built on this principle. Sections 24(a) and (b) indicate that "everyone has the right to an environment that is not injurious to their health or wellbeing; and the right to have the environment safeguarded, for the benefit of current and future generations, by appropriate legislative and other measures that are effective are:

Avoid environment pollution deterioration;

- Encourage conservation; and
- Ensure ecologically sustainable development and utilization of "natural resources."

On the basis of this provision of the South African constitution, a number of rules and regulations have been adopted, which serve to lead both the public and commercial sectors in their everyday operations toward enhanced environmental governance (Figure 2.5).

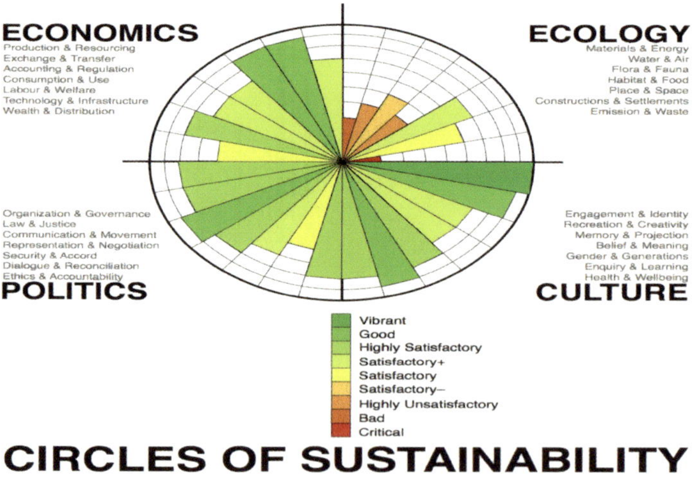

Figure 2.5. Circles of sustainability.

Source: Image by commons.wikimedia.com.

South Africa's National Water Act, for example, which transfers water rights from private to governmental ownership, is supposed to encourage sustainable growth in terms of environmental resources. Despite the passage of these laws and programs, the general condition of South Africa's environment continues to deteriorate.

The Millennium Development Goals (MDGs), established during the Millennium Conference in September 2000, are one of the measures designed by the global community to accomplish sustainable development principles, particularly in poor countries, including those on the African continent.

According to the 2014 UN report on the state of the MDGs, there has been great progress in achieving all objectives, with certain targets already completed before the 2015 deadline. Some nations made great progress toward some MDG targets, whereas Sub-Saharan Africa lags far behind.

The issue is exacerbated by the progressive degradation and pollution of Sub-Saharan African countries' natural resource bases (forests, fisheries, soil, and water). Since 2000, the number of people living in extreme poverty in developing nations has decreased by 700 million.

The MDG of halving global poverty was met in 2010, despite inconsistent and insufficient progress; in reality, the proportion of people living on less than $1.25 per day fell from 47% in 1990 to 22% in 2010, with the bulk of the extremely poor living in southern Asia and Sub-Saharan Africa. However, some progress has been made, as the number of severely poor individuals in Sub-Saharan Africa has decreased and the relative poverty ratio has decreased, which is noteworthy because poverty in Africa is related to substantial income inequality.

One of the MDGs that South Africa focused on was halving poverty and unemployment rates by 2014 (Burns and Weaver, 2008); nevertheless, this objective is still far from being met. Achieving MDG 7, which focuses on environmental sustainability, will aid in the achievement of MDGs related to poverty, health, and gender equality, which come within the social and economic domain.

Environmental assessment is a crucial instrument used to promote sustainable development concepts across the world, with an emphasis on the environment as an intrinsic link to human wellbeing (Sadler, 1996). Although the primary goal of this instrument was to guarantee that the biophysical implications of any changes were recognized in decision-making rather than focusing on sustainable development.

The United States of America was the first country to enact environmental law in the form of environmental impact assessment (EIA) with the National Environmental Policy Act (NEPA) of 1969. Following that, several other countries enacted similar legislation. Furthermore, as an extension of EIA, a strategic environmental assessment (SEA) was developed in order to incorporate sustainability principles through the formulation of long-term goals, indicators, and targets to direct human activities.

According to a United Nations Environment Policy (UNEP) study, certain poor nations have had success with their sustainable development strategies. China, Kenya, and Tunisia, for example, are putting more emphasis on renewable energy and energy efficiency.

Uganda has made significant progress from convectional agricultural production to an organic farming system that uses the least amount of artificial fertilizer in the world; and Brazil is investing in sustainable urban planning through a combination of land-use zoning and public transportation infrastructure, which has reduced traffic congestion and pollution.

Nepal, Ecuador is concentrating more on forest management, which has resulted in forest conservation and improved soil and water management, and Ecuador is conserving ecosystem services through watershed protection programs. These nations' sustainability programs benefit not just the environment, but also the socioeconomic element, by generating jobs and decreasing poverty.

2.10. STRATEGIES FOR PURSUING SUSTAINABLE DEVELOPMENT

The United Nations' Agenda 21 underlined the interdependence of the three elements of sustainable development. Its actual execution, however, may not have occurred in an integrated manner intended. While the MDGs focused on specific social and human development priorities, the world today is witnessing the emergence of new challenges, exacerbated by multiple financial, economic, food, and energy crises that have threatened all countries' ability to achieve sustainable development. The United Nations Conference on Sustainable Development reaffirmed the international community's political commitment to promote sustainable development in accordance with Agenda 21, particularly the idea of shared but differentiated responsibilities.

2.10.1. Implementation Process of Agenda 21 and the United Nations Conference on Sustainable Development

It is now obvious that economic, social, and environmental implementation efforts must be reintegrated, and the debates currently taking place under the banners of the MDGs and future sustainable development goals (SDGs) must be viewed as dimensions of the sustainable development paradigm.

Unsustainable consumption and production habits in wealthy nations, which are rapidly being copied by developing countries, pose a significant obstacle to sustainable development. In wealthy nations, for example, per capita, greenhouse gas emissions are 20–40 times more than what is required to stabilize atmospheric greenhouse gas concentrations (Figure 2.6).

Figure 2.6. UN agenda conference on sustainable development.

Source: Image by commons.wikimedia.com.

In affluent countries, per capita, ecological footprints are 4–9 times bigger than bio-capacity. The high level of inequality that accompanies and fosters these patterns renders them socially unsustainable and limits the attainment of human development goals. High-income families in both developed and developing nations are likely to continue to engage in unsustainable consumption behaviors in the absence of an effective global agenda.

2.11. NEED FOR INCLUSIVE STRATEGIES AND TECHNOLOGY INNOVATION

The United Nations Conference on Sustainable Development outcome statement gives recommendations for attaining sustainable development as a method of promoting the wellbeing of present and future generations in all nations.

Sustainable development initiatives must be inclusive and prioritize the needs of the poorest and most vulnerable people. Strategies must be aspirational, action-oriented, and collaborative while accounting for various country situations.

They will need to shift consumption and production patterns systematically, which may imply large price adjustments, as well as support the preservation of natural endowments, decrease inequality and enhance economic governance. This approach will need to decrease the forms of consumption and output that have negative externalities while simultaneously attempting to maximize the sorts of consumption that have Positive externalities created through consumption and production. Examples of limiting negative externalities include environmental pollution reduction, whereas examples of positive externalities include technological adaption, food waste reduction, and increased energy efficiency (Figure 2.7).

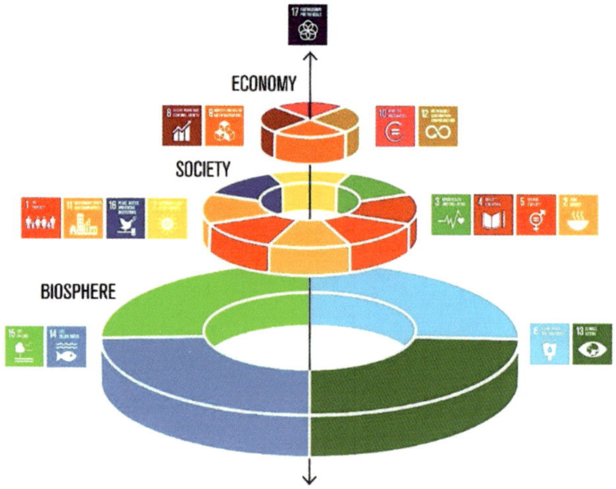

Figure 2.7. Economy and sustainability.

Source: Image by commons.wikimedia.com.

Technology will undoubtedly play a significant part in this shift. Changes in consumption patterns can spur the development of new technologies required for sustainability, as well as their acceptance and dissemination at the optimum rate.

To be successful in bringing about these changes, significant rearrangement of the economy and society, as well as lifestyle adjustments, will be required. Incentives for the development and implementation of new technologies will be required, which may include creative legislative reforms.

Poverty eradication, changing unsustainable and promoting sustainable patterns of consumption and production, and protecting and managing the natural resource base of economic and social development are the overarching objectives of and essential requirements for sustainable development.

In this large context, protection of climate and environment will need to be pursued as a universally shared goal. The global relocation of manufacturing and services sectors will also mean that appropriate technical regulation and social standards need to be adopted by developing and developed countries, with technical and financial support for developing countries.

The global sustainable development transformation entails, inter alia, significant price corrections, a strong commitment to preserving natural endowments, a reduction of inequalities, introduction of environmental accounting, strengthening of public spheres of life, redirection of the financial sector to the real economy and sharing of profit and employment.

Transformation along these lines may be expected to increase the wellbeing of people, especially the poorest. The contribution of the financial industry to the actual economy, as well as profit and employment sharing Transformation along these lines may be anticipated to improve people's wellbeing, particularly the poorest.

Human development will continue to be prioritized in developing nations' sustainable development programs, with poverty eradication as the primary aim. Human growth necessitates increased attention being paid to quality concerns as well as national coherence.

The success of human progress is heavily reliant on maximizing the possibilities given by globalization while limiting its negative consequences. Better management of capital flows and macroeconomic rules may be required in this setting, and coordination between national development objectives and global decision-making is critical.

Global institutions must address the unique demands of developing nations, particularly the least developed countries, small island developing states, landlocked developing countries, and post-conflict countries. The global agenda will change Human rights, conflict avoidance, good governance, and inequality reduction must all be prioritized.

Both rich and developing nations may enter a virtuous circle of collaboration and participation to secure global sustainable development.

2.12. GLOBAL TRENDS FOR SUSTAINABLE DEVELOPMENT CHALLENGES

The obstacles to sustainable development are impacted by socioeconomic, demographic, technical, and environmental developments, which are regarded as the major factors that shape society and have a significant influence on individuals. The recent technological innovation, along with the unexpected global economic fluctuations, has resulted in the following patterns;

In the midst of a global financial crisis, the international community must devise development plans to combat poverty and promote long-term development. If socioeconomic advancement remains unequal, more expenses will be spent due to environmental damage.

Inequality, globalization, environmental degradation, and demographic diversity are among the socioeconomic, social, technological, and environmental developments producing sustainable development issues.

These tendencies complement one another in a way that creates a number of issues. Rapid urbanization in emerging countries, financialization, and globalization are recipes for inequality, exposing nations to significant food and nutrition risks, environmental degradation, and energy security due to increased demand for land and water.

Since environmental deterioration has progressed to a critical point, the casual business as usual attitude is strongly discouraged in order for revolutionary change to occur at the community, national, and even global levels in order to achieve sustainable development.

2.13. STRATEGIES FOR SUSTAINABLE INCLUSIVENESS

The conclusion document of the United Nations Conference on Sustainable Development provides guidance for achieving sustainable development progress as ways for boosting the prosperity of current and future generations. Sustainable development strategies should be comprehensive and take into account the needs of the poor and disadvantaged.

Strategies should be goal-oriented, action-oriented, and community-based, taking into account unique country situations. The measures should systematically modify usage and production structures and may involve, among other things, massive price adjustments, enabling the protection of traditional blessings, reducing inequities, and strengthening the fiscal organization.

Such a plan should limit negative externality-producing usage and production while attempting to boost positive externality-producing use and creation. Examples of how to limit negative externalities include a reduction in environmental pollution, while also attempting to broaden the types of consumption and development that generate positive externalities

Examples of limiting negative externalities include reducing environmental pollution, whereas examples of positive externalities include, innovative adaptation, reducing food waste, and improving total nutritional value.

Technology will play a key role in addressing consumption habits in order to stimulate the development of innovations and improvements that are critical for sustainability. Achieving these advancements will necessitate a fundamental restructuring of the economy and society, as well as changes in lifestyle.

Economic and financial push for the development and acceptance of new technical developments will be necessary, as will creative policy adjustments. Combating poverty, unsustainable consumption and production, and ensuring that natural resources are adequately managed and conserved are the overarching goals of the key prerequisites for sustainable development.

Climate and environmental conservation must be seen as a universal aim by everybody in today's global globe. The present tendency of shifting manufacturing and other services to emerging countries asks that wealthy countries provide both technical and financial assistance to poorer countries.

Sustainable development transformation entails, among other things, significant value redresses, a firm commitment to safeguarding natural endowments, a reduction in inequalities, environmental accounting, public sector strengthening, and investment for development and profit-sharing, thereby improving poor people's livelihood and socio-wellbeing. Sustainable development initiatives in underdeveloped countries will continue to meet human development needs, with an emphasis on poverty reduction.

While human development requires increased attention to people's quality of life and other challenges at the national level, its success is mostly dependent on capitalizing on globalization's opportunities while limiting its negative consequences. In this situation, stronger capital-flow organization and macroeconomic principles may be required, as well as sufficiency between country-specific development strategies and global decision-making is important.

Overall, organizations must accommodate the innovative demands of emerging countries, particularly those of developing countries. The worldwide strategy will also need to prioritize avoiding confrontations, and human rights violations, ensuring big administration successes, and reducing inequality.

2.14. CHALLENGES FACING THE ADVANCEMENT OF SUSTAINABLE DEVELOPMENT PRINCIPLES

Several countries' governments that are actively pursuing sustainable development are confronted with the issue of establishing the best methods to balance the difficulties and possibilities connected with growth, as well as strategies to encourage growth in the economy that does not have severe environmental consequences.

Most nations' policies target the three pillars of sustainable development independently and in isolation, which can result in unfavorable outcomes; an integrated strategy would lead to better outcomes. Some nations' practices, which have been entrenched in regulations and legislation, rely on fast fixes and do not lead to long-term solutions.

One example is carbon trading, in which one company is permitted to emit more emissions if another one does not. Another industry is compensated for producing less of the same pollutant. This approach simply shifts the damage from one location to another; occasionally, the impact is moved from one environmental medium (air, water, or land) to another, which may intensify the impact.

Poverty, political instability, conflict concerns, unemployment, and inadequate infrastructure are key hurdles to achieving the goals of sustainable development in many developing nations. Instead of addressing the fundamental cause of these issues, just the symptoms are handled, creating a cycle of recurring incidents. In many nations, societal expectations exacerbate the issue by placing pressure on people and encouraging excessive use of resources, wealth accumulation, and a strong drive to achieve power at any cost.

Poverty has been linked to environmental deterioration in studies; poverty is both a cause and a result of environmental degradation. This is because the poor are disproportionately harmed by environmental deterioration as a result of their reliance on the environment via direct usage of natural resources People who do not have access to these services have few options for coping. It has also been demonstrated that nations experiencing internal or cross-border conflict do not prioritize the environment owing to a lack of economic resources or political will (Figure 2.8).

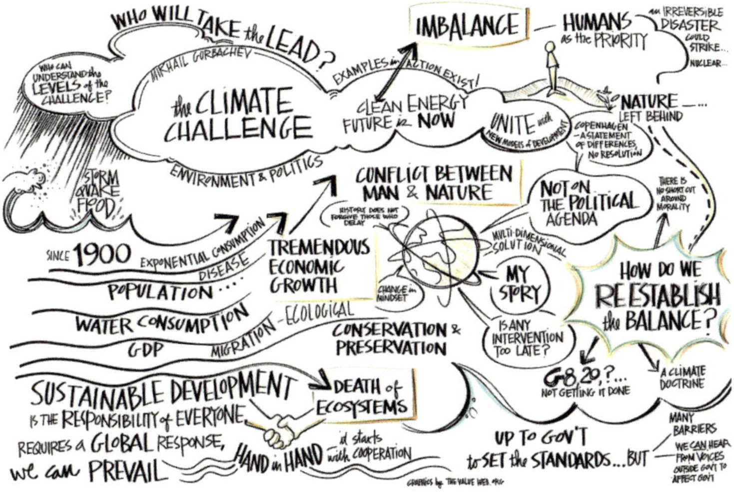

Figure 2.8. Challenges in attaining sustainability.

Source: Image by flickr.com.

Rapid population increase, food security, desertification, and troubling health trends such as the spread of HIV/acquired immune deficiency syndrome (AIDS) all impede developing nations' accomplishment of SDGs. For example, rising population pressures the agricultural sector to expand food production, which, although utilizing fewer employees and less land, must compete for resources with other sectors, eventually requiring more water, chemicals, and technology.

This action adds to rising levels of environmental pollution, homogenization of landscapes, and habitat destruction for species. There is hence a need for policies and management efforts that can increase the agricultural sector's positive contributions to society while reducing its negative effect.

In developing nations changes in land-use patterns in developing nations have resulted in decreased water access, erosion, land degradation, overgrazed, and deteriorating rangelands, deforestation, and biodiversity loss. Land-use changes have also led to changes in land tenure and ownership patterns, shifting from communal and open-access ownership to private ownership, with an increased proclivity for land sales, particularly in African nations.

These methods frequently result in disputes and are suboptimal land usage. In addition to the aforementioned consequences, there is the issue of urban sprawl and the development of informal settlements, which occur in the absence of proper land use plans, resulting in forest cover loss and significant environmental degradation.

2.15. SUSTAINABLE TRANSFORMATIONAL RESEARCH STRATEGIES

By 2030, the two blocs—developing and developed nations—will now have to adopt key transformational strategies toward developing sustainable socioeconomic frameworks and balanced ecosystems by reforming policies and governance systems; changing human behavior, societal norms, and beliefs; improving data analytics through machine learning (ML) and artificial intelligence (AI); and raising community awareness of these key sustainability drivers.

Understanding the significance of addressing global sustainability challenges necessitates coordinated research and the integration of contradictory sectors of society such as production and consumption with biodiversity and ecosystem services in order to build resilience at the expense of inequality. To do this, an integrated strategy that pulls all of these sectors together will be required. synergies across seven main driving areas to aid in the development of sustainable systems approaches (Figure 2.9).

Figure 2.9. Sustainability logo. Source: Image by pixabay.com.

2.16. SYSTEM APPROACHES FOR SUSTAINABILITY

2.16.1. Governance and Institutional Establishment

The primary and secondary sustainability drivers While an adaptable multi-model approach is concerned with conventional organizational system models at the primary level, governments are expected to adapt models for theory testing, predictability models to investigate the soundness of societal system dynamics, and policy assessment before deployment.

To achieve complete sustainability, the strategy may also incorporate secondary constraints such as equality and resilience, biodiversity, and ecosystems, and production and consumption at a higher level. In further depth, all seven social factors are required to aid in the development of cutting-edge model methods that are country-specific and capable of resolving sustainability concerns.

A fundamental rethinking of its logical techniques, scientific communication and commitment strategies, and perceived role in the public sphere—giving rise to the new realm of "transformative science."

2.16.2. Innovation and Technology Development

New breakthroughs and technological advancements, such as digitization, are now having a substantial impact on several subject areas of the global economy. They not only have an impact on equality, work, production, recreation, behavior, education, and government, but they are also widening cultural and social divides.

Understanding how new technologies interact with and are used by society, as well as the consequences of this, is critical to equipping innovations to help social orders and inhabitants' prosperity. The main difficulty is determining how governments can maximize the benefits of innovation and technological growth as the world moves toward ultimate sustainability.

2.16.3. Economy and Society

Modern society is focused on the manner in which social orders organize their economic activities, as well as the significance of this process for long-term growth. The socio-economic framework is directly implicated in sustaining a worldwide quandary such as inescapable and expanding societal disparities, widespread hardship, and restricted social and cultural flexibility. Furthermore, the manner in which the social sector prepares and promotes its economic activities has substantial consequences for the transition to dematerialized production and consumption patterns, as well as the sustainable use of land, water, and natural resources.

Because the economy is deeply embedded in both social and biophysical systems, it must be analyzed holistically. This necessitates a systems examination strategy and interdisciplinary research structures incorporating a variety of various logical ways and procedures to depict grasp and explain, as well as illustrate economic, political, and environmental advancements.

Given the present societal concerns that are being pushed by dominating economic frameworks and structures, it is critical to identify alternative solutions to these issues and demonstrate the power of system thinking in advancing various socioeconomic points of view and possibilities.

2.16.4. Population and Behavioral Change

Over the last decades, socioeconomic, and technical advancements have considerably improved human living standards and wealth. In any event, these benefits are not dispersed evenly between nations, regions, and communities, and population groupings. Such inequities impede economic development, progress, and, ultimately, the achievement of sustainability.

Furthermore, many of the new challenges we confront now are the result of previous efforts to enhance and improve the human situation. Not only did socioeconomic improvement lead to lower birth rates and longer life spans, resulting in population aging; it also prompted lifestyle and nutritional modifications, resulting in upward or downward swings in death rates from chronic, non-transmittable, and degenerative illnesses (Figure 2.10).

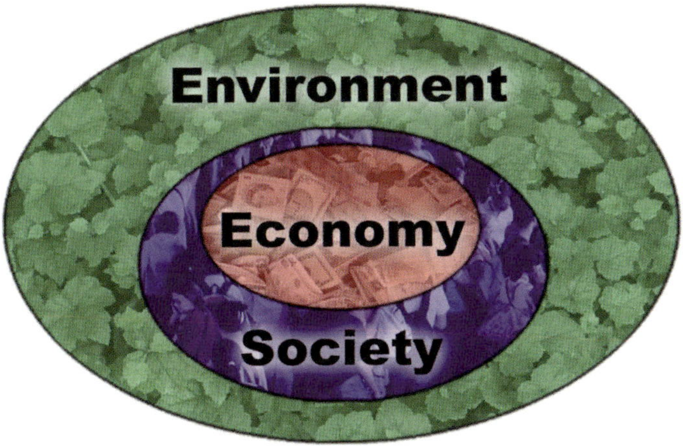

Figure 2.10. Relation between economy society and environment.

Source: Image by pixabay.com.

Such changes in lifestyle and consumption aggravate global climate change, whereas environmental change has an impact on human and social prosperity. Transformations in economic and social systems need changes in personal behavior, which has tremendous potential for advancing toward sustainability in cost-effective ways, as well as larger and coming technology advancements like those from the COVID-19 pandemic.

Apparently, the best method to deal with such changes is to Figure out how to inspire the necessary large-scale and prevalent behavioral change by investigating holistic and blended approaches that include social sciences, natural sciences, and engineering.

2.17. SECONDARY APPROACHES

2.17.1. Equity and Resilience

Humans are both the cause and the effect of the majority of global developments. This confirms the presence of system dangers that are likely to spread across interrelated socioeconomic systems and impose insurmountable burdens on the poor and vulnerable people.

Extreme weather conditions, forced people movements, food, and water shortages, pandemics, marine, and air pollution, biodiversity loss, and financial instabilities that may lead to a financial crisis are all potential sources of these dangers. Projections show that these hazards will increase significantly, resulting in a predicted loss in social resilience.

Based on this context, it is critical to understand how population and socioeconomic pressures, individual, and group activities (i.e., values, beliefs, norms, and cultures), and community diversity (e.g., rural, and urban) influence potential intercessions to improve the versatility, equality, and manageability of human societies.

Furthermore, it is often assumed that societal division mostly results in policy check or reformulation, a scenario that must be remedied by stronger partnerships between socioeconomic systems and governance systems.

2.17.2. Production and Consumption

Inequality and unsustainable consumerism define patterns of resource use and the creation of products. The test for civilizations is to modify the existing model of creating products and consuming commodities, which causes the economy to divorce economic progress and social wellbeing for people from environmental deterioration while also depleting the earth's resources.

This necessitates a concerted effort on the part of public and private sector executives. Patterns such as digitization can either favorably or adversely contribute to sustainability by increasing productivity or increasing resource consumption in the manufacturing, transportation, and commerce sectors. It is critical to enhancing end-user designs on a vast scale throughout the world.

More integrated technologies are needed to promote circular economies that are defined by using fewer raw materials, components, and products to cut costs and possibly transition to renewable resources.

2.17.3. Biodiversity and Ecosystems

In the face of changing climate and high resource consumption pressures by humans and animals, particularly on food, fiber, fodder, and other bio-products, current unsustainable land use and water consumption are reducing the quality and levels of fresh-water and ground-water levels, contributing to land degradation, biodiversity losses, unbalanced ecosystems, and contributing 25% of global greenhouse gas emissions.

Warm-blooded and cold-blooded creatures on land and in water have declined by roughly 60% in the last 40 years and may risk extinction. Furthermore, about 800 million people are still hungry and lack access to safe water.

According to the United Nations, food production should be increased by 50% to meet the demands of projected population growth by 2050 to land, water, food, and biodiversity across all sectors and strategy levels are critical to solving climate change-related difficulties caused by biodiversity and ecosystem losses.

2.18. CONCLUSION

Sustainable development is a central concept for our age. The term sustainable development is usually used to refer to practices that are reputed to be more environmentally sound than others (Heinberg, 2007). Achieving sustainable development on our crowded, unequal, and degraded planet is the most important challenge facing our generation.

Thus, we arrive at sustainable development. As the concept developed, it shifted its focus more towards economic development, social development and environmental protection for future generations. It seems that the super-rich also jostles for their place on the world's rankings of richest people. It's a lot to ask for, and there is no shortage of challenges to achieving sustainable development in practice.

There is much debate about the concept of sustainable development with diverse sectors of the economy ascribing different meanings to it. Notice that sustainable development recommends a holistic framework, in which society aims for economic, social, and environmental goals. These billions of people are looking for their foothold in the world economy.

The world economy is not only remarkably unequal but also remarkably threatening to the planet itself. Is there a way to change course, a way to combine economic development with environmental sustainability? The world's multinational companies are often the most powerful actors.

While the modern concept of sustainable development is derived mostly from the 1987 Brundtland Report, it is also rooted in earlier ideas about sustainable forest management and twentieth-century environmental concerns. In truth, such a comparison is not all that meaningful, since most of the world economy today consists of goods and services that did not even exist 250 years ago.

REFERENCES

1. (2013). *World Economic and Social Survey 2013: Sustainable Development Challenges.* [e-Book] United Nations publication. Available at: https://sustainabledevelopment.un.org/content/documents/2843WESS2013.pdf (accessed on 21 June 2022).
2. Gautam, P., Kumar, S., & Lokhandwala, S., (2019). Energy-aware intelligence in megacities. *Current Developments in Biotechnology and Bioengineering,* 211–238. [online] Available at: https://www.sciencedirect.com/science/article/pii/B9780444640833000117 (accessed on 21 June 2022).
3. Gilberto, G., (2003). *A Systems Approach to Sustainability and Sustainable Development.* [e-Book] Santiago, Chile: United Nations Publication. Available at: https://repositorio.cepal.org/bitstream/handle/11362/5759/S033119_en.pdf (accessed on 21 June 2022).
4. Imasiku, K., (2021). Organizational insights, challenges and impact of sustainable development in developing and developed nations. *Sustainable Organizations-Models, Applications, and New Perspectives.* [online] Available at: https://www.intechopen.com/chapters/73366 (accessed on 21 June 2022).
5. Newton, A., (2012). A systems approach for sustainable development in coastal zones. *Ecology and Society, 17*(3). [online] Available at: https://www.researchgate.net/publication/231547736_A_Systems_Approach_for_Sustainable_Development_in_Coastal_Zones (accessed on 21 June 2022).

CHAPTER 3

ECONOMIC EMPOWERMENT MODELS

CONTENTS

The Circular Economy (CE) method has been led by research, which depicts the world as a circular, closed system with finite resources, in which the economy and the environment should coexist. CE has garnered considerable attention from scholars, politicians, and businesses because of its relevance and predicted influence on sustainability.

The European Circular Economy package demonstrates the EU's commitment to a CE. On the other side, entrepreneurs are becoming aware of the CE's business model prospects. At the same time, they emphasis the "need to promote a bigger contribution of researchers from the Business and Economics sector to investigate the viability and profitability of CE strategies and related managerial practices to solve related difficulties."

3.1. INTRODUCTION

The circular economy (CE) is regarded as a critical paradigm for industrial economics pursuing long-term growth. CE is recognized "as a strategy for balancing objectives for economic expansion and environmental conservation" in relation to the restrictions of the take–make–use–dispose of linear economy.

Despite the fact that CE's global pursuit requires additional engagement, it is claimed in that "CE provides a reliable framework towards radically improving the current business model towards preventive and regenerative eco-industrial development as well as increased wellbeing based on recovered environmental integrity."

To shift an economic paradigm from production—consumption—waste to production-consumption—reuse, numerous stakeholders, including producers, consumers, and legislators, must be involved and committed. Value co-creation between various players is important to the success of this economic model, which is intended to have a good influence on the social life of the community, the sufficiency of the economy, and the natural environment (Figure 3.1).

Figure 3.1. High-level political forum (HLPF) side event—high level panel on women's economic empowerment.

Source: Image by flickr.

According to their comprehensive literature review, the CE "is seen as a requirement for resilience, a favorable relationship or a trade-off" The authors define CE as a "regenerative system in which resource input and waste, emission, and energy leakage are minimized by slowing, closing, and narrowing material and energy loops," and they define sustainability as "the balanced integration of economic performance, social inclusion, and environmental adaptability, for such benefit of present and future generations."

Most academics have focused on assessing the influence of a CE on natural environment progress. Other academics have concentrated on examining the CE in terms of an integrated view of sustainability, which includes not just the environmental effect, but also the social and economic impact.

When assessing the enhancement of the community's social life, several researchers include expanded career prospects. Other scholars have expanded on other aspects of the CE's influence on social life, such as an efficient tax system or changes in consumer behavior.

Many experts have examined and investigated the CE's influence on society, the economy, and the environment, as well as boosting consumer awareness and advocating the creation of circular creative business models and governmental laws to support them.

Collaboration via the quadruple helix is another facilitator of CE, in addition to business model innovation and responsible consumers. The suggested conceptual framework of the integrated CE, which is a theoretical framework made of two complimentary structures, is the study's uniqueness.

The first structure is dedicated to the importance of a quadruple helix model in CE support. This has been generated and substantially supported by literature findings, but is not considered to be assessed in this article, whereas the second structure includes the three-tiered concept of sustainable development—social–environmental–economic—with innovation at the core as a crucial driver to CE.

The innovation of this article, in addition to the suggested framework of an integrated CE, is the linkage of the CE variables with each of the sustainable development aspects: social–environmental–economic. Although some limited studies have used panel data to quantify the influence of CE on GDP, such as, none of them have examined the CE variables to be connected with the three pillars of sustainable development.

Finally, to cross-check the results and enhance the conclusions, this study employs two distinct approaches: the fixed effect method and generalized methods of moments (GMM). If the fixed effect technique is extensively used but occasionally challenged, the GMM employing the Arellano–Bond criteria is a more robust method.

Anticipating the possible economic, environmental, and social consequences of proposed policy is a critical stage of SIA. This is only possible for long-term and complicated policy issues using mathematical or computer-based models. However, there are various techniques to economic–environmental or integrated modeling, and it is difficult for policymakers to determine which is best suited for any given setting.

Our goal here is to assist users in selecting the best modeling tool for a certain sustainable development challenge and in better understanding what type of information can be expected from the models. This topic has received very little attention in the literature (Figure 3.2).

Figure 3.2. 2018 women's empowerment principles forum.

Source: Image by flickr.

The only work in this journal that addresses a comparable subject is van den Bergh and Nijkamp (1991), but there is no standard technique for evaluating the strengths and limitations of various modeling systems for sustainable development policy-making. Our contribution is to develop a formal methodological framework to address this challenge, which we will then apply to existing modeling paradigms and two policy sectors.

This is a decision-making dilemma. It is concerned with the identification of possible alternatives (the various modeling approaches and tools), the selection of criteria to assess them, the assessment itself in relation to the criteria, the weighting of the criteria, and, finally, the aggregation of the partial assessments (on each criterion) in an overall assessment. This is, roughly, how we will go in this article.

Several modeling methodologies will be evaluated in two stages: first in terms of generic criteria closely connected to sustainable development, and then in terms of policy issues (energy, land use, and transportation regulations) viewed through the lens of sustainable development. Six modeling paradigms will be evaluated, initially on an a priori basis.

Six modeling paradigms will be evaluated, first on an a priori and general basis, and then in relation to two specific policy contexts (energy policy and land use and transportation planning). To determine the most applicable evaluation criteria, we begin by emphasizing what is unique to sustainable development. The modeling paradigms are then purely a priori compared to these criteria and graded in terms of their prospective effectiveness in dealing with sustainable development concerns.

This ranking's robustness is then tested in two particular policy contexts: energy policy on the one hand, and land use and transportation policy on the other. These policy areas are viewed as groupings of more tangible challenges (such as resource exhaustion and energy reliance in the case of energy), each representing the essence of sustainability at different levels. The comparative suitability of the varied modeling techniques to these policy areas is considered as a function of:

- The degree to which the policy domains embody sustainable development characteristics; and
- The degree to which the modeling paradigms are capable of dealing with these characteristics. Finally, we examine actual modeling techniques in the two policy sectors to determine if they support our findings on the utility of various modeling paradigms.

3.2. METHODOLOGICAL ANSWERS TO DECISION-MAKING IN SUSTAINABILITY

As a type of objective decision-making, policymaking combines two distinct types of intellectual movement: knowing and assessing. In its most basic form, it expects us to:

- Recognize prospective options, activities, plans, or initiatives;
- Select major guidelines for evaluating their performance;
- Alternatively, assess the measurements in terms of their relative exceptional quality;
- Assess the various possibilities for measures in relation to the criteria;
- Alternatively, interpret the evaluation as an incomplete utility worth;
- Sort the alternatives based on their overall utility; and

- Select the best option or, alternatively, restart the interaction procedure from the beginning.

The goal of these models in the decision-making process is to predict how the system will react to policy instruments given behavioral and structural limitations. Policymaking for sustainable development is a unique type of decision-making for three reasons. First, the objectives are not provided in advance, as the definition of the aims and objectives is part of the decision-making problem.

Second, there is no single decision-maker, but rather a group of decision-makers, each with their own preferences, goals, expectations, and beliefs. Third, determining the costs and benefits of sustainability concerns is far more complicated than it is for regular firms.

This third reason is of special relevance to us since it is connected to three important characteristics that are present in all sustainability challenges, namely the presence of externalities, the presence of uncertainties, and the interaction of humans and nature. Externalities can be of several forms, including geographical (e.g., for a global contaminant), intertemporal (e.g., across generations), and social (e.g., between social categories) (Figure 3.3).

As a result, sustainable development challenges arise when certain human groups do not bear the full cost of their production and consumption practices, but instead pass the costs on to other human groups that are socially, physically, or temporally distant, with inadequate, if any, recompense. The presence of pervasive uncertainty is the second characteristic.

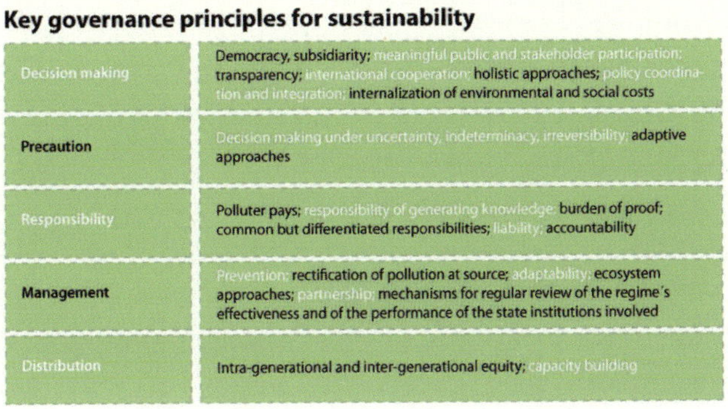

Key governance principles for sustainability

Decision making	Democracy, subsidiarity; meaningful public and stakeholder participation; transparency; international cooperation; holistic approaches; policy coordination and integration; internalization of environmental and social costs
Precaution	Decision making under uncertainty, indeterminacy, irreversibility; adaptive approaches
Responsibility	Polluter pays; responsibility of generating knowledge; burden of proof; common but differentiated responsibilities; liability; accountability
Management	Prevention; rectification of pollution at source; adaptability; ecosystem approaches; partnership; mechanisms for regular review of the regime's effectiveness and of the performance of the state institutions involved
Distribution	Intra-generational and inter-generational equity; capacity building

Figure 3.3. Key governance principles for sustainability.

Source: Image by flickr.

The higher the likelihood that the intended policy will have a long-term and/or unanticipated impact, the greater the uncertainty around its cost-benefit balance and the greater the chance that it will have far-reaching and long-term negative implications.

The third fundamental aspect is the interaction between natural or environmental processes and human activity because there is a conflict between human behaviors and natural processes in practically every sustainability issue. Many scholars contend that this is the primary, if not the only, definition of sustainable development.

Actually, because the first two qualities are present, the third is merely one of the characteristics of a sustainability challenge. What is critical for our research is that each characteristic necessitates a distinct methodological response; these responses are precisely the criteria we seek to assess the fitness of the modeling techniques.

It is vital to clarify what models demand sustainable development from a modeling standpoint, and what conditions must be met for models to be more adapted to sustainable development only then would it be feasible to assess the advantages and disadvantages of various modeling paradigms.

3.3. FIVE METHODOLOGICAL CRITERIA

3.3.1. Interdisciplinary Approach

Interdisciplinary' has multiple meanings in the area of applied modeling. To begin with, it implies that the model's state variables must be relevant to more than one scientific subject. To put it another way, it is not enough to consider the influence of changes in state variables belonging to a particular field on, say, environmental indicators to be credited with an interdisciplinary approach.

A truly multidisciplinary model should remove the black box that exists between core variables and impact indicators and include the impact indicators into the model's kernel. In other words, the model should provide feedback between variables of varying ontological natures.

Adopting a meta-theoretical vocabulary in which every discipline statement may be recast is another strategy to assure interdisciplinarity. The most significant contender is general system theory (Bunge, 1977). It may be viewed as a trans-disciplinary framework, that is, one in which assertions and variables from several disciplines can be merged rather than simply placed side by side.

Furthermore, from a pragmatic standpoint, a truly interdisciplinary approach necessitates the development of situations as well as the interpretation of outcomes to be the product of an interdisciplinary discourse in which all important disciplines own a say.

3.3.2. Uncertainty

In a modeling context, epistemological ambiguity could be divided into three categories: lack of certainty about a model's quantities (the parameters and initial conditions); uncertainty about a model's structure (the relationships among factors, functional forms, causal influences, delays, and so on); as well as indecision about a model's pertinence (it is a level of granularity, selection of variables, closeness, time scale, etc.).

Sensitivity analysis and traditional statistical approaches are only useful when dealing with quantitative uncertainty. This is also true for scenarios, which are defined as collections of coherent hypotheses about the likely values of various parameters considered together.

Except for fairly modern statistical approaches such as Bayesian model averaging, the only option to lessen the two main types of uncertainty is to expand our scientific understanding.

3.3.3. Long-Term Perspective

A long-term view does not always imply that models should have a time range of several hundred years. What is more crucial from the standpoint of modeling is that diverse time spans be completely integrated and that a time period long enough to allow the unfolding of the system's whole dynamics (natural cycles, business cycles, etc.) be used (Figure 3.4).

Figure 3.4. Inhabitants of Plachimada protest outside the Coca-Cola factory in their village.

Source: Image by blogs.sussex.ac.uk.

Because what counts in terms of sustainable development is intra- and intergenerational fairness, the generation (however, defined) is a suitable duration unit for assessing sustainability. In economics, for example, overlapping generation models are beneficial in this regard without requiring adopting a long-term perspective.

3.3.4. Global–Local Perspective

At the political level, the global-local approach, or g-locality, is connected to the well-known adage to think globally and act locally. As previously stated, the requirement for a multi-level approach derives from the fact that spatial externalities are ubiquitous. However, from a methodological standpoint, it is also related to the pervasive difficulty of the micro-macro connection.

Most scientific fields, including theoretical physics, still lack comprehensive or totally adequate solutions to problems such, as "How does the macro-level originate from micro-level processes?" T, how does the macro-level shape or restrict micro-level processes? d and t how much autonomy do the various hierarchical levels have?

3.3.5. Participation

Stakeholder engagement cannot be regarded a methodological necessity for modeling activities in a strictly scientific environment. However, applied modeling in a policy-making environment is not the same as pure science.

Bunge (1995) first advocated for participation in such a context, arguing that the design of any effective economic policy cannot be left in the hands of economic specialists, but must result from the collaborative efforts of experts in a number of related disciplines, as well as representatives of the sectors likely to be affected by the plan's implementation.

This quotation becomes even more relevant when the word 'economic' is substituted by the phrase sustainable development.' To enable public engagement, a model must be as simple as possible., allowing for the incorporation of stakeholders' values and objectives, and enabling simulation output communication.

3.4. CANDIDATE MODELS FOR SUSTAINABLE DEVELOPMENT POLICY-MAKING

Six types of models commonly used in socioeconomic policy-making have been chosen for consideration: macro-econometric models, computable general equilibrium models, optimization models, system dynamics models, probabilistic or Bayesian network models (this category also includes risk assessment models based on influence diagrams), and multi-agent simulation models (Figure 3.5).

Figure 3.5. World leaders at the United Nations conference on sustainable development.

Source: Image by Wikimedia commons.

The first three are mainstream, well-known economic or technical models that are commonly employed in policymaking. The remaining three are less prevalent, with the exception of system dynamics models, which are common in environmental science and natural resource management. Let us simply outline the major characteristics of these models.

- For roughly twenty-five years, macro-econometric models have been widely used to simulate national economies in order to anticipate short- or medium-term profiles and to evaluate economic policy.

A macro-econometric model is a simulation system of simultaneous equations (usually with a neo-Keynesian flavor) evaluated using statistical processes on time series or cross-sectional data. They have been expanded to include environmental characteristics, particularly those related to energy use and production.

- Neoclassical economic theory underpins computational general equilibrium (CGE) models. National economies are shown as interconnected markets in equilibrium, with prices assuring the clearing of demand and supply in each.

The interrelationships between productive sectors are depicted using an input-output matrix, just as in macro-econometric models, however, unlike macro-econometric models, CGE models are calibrated rather than experimentally tested.

CGE models are long-term in nature, with the primary goal of policy analysis rather than forecasting. The European GEM-38 model, as well as EPPA, GTAP, and MERGE, are well-known examples of CGE modeling in the energy market.

- Centralized optimization models are primarily used to make technology selection decisions: considering an objective function (generally the minimization of operational and fixed costs) and some constraints on technological availability, prices, and so forth, the model recognizes that what technologies must be selected to get it as close towards the objective as possible.

Therefore, unlike simulation models, optimization models are essentially normative rather than descriptive. MARKAL-TIMES12 is a good example of energy policy.

- All models based on general system theory are classified as system dynamics. In reality, the majority of system models in the literature are expressed in terms of levels (stocks), rates (flows), and auxiliaries, i.e., in the Forresterian dialect of general system theory. This is most likely due to the fact that the most widely used and least priced system simulation software (Stella, Powersim, Vensim, and so on) are written in this dialect.

The system dynamics method is far more common in environmental sciences than in economics or political science, where it has a negative image as a result of certain early unethical implementations. Systems dynamic models, on the other hand, have several applications in management sciences as well as climate and energy policy.

- Multi-agent simulation is a relatively recent modeling method. It differs from other types of models in that it is stated in terms of agents, objects, and environments rather than variables, functions, or equations. The components of multi-agent models are autonomous entities that interact with one another and with an artificial environment.

Multi-agent models are frequently portrayed as artificial communities or artificial ecosystems (Epstein and Axtell, 1996). Many multi-agent modeling applications may be seen in the online Publication of Artificial Societies and Social Simulation.

- Bayesian networks (Jensen, 1997) are risk-adjustment models that are based on influence diagrams (acyclic directed graphs) and probability theory.

The combination of a graphical representation of causal chains between events or variables and an inference mechanism that allows information to be processed from (the probability of) causes to (the probability of) effects (or the other way around) makes the Bayesian network a useful tool for a variety of tasks in a probabilistic framework, including early warning, diagnosis, prediction, and simulation.

Boulanger et al., (2004) discuss applications of Bayesian networks to food security and famine early warning, and Bacon et al., (2004) discuss applications to land use management (2002). However, Microsoft's Office assistance system is the most frequently utilized but generally unrecognized Bayesian network.

3.5. MODEL IMPLICATIONS OF INTERGENERATIONAL CONSIDERATIONS

The time horizon is one of the elements of models that can contain intergenerational issues. the social welfare and bequest functions, the social rate of discount, and any applicable limitations Stocks, controls, stock changes, and integrals are all classed as stocks.

3.5.1. Time-Horizon and Intergenerational Welfare Comparison

In general, the time horizon in a sustainable development study is long, spanning at least two generations. Long-term behavior—trends and structural changes—and stability concerns at both the economic and ecological system levels are important for long-term results in sustainable development.

Unfortunately, it is difficult to incorporate short-term adjustment processes after deviations from equilibrium with long-term equilibrium trends and structural change in a single modeling framework. Models are either suited to short-term data and are only capable of representing short-term processes, or they are oriented toward long-term data gathered in the most precise manner. The second sort of model will almost certainly include highly unpredictable parameter values, functional forms, and even relations, which must be compensated for via scenario analysis. These models must be viewed qualitatively rather than predictably. A social welfare function acts as an assessment criterion for the identification of social decisions, which may rank all feasible states in an ideal setting (Figure 3.6).

Figure 3.6. UN media forum on sustainable development goals (SDGs) in Addis Ababa, Ethiopia.

Source: Image by flickr.

To combine individual utility functions allowing intergenerational comparisons, the cardinal significance condition on utility functions is required, as does the selection of a discount factor. The additive, the separable utility function is one possible option of an aggregate welfare function that is justified by several moral theories [namely, Classical Utilitarianism and Intuit ideas (Dasgupta and Heal, 1979)].

To represent the unpredictable exogenously determined period of extinction of the human species on Earth, the temporal horizon for continuous time could be defined as a distribution with a probability density function p(T).

3.5.2. Discounting for Intergenerational Comparisons

Discounting is a recurring topic in talks about intergenerational equality. Ethical concerns with high or positive discount rates have centered on the impact of pushing expenses to future generations and providing fewer incentives for long-term initiatives (especially environmentally favorable projects). However, the third effect of low-interest rates is slow growth as a result of insufficient investment in general.

This may be helpful to the environment due to the negative impact on resource consumption and residual emissions. As a result, the intergenerational equity and environmental goals do not appear to be perfectly aligned in this case. Discounting may be used only if the criterion for intergenerational evaluation is an additive, separable utility function (benefit-cost analysis in an operational context).

As a result, classical utilitarianism is the foundation of discounting. Discounting cannot be coupled with minimax criteria or with social welfare functions that include nonlinear or interaction utility components. Time preferences, investment possibilities, and uncertainty concerns all play a role in determining a societal discount rate.

If a social rate of time preference (consumption rate of interest) and a social opportunity cost rate can be calculated, the social rate of discount may be calculated as a weighted average of the two, adjusted for risk by adding a social risk premium..' Then two issues occur. First, it is unclear how a given weighting scheme should be justified.

Second, calculating the social time preference rate, social opportunity cost rate, and social risk premium presents some conceptual and practical challenges. When a society is not perceived to be impatient, the social time preference might be regarded to be meaningless. Individual pure time preferences are hence considered non-transferable to communities.

Furthermore, there is a conceptual distinction between discounting over relatively short time periods (shorter than the normal lifetime) and depreciating across multigenerational time spans Therefore, one may argue that predicted consumption growth rates, as well as the elasticity of the marginal utility of consumption, should be included in order to get a positive time preference.

In a perfect market, the opportunity cost will tend to be equal to the time preference rate, i.e., the market interest rate. This is one of the reasons for focusing on opportunity costs. The difficulty of deviating from the opportunity cost rate is one argument for focusing on it for social discounting: a higher rate implies that fewer projects will be approved; a lower rate may result in too many projects being financed.

The opportunity principle may also establish a link between the discount rate and the method of funding an investment.as part of a specific project as a result, the discount rate can be fixed to be equal to

- The social opportunity cost rate, compensated for imperfect markets and inefficiencies, if project funds are acquired through the capital market; or
- The social time choice rate (interest rate on consumption) when consumption is sacrificed (taxes).

Costs and benefits may also be utilized, with presumably differing societal rates of subjective value. However, variable rates across various investment projects may result in financial crowding out. Finally, the opportunity cost concept may only apply to small-scale, short-term initiatives; if used in large-scale, government, or long-term projects, it should only be compared to other long-term projects, resulting in reduced opportunity cost rates.

Both sorts of initiatives must be completed and must not compete with one another. It may suggest that the discount rate plays just a minimal influence. Incorporating 'pure' risk into the discount rate is quite restricted (and even more so for other forms of uncertainty), as it provides just one method of dealing with risk, namely as a negative exponential path (Figure 3.7).

Figure 3.7. International collaboration in science and technology for sustainable development.

Source: Image by flickr.

Even if risk 'increases monotonically,' a negative exponential pattern is extremely implausible. As a result, more adaptable frameworks are required. Discount rates have the potential to be overlooked in considerations of intertemporal and intergenerational distributions. Then we must accept that temporal preference only applies to people, not groups, and certainly not for multigenerational assessment.

Risk can be addressed in more suitable ways than just adjusting discount rates. Thus, just the opportunity cost concept must be considered, taking into account the comments stated above about its application. The other factors stated might be left out or included in different ways, including external and intangible consequences. A multi-purpose discount factor has the primary advantage of simplifying the model structure.

3.5.3. Intergenerational Constraints

Intergenerational considerations, in addition to an assessment criterion, may necessitate the inclusion of constraints in a model, referring to, for example, values of state variables at T; stocks, stock changes, or controls; and integrals or sums across the time of variables or functions of variables. Stock conditions can be used to calculate flow conditions.

The unit of time is significant for intergenerational comparisons. If one unit corresponds to a human generation, the dynamic system is plainly not flexible enough to explain smooth adjustment processes. Of course, processes in actuality are susceptible to varying rates of internal dynamics and feedback loops, so the difference between stocks and flows is rather arbitrary.

Because this is especially important when using long-term perspectives, different forms of flow can be used in intergenerational models. In a model, ions on the beginning and ultimate values of state variables. If the time-horizon T is finite, a condition for acceptable state values at time T can ensure that future generations have the endowments and skills to meet their demands to an acceptable level.

Every generation may optimize societal welfare over a finite time span using a moving forward approach. The previous generation would then decide the conditions on the starting states, while the current generation would define the end conditions and act as starting conditions on states for the following generation.

As a result, the optimization issue with an indefinite time horizon may be approximated progressively using a combination of sub-problems with limited horizons linked by the beginning and end-state conditions of the corresponding dynamic equations the issue is transferred to the ethical quandary of determining stock conditions at some future point in time.

3.5.4. Regional Models for Sustainable Development

A meso-level of analysis that is also in harmony with administrative possibilities is important in light of the necessity for operational policies. A meso-level has the following advantages: interactions and feedback mechanisms are more easily traceable than at the global level; environmental decision-making can be guided more easily by a regional governmental agency, and regions have specific problems or capacities that should be addressed in their appropriate context and level of detail.

In general, the term "sustainable development" refers to rather large geographical units (e.g., continents, countries). The geographical delineation of a region from the standpoint of sustainable development is far from simple since a balance between functional economic and ecological sectors must be reached.

The choice will be influenced by data availability: if economic data at various levels are plentiful. It is feasible to allow ecological coherence to influence regional delineation and vice versa. To integrate the two, one may aim to limit cross-border economic-demographic and physical-ecological fluxes. The major distinction between a global or closed system and a regional or open system is that the latter is exposed to cross-border flows and has external drivers of internal processes. Cross-border flows can be classified as monetary-economic or physical-ecological. External influences have an impact on regional development. One region may be simulated individually, subject to specific assumptions about these flows and drivers.

- There is a balance of material cross-boundary flows;
- Internal and external flows are closed through cross-boundary flows; and
- There are no cross-boundary flows.

External determinants might be based on certain growth patterns anticipated outside the region that fit into the structure of a multiregional system's sustainable development. Moreover, in a multinational context, one is free to pursue inter-regional distribution policies or to extend compensation for negative impacts on the environment of regional growth to a multiregional setting (leading to the notion of complementary development).

If additional areas participate in this manner, we have a top-down model in which supply and demand are resolved at the national scale. Spatial spill-overs are an issue that develops when a regional utility measure (e.g., regional welfare) is maximized. For example, from a national perspective, the shadow costs of, say, pollution do not accurately represent scarcity (Figure 3.8).

Figure 3.8. The different elements of sustainability according to the definition used by the sustainability week Switzerland.

Source: Image by Wikimedia commons.

This will result in various places overusing or underusing products and services in production and consumption, resulting in an unfavorable dispersion of pollution. For an operational example, national limits on the behavior of regional authorities may compel a solution, as may negotiation between regions.

To address the spatial equality issue, one can establish a minimal level of overall regional wellbeing by employing relevant indicators (e.g., income, natural vegetation, resources, and pollution per capita or per m^2 regional area).

3.5.5. Multiple Use and Models

Since populations, natural resources, or ecosystems may serve many roles, economic players can exploit them in multiple ways at the same time. When such activities do not conflict in both economic and ecological terms, they can be treated separately. Nevertheless, activities frequently interfere, whether in a competitive or complementary manner.

We are discussing the notion of multiple usages, which can take several forms. For starters, ecosystems, people, and resources may provide comparable services for both natural and commercial activity. A species that serves as both a natural and a human predator (e.g., some fisheries) is an example. Second, numerous individual human players may use resources in a similar fashion.

Congestion and inefficient results, such as in open-access or common-property usage of an area, environment, or population, may then occur. Their solution may need the creation of a social agency that regulates the resource and its use. Third, the services provided by natural systems or resources to human actors might vary greatly.

As a result, conflicts between users with quite diverse agendas may arise. Conflicts between recreational and commercial users of lakes, woods, or fisheries are common examples. The social benefits of such activities might then be compared to arrive at a solution. Finally, a resource system may derive a variety of roles and traits that are potentially useful to both human actors and natural processes.

A forest, for example, supplies timber, recreational opportunities, and a stable flora and fauna. Water precipitation and evaporation management, assimilation functions, a pollutant reservoir, and so forth. Economic activities and natural processes can be autonomous, competing (the most severe situation is mutual exclusivity), complimentary, or commutative when consuming or altering a resource base.

Many of these multiple-use occurrences may be addressed by developing models that take into account the various potential uses as well as the potential ecological and economic consequences. As a result, possible conflicts between uses and the possibility of trade-offs between them are effectively depicted. A generic form can be presented by merging the economics and ecology of a multiple-use situation.

One method is to find the best combination of human activities (using benefit-cost analysis) while keeping in mind the needed levels of natural functions, the interacting economic-ecological flows and consequences, and the ecosystem's internal dynamic processes. A multi-objective programming issue is a second generic formulation of multiple usages, with each economic and ecological activity or function generating one or more objectives.

Multiple uses are a transitional strategy to sustainable development that exists between the single use of a single resource and the economically and environmentally intertwined patterns of numerous uses of multiple resources.

3.6. ECONOMIC-ECOLOGICAL INTEGRATION: DYNAMIC MODELS

Economics and environment are not only distinct subjects of study but have also given rise to distinct fields. As a result, many of their theoretical notions and approaches disagree. Furthermore, the approaches utilized to operationalize theoretical concepts, conduct empirical investigations, and test hypotheses are not necessarily the same.

However, some relationships may be seen, for example, between the sub-disciplines dealing with a more aggregate treatment of subjects of research, namely macroeconomics and synecology, in both of which the deductive technique has prevailed. Moreover, although both professions have limited opportunities for experimentation, ecology has more than economics.

The use of formal models to explain and link processes in different domains is a sensible approach to integration. To some extent, methodological distinctions are avoided in this manner, although specialized collected discipline knowledge is employed to construct the structure of the model, choose the elements, and characterize their interactions (Figure 3.9).

Figure 3.9. 8th session of the Africa regional forum on sustainable development.

Source: Image by flickr.

It is obvious that concurrent study of environmental concerns or economic-environmental interconnections is now conceivable. A model that is relevant for gaining insight into sustainable development concerns or tracking sustainable development routes must meet a set of minimum requirements. The following factors may help to clarify this:

- A comprehensive or broad strategy, as opposed to a partial one, should be used since it is relevant for long-term horizons. In the long run, the entire economic system should be represented in some form, and the description of the natural environment should be consistent with it.
- Economic productive and consumptive activities have an influence on the natural environment in terms of material extraction, waste emission and pollution, and non-material disruptions. More specifically, one must consider:
  - the extraction of non-renewable, biotic, and abiotic renewable resources;
  - agricultural activities affecting groundwater and soils such as fertilizing, pesticide use, irrigation, drainage, and plowing;

  - the use of terrestrial and aquatic ecosystems for recreational purposes;
  - land use and the patterns and infrastructure involved; and
  - pollution and waste disposal, with a special focus on toxins, reactiveness, and dioxins.
- The presence of a feedback loop from the environment to the economy. This comprises a variety of characteristics such as recreation and tourism, landscape values, tranquility, and irritation. In order to adequately describe long-term processes in economic systems, feedback on ecological repercussions of general economic activity on the economic system must be included.

Feedback to decision-making on productive activities, for example, may be included, among other things. via perceptions of resource scarcity and pollution levels, or overall destruction of nature.

- Additional services, including productive conditions (e.g., soil quality) and amenity services, should be provided as much as feasible, in addition to material or priced services. The latter may be incorporated into the assessment or welfare function, but also through behavioral feedback mechanisms. Thus, all multifunctional features of ecosystems may be addressed.
- Responsibility for coming generations must always be taken into account. For starters, this may mean that a judgement criterion is used to evaluate intergenerational distributions. Various circumstances may also assure fair intergenerational distribution.

If the consequences of intergenerational concern are viewed as behavioral rather than evaluative or restricting, it suggests that behavioral or policy feedbacks aimed at intergenerational equity are endogenous.

- A long-time horizon follows logically from the preceding argument. It means that short-term activities are eliminated wherever feasible to simplify the image. It also means that linear models will not be enough to describe all processes, and that scenario analyzes may be employed to cope with numerous conceivable tactics and policies.

Further. In the context of sustainable development, comparing static and dynamic studies are useful. Changes in preferences, for example, may be indicated by shifts in welfare function parameter values, or biological and ecological evolution by altering ecosystem characteristics.

- The ability to describe qualitative (structural) change, either implicitly or explicitly, should be possible. This implies that irreversible processes, thresholds, nonlinear structures, and time delays must be described. These methods can be augmented by risk analysis to deal with uncertainty openly in a number of ways.
- Physical restrictions should not be in contradiction with model assumptions. Limitations on replacement in production and utility functions should be considered. Furthermore, the interdependence of production factor substitution, investment, and technical growth must be evaluated concurrently. The assumptions of the model should not contradict thermodynamic rules. Material balances might be expressly included.
- In terms of specialized circumstances for long-term development. Over generations, we distinguish between limits on the amount of wellbeing (for an entire generation or per capita) and constraints on physical-ecological stocks and fluxes. In the first scenario, one may select between two kinds of conditions:
  - requiring welfare to always surpass some minimal level (e.g., a subsistence level); or
  - requiring a monotonous non-decreasing flow of benefit over time.

The second sort of circumstance may entail stock limits or fluxes in and out of economic and environmental systems. For example, the idea of stock constancy (or non-decreasing stocks) can be extended to the total of man-made economic and natural stocks, a stock concept such as environmental quality or environmental deterioration, the sum of all natural stocks (compensation principle), or each stock individually.

Instead of explicitly applying such stock conditions to a model, derived flow conditions might be used. These considerations highlight the importance of the dynamic aspect. A second significant aspect is a requirement for these models to incorporate environmental-ecological and economic phenomena.

The term 'economic-ecological' has been applied to models that employ quite diverse integration approaches it's been used in economic processes that include environmental variables (such as waste discharge or resource exploitation) as well as ecological process models which include economic variables (e.g., stress factors).

The above factors suggest that a more robust paradigm is required to deal with sustainable development, specifically one that integrates economic and ecological processes rather than an economic process and an isolated external ecological variable (or the contrary).

Many relationships may need to be included when modeling sustainable development. For starters, it includes subjective judgements on critical aspects. Second, any relationship is surrounded by ambiguity due to a lack of knowledge and facts. With numerous connections, this may have a detrimental influence on the overall model's dependability.

Finally, it is obvious that some processes and challenges inherent in sustainable development cannot be adequately addressed using mathematical modeling analysis. However, in many circumstances when well-executed modeling studies fail to further our understanding, alternative techniques frequently suffer from the same shortcoming.

3.7. TRANSFORMATION, CHANGE PROCESSES (AND BUSINESS MODELS)

It is believed that business transformation is the process of transforming an organization from its current state to a future one in accordance with a certain strategic goal (Hoyte & Greenwood, 2007). According to this viewpoint, process research focuses on changing phenomena, taking into consideration the significance of time and the nature of the process(es) of change (Langley, Smallman, Tsoukas, & Van De Ven, 2013).

From this vantage point, we believe it is critical to consider the practices and outcomes that underpin any BMfS; it is critical to comprehend and theories the dynamics of transformation and change that shape BMfS and how they are linked to business transformation and, ultimately, sustainable development.

This is significant because BMfS that contribute significantly to sustainable development must, by definition, involve continuous adaptation to the interaction between the socio-economic-technical-technical system of which the company's activities are a part and the conditions of the ecological contexts in which such a system works.

The literature on marketing strategies and BMfS has frequently invoked a stable model once developed rather than envisioning a business model's adaptation to different circumstances or the continuous change required by changing circumstances that are associated with the adaptive transformations that characterize sustainable development.

Cavalcante et al., (2011) propose four paradigms for business model transition. Business models can be formed where there is none previously existed; business models could be stretched in which businesses maintain their own existing model (s) whilst also introducing a new approach to complement it (them); business models can be revised to replace an existing model, and business models can be terminated to abandon an existing approach. The decision to terminate a business model is a highly strategic move in a corporation since it affects what the firm does and changes the status of management linked with the terminated model. By definition, business model alteration is always followed by closure.

This article focuses on the business model revision or the replacement of a current business model with a new model, and we investigate it in the context of businesses that have undergone significant, strategic whole-company transformational changes in order to combine economic performance with a contribution to sustainable development, which previously did not exist.

The redesign of a business model necessitates fundamental changes and is likely to face significant problems due to uncertainty and ambiguity, as well as a lack of information and skills (Cavalcante et al., 2011). Revision is inevitably linked to the dangers and uncertainties that come with a more dramatic change.

3.8. A FIRST APPLICATION: LAND USE AND TRANSPORT

The long-term effects of land use regulations are complex and all-encompassing. Mostly every land-use decision involves economic, environmental, and social ramifications. It has an impact on water, soil, air, biodiversity, transportation, energy, human health, safety, and wellbeing, social stratification and poverty, and amenities.

An evaluation of the influence of land use policies on each of these several systems or situations necessitates an interdisciplinary approach, uncertainty management, long-term views, dg-locality, and engagement. However, certain applications demand more from some characteristics than others, or, to put it another way, not every criterion is equally important for each of these systems or situations.

However, determining the proportional relevance of each criterion for any system is a challenging process. The results of a participation exercise, a discourse involving scientists from various fields and public employees from various administrative departments. They are only suggestions and should not be considered final. Furthermore, the statistics have no intrinsic worth; only the relative ordering of criteria and systems/problems as indicated by them should be taken into account. An evaluation of row totals provides us with a relative rating of challenges and systems in terms of sustainable development. Thus, water management and biodiversity (from a land-use policy standpoint) may be regarded as highly indicative of sustainable development issues because they score well on average for each criterion. Poverty, on the other hand, is a less common sustainable development issue (from a land use policy stance).

3.8.1. Current Practices in Land Use and Transport Modeling

Do existing modeling approaches in the field support these findings? They surely do in terms of centralized optimization methods: with the exception of a few transport-only models, such models are essentially non-existent in land use research. This is also true for Bayesian networks, maybe because of their novelty. There are no pure macro-econometric or CGE land use and transportation models, although many models blend these two techniques. The most often used tools (such as TRANUS21, MEPLAN22, DRAM/EMPAL (Putnam, 1992), and IRPUD23) integrate macro-econometric tools (input-output matrices, random utility models, entropy maximization, and so on) with a spatial (partial) equilibrium framework.

They are unquestionably cutting-edge in their area, yet they do have certain known flaws, most notably in terms of research methodologies. Furthermore, most land use and transportation models are woefully inadequate in terms of combining water management, biodiversity impacts, health, wellbeing, and poverty concerns. Energy is the only non-purely commercial sphere in which they integrate more or less successfully. This is a known issue, so much so that the European Commission has commissioned two major research projects to try to improve these models' capacities in addressing the environmental and socioeconomic implications of land use and transportation. The SPARTACUS and PROPOLIS24 projects attempt to integrate social, environmental, and economic variables into the MEPLAN model in order to examine the implications of land use decisions on sustainable development.

The simple inclusion of output indicators, on the other hand, does not correspond to our definition of interdisciplinarity as providing feedback between state variables of various ontological natures.

3.9. A SECOND APPLICATION: ENERGY

Over the years, the issue of energy has given birth to a significant number of researches on related areas of importance. The European Commission's recent perspective (2003) gives clear examples of the issues at stake and how they might be evaluated from a policy standpoint. However, there has been little consideration of the significance of these difficulties for policy-making on sustainable development.

The topics at stake in the energy discussion must be disentangled in our methodological framework. We thought about the following: Exhaustible resources, nuclear power, renewable resources, energy utility access, climate change, energy efficiency, and the influence on health.

The main point in our technique for the land use policy issue is that some of these concerns are more demanding than others on specific criteria and that each criterion does not have the same relevance for each of these difficulties. Both of these problems are addressed in terms of sustainable development (Figure 3.10).

Figure 3.10. Renewable energy–solar cell panels in the foreground, wind turbines in the middle ground, and electricity pylons in the background.

Source: Image by Wikimedia commons.

The ratings in the land use example originate from a participation exercise, although they should be viewed as mostly suggestive. Researchers have focused on five methodological features that are equally important in decision-making for sustainable development: multidisciplinary potential, long-term, and intergenerational concern, uncertainty management, local-global interaction, and stakeholder involvement.

Macro econometric models, computable general equilibrium models, optimization models, system dynamics models, multi-agent simulation models, and Bayesian network models have all been investigated. During interactive workshops attended by model users and builders, all were graded on an ordinal scale. What is novel is how we proceeded to evaluate the potential of the six alternatives for policy decisions in energy and land-use concerns.

Whatever arises is that not every modeling methodology are equally useful for policy-making on sustainable development. Most importantly, we explain why we ranked the way we did. Naturally, each model has its own usefulness, and there will never be a one-size-fits-all model.

What is vital is to understand how the models may be enhanced for sustainable development and utilized to aid decision-making. In this regard, the models discussed in this work can be divided according to their level of engagement in the decision-making process to date.

The fact that the most extensively used models are not the best for sustainable development objectives proposes two lines of research: first, how to employ the best-performing models in decision-making; and second, how to enhance the goodness-of-fit. of the modeling tools that are currently in use Our methods may aid in finding the main traits.

The multi-agent simulation model appears to be the most effective modeling technique. It has several potential strengths to its credit. To begin with, such models avoid most mathematical jargon and directly imitate scientific ideas or even common-sense information without previous mathematical translation.

Second, they enable intuitive depiction of the environment as well as the embedding of actors in a spatial and natural setting. Finally, they truly exhibit a bottom-up structure, allowing for an accurate portrayal of micro/macro interactions.

3.10. CONCLUSION

Let's begin by stressing what is specific in sustainable development in order to decide on the most relevant assessment criteria. The CE is perceived as a crucial model for industrial economics to pursue sustainable development. An essential stage in SIA is anticipating the likely economic, environmental, and social impacts of the planned policy.

The modeling paradigms are then compared against these criteria on a purely a priori basis and ranked with respect to their potential performance in dealing with sustainable development problems. The robustness of this ranking is then checked in two concrete policy contexts: energy policy, on the one hand, and land use and transport policy, on the other hand.

Our objective here is to help users choose the most suitable modeling tool for a particular sustainable development problem and better understand what kind of information can be expected from the models. Six modeling paradigms will be assessed, first on a purely a priori and general basis, and then against two specific policy contexts (energy policy, and land use and transport planning).

The only paper addressing a similar question is by van den Bergh and Nijkamp (1991) in this journal, but there is no standard procedure for evaluating the strengths and weaknesses of different modeling approaches for sustainable development policy-making.

However, there are several different approaches to economic–environmental or integrated modeling and it is not easy for the policy-maker to decide which is the most appropriate for any context. Due to its importance and the expected impact on sustainability, CE has received a lot of attention from researchers, policymakers, and entrepreneurs.

The European CE package is an indication of the EU's commitment to a CE. In addition to the proposed framework of an integrated CE, the novelty of this paper is the association of the CE variables with each of the sustainable development aspects: the social–environmental–economic.

REFERENCES

1. Boulanger, P., & Bréchet, T., (2005). Models for policy-making in sustainable development: The state of the art and perspectives for research. *Ecological Economics, 55*(3), 337–350. [online] Available at: https://sci-hub.se/10.1016/j.ecolecon.2005.07.033 (accessed on 21 June 2022).
2. Hysa, E., Kruja, A., Rehman, N., & Laurenti, R., (2020). Circular economy innovation and environmental sustainability impact on economic growth: An integrated model for sustainable development. *Sustainability, 12*(12), 4831. [online] Available at: https://www.mdpi.com/2071-1050/12/12/4831/pdf (accessed on 21 June 2022).
3. Roome, N., & Louche, C., (2015). Journeying toward business models for sustainability. *Organization & Environment, 29*(1), 11–35. [online] Available at: https://sci-hub.se/10.1177/1086026615595084 (accessed on 21 June 2022).
4. Van, D. B. J., & Nijkamp, P., (1991). Operationalizing sustainable development: Dynamic ecological economic models. *Ecological Economics, 4*(1), 11–33. [online] Available at: https://libgen.rocks/ads.php?md5=0ea56653683ac7e8eaae73814189811c&key=AUEGCB66PTN1SO0X&doi=10.1016/0921-8009(91)90003-w (accessed on 21 June 2022).

CHAPTER 4

SUSTAINABLE DEVELOPMENT: POLICIES AND PRACTICES

CONTENTS

This chapter on the policies and practices of sustainable development explores the general strategy and specific issues to focus on. It examines the significant bottlenecks where government initiatives in member countries can better their integration of environmental, economic, and social goals. A complex and comprehensive agenda for sustainable development is advocated.

It covers the important elements of sustainable development policies, key obstacles in isolating environmental concerns from economic growth, the social aspect of sustainable development and how to make markets function around it, harnessing science and technology, managing linkages with the global economy, responding to climate change, managing natural resources, policies, and strategies for sustainable development, planning for sustainable development, environmental policies and strategies of governments and Strategic Environmental Assessment.

4.1. INTRODUCTION

The Sustainable Development (SD) Policies lay out the general strategy and important issue-specific sustainability areas of focus, as well as the basic requirements that define our position on sustainability. The Sustainable Development Management System (SDMS) is a framework for ensuring excellent corporate governance in the field of sustainability, which is a significant risk and potential for a company's future development.

Policies aiming at ensuring long-term economic growth, a healthy environment, or a more inclusive social development are all crucial for long-term development. Organization for Economic Co-Operation and Development (OECD) documents on economic growth (OECD, 2001b), an environmental plan for the next decade (OECD, 2001d), and guidelines for poverty reduction in developing countries (OECD, 2001a) contribute to the study of policies in these other areas. These findings are also extremely important for the larger conversation on sustainable development.

Economic growth is frequently used in OECD countries as a metric of improving human welfare. It's hardly unexpected that economic growth is used as a proxy for welfare. After all, consumption options are a big part of what people think of when they think of welfare.

However, that same public recognizes that economic growth alone is insufficient to meet its needs and desires. Some of the negative effects of economic activity, such as health concerns from transportation emissions and ozone depletion, decreased biodiversity due to habitat loss, and new forms of inequality linked to changes in technologies and production patterns, serve as reminders.

This is the background in which the concept of sustainable development—that is, connecting the economic, social, and environmental goals of societies in a balanced way—has taken root. The Brundtland Commission defined sustainable development as "development that meets current demands while not jeopardizing future generations' ability to meet their own needs" (WCED, 1987).

Many people will be motivated to look beyond economic progress as a measure of wellbeing because of their concern for future generations. There are, however, other causes. Maintaining essential ecosystem services, a healthy environment, and cohesive societies are all necessary for long-term economic prosperity.

Because risks of disintegration and exclusion affect all countries, as do opportunities to benefit from participation in a growing global economy, balancing these elements will require stronger cooperation with developing and transition countries—which already account for over 80% of the world's population and will account for virtually all of its future growth.

As a result, it is critical to have a larger view of what welfare includes, to consider the long-term effects of current activities, and to place a greater emphasis on international cooperation in order to find feasible solutions. The concept of sustainable development is firmly anchored in normal economic analysis ten years after the Rio Conference on Environment and Development (Figure 4.1).

Despite all of the conceptual effort, implementation in practice remains sporadic and inconsistent. Why have tangible efforts lagged behind the urgency with which the case for sustainability is frequently made?.

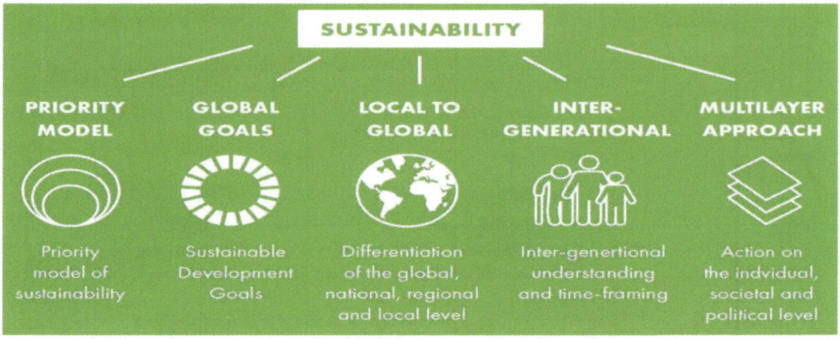

Figure 4.1. Sustainability.

Source: Image by commons.wikimedia.com.

The policy paper addresses some of the major conceptual and practical roadblocks to development, as well as areas where real government initiatives in Member countries could improve the integration of environmental, economic, and social goals. Sustainable development advocates a complicated and comprehensive agenda.

As a result, it's critical to concentrate solely on a few essential areas—those with the greatest risk of non-sustainability. This paper focuses on the dangers of irreversible depletion and deterioration of a variety of natural and environmental resources, as well as a comprehensive set of countermeasures.

While potential to contribute to long-term sustainability through economic and social policies are undoubtedly significant, full sets of policies in these two domains are rather well established—at least in OECD countries. The connections between economic and social policies are also important. Environmental policies, on the other hand, and their connections to both economic and social policy, are less well understood.

To support long-term development, these ties must be strengthened. Because of these factors, the policy study focuses heavily on the environment-economic link, partly because the stakes are particularly high in this area, and partly because little is known about the environmental-social link.

Improving the alignment of economic and environmental policy would help to eliminate the inefficient incentives that lead to unsustainable resource depletion and environmental deterioration.

4.2. IMPORTANT ELEMENTS OF SUSTAINABLE DEVELOPMENT POLICIES

4.2.1. Delivery of Public Goods

Many of the benefits of government actions that are required to support sustainable development are public goods (basic research, information, health, and education). Many of these public goods are also global in nature, as they will benefit multiple countries (e.g., information on the state of global ecosystems).

Effective delivery of these public goods necessitates overcoming barriers to coordination through burden-sharing policies that recognize individual countries' varying obligations and response capacities.

4.2.2. Cost-Effectiveness

The cost of policies should be kept as low as possible. This will necessitate ensuring that the costs of each additional resource spent are equal throughout the spectrum of actions. Cost-effectiveness allows for the reduction of overall costs and the future setting of more ambitious goals.

4.2.3. Environmental Effectiveness

The following are things that policies should protect:

- Regeneration—renewable resources should be used efficiently, and their use should not be allowed to exceed their long-term rates of natural regeneration;
- Substitutability—non-renewable resources should be used efficiently, and their use should be limited to levels that can be offset by renewable resources or other forms of capital;
- Assimilation—releases of hazardous or polluting substances to the environment should not exceed its assimilative capacity;
- Assimilation: When assimilative capacity is effectively nil, zero discharge of such compounds is required to avoid environmental buildup; and
- Avoiding Irreversibility—human activities should not have irreversible negative effects on ecosystems, biogeochemical cycles, or hydrological cycles (Figure 4.2).

Figure 4.2. Sustainable development poster.

Source: Image by ndla.zendesk.com.

Natural processes capable of preserving or restoring ecosystem integrity should be protected against the negative effects of human activity. Ecosystems with varying levels of resilience and carrying capacity should be considered in order to protect threatened, endangered, and vital species populations.

4.2.4. Policy Integration

Inconsistent policies across domains might lead to unsustainable activities. Sectoral policies, in particular, are frequently implemented without sufficient consideration for the externalities that environmental policies seek to address, resulting in inconsistencies and spillover effects. Better integration of economic, environmental, and social goals in various policies is required to improve policy coherence.

4.2.5. Precaution

The dangers of breaching crucial thresholds in the environment's regenerative capacity are unknown. As a result, in instances where scientific certainty is lacking, countries should exercise prudence when developing policies for sustainable development.

4.2.6. International Co-Operation

Spillovers become increasingly common as international interdependence grows. When countries are confronted with a variety of environmental and socioeconomic concerns with global repercussions, a narrow emphasis on national self-interest is not possible (Figure 4.3).

Figure 4.3. UN international conference on sustainability.

Source: Image by flickr.com.

4.2.7. Transparency and Accountability

Because the criteria for sustainability cannot be defined solely in technical terms, a participative approach is critical to successfully meeting the challenge of sustainable development. This necessitates a decision-making process that is informed by the whole range of possible repercussions and transparent to the public.

4.3. DE-COUPLING ENVIRONMENTAL PRESSURES FROM ECONOMIC GROWTH: KEY CHALLENGES

Are we on the right track? Not without significant adjustments aimed at decoupling a variety of environmental pressures from economic growth, in order to avoid further environmental degradation as a result of sustained economic growth.

At the heart of sustainable development is the relationship between economic progress and the natural environment that supports it. Economic growth promotes human well being and offers the resources necessary to meet a variety of environmental goals.

However, when incentives to exploit natural resources are improper and external effects are not internalized, economic growth can lead to unsustainable destruction of the environment and natural resources. Economic expansion has always entailed converting most of a society's natural resource stock into other forms of capital.

Maintaining functioning ecosystems that can support economic and social development is now recognized as critical for long-term development, especially where there are no alternatives. Economic and demographic projections emphasize the need for more ambitious initiatives to address the decoupling dilemma.

Between 1995 and 2020, global GDP is expected to grow by 75%, with two-thirds of the growth occurring in OECD countries. Over the same period, global energy demand is expected to rise by 57% (IEA, 2000) and motor vehicle kilometers travelled by around 80% (OECD, 2001c), with non-OECD nations accounting for around three-quarters and two-thirds of these increases, respectively.

On the demographic front, the global population, which has tripled in the last 50 years, is expected to grow by another 20–75% over the next 50 years, according to various UN estimates of fertility and mortality rates, with much of this growth occurring in less-developed countries' metropolitan areas.

Because of their growing economic clout, non-OECD countries will play an increasingly important role in influencing global environmental circumstances. Through demands for food and other natural resources, consumption habits in OECD countries are already putting a significant strain on the global environment.

The threat of increased competition for scarce resources and increased environmental constraints as a result of expanding these consumption patterns to the entire world population emphasizes the significance of attaining more sustainable consumption patterns globally.

Key governance principles for sustainability

Decision making	Democracy, subsidiarity; meaningful public and stakeholder participation; transparency; international cooperation; holistic approaches; policy coordination and integration; internalization of environmental and social costs
Precaution	Decision making under uncertainty, indeterminacy, irreversibility; adaptive approaches
Responsibility	Polluter pays; responsibility of generating knowledge; burden of proof; common but differentiated responsibilities; liability; accountability
Management	Prevention; rectification of pollution at source; adaptability; ecosystem approaches; partnership; mechanisms for regular review of the regime´s effectiveness and of the performance of the state institutions involved
Distribution	Intra-generational and inter-generational equity; capacity building

GRID-Arendal

Figure 4.4. Key governance principles of sustainability.

Source: Image by flickr.com.

One area where de-coupling is particularly relevant is human intervention with the climate system. Many of the climatic services given by nature have no substitutes, and several of the changes caused by rising greenhouse gas concentrations in the atmosphere may be irreversible.

The combustion of fossil fuels (which account for around 85% of world emissions) and a variety of other economic activities have all contributed to rising greenhouse gas concentrations. According to new scientific findings, human activities are responsible for the majority of the recent warming (IPCC, 2001a).

If current trends continue, greenhouse gas concentrations might quadruple by the end of the century, raising temperatures, changing precipitation patterns, raising sea levels, and interfering with atmospheric and oceanic circulation.

Inundation of coastal areas, loss of forests and coral reefs, extinction of species, crop production reductions, irrigation impacts, increased air pollution, health effects of heat waves, and the spread of infectious diseases are all possible consequences (IPCC, 2001b).

In the short term, most OECD countries have committed to considerably lowering their greenhouse gas emissions. In the long run, developing countries' engagement in the mitigation effort will be critical to limiting climate change. Even if OECD countries cut their emissions to zero, the global concentration of greenhouse gases would continue to rise unless other countries lower their emissions.

Because of the disparity between past responsibilities for greenhouse gas emissions (primarily in developed countries), future pressures (which include some large non-OECD countries), and vulnerability to climate impacts (in some of the poorer developing countries), issues of equity between countries are at the heart of climate policies.

The dangers that current production and consumption patterns pose to the life-sustaining services that humans rely on also extend to other components of the global ecosystem. Traditional resource management in OECD countries has focused on market-based natural resource values while generally disregarding values not captured by markets.

All ecosystem services are a result of both the quantity (total stock) and the quality (resilience) of the resources involved in sustainable development. Most countries' management systems are gradually recognizing this broader perspective, particularly in sectors such as biodiversity, cropland, forests, water, and living marine resources.

Over the last two decades, the international community has enacted a number of conventions and treaties aimed at addressing these issues. Non-ratification, on the other hand, has frequently harmed the legitimacy of the treaty-making process.

It's difficult to quantify the importance of ecosystem changes, but an analysis of selected vertebrate species found in forests, freshwater habitats, and marine ecosystems reveals that their populations have decreased by around one-third in the last thirty years.

Marine resources are particularly vulnerable to stresses. In 1996, approximately one-quarter of major fish stocks were over-exploited; while they are currently recovering in some regions, they will not recover to levels compatible with their single-species maximum sustainable yields unless fishing activity is reduced further (OECD, 2000).

Overexploitation of native species, habitat degradation, and the introduction and spread of invasive species are all factors that contribute to biodiversity loss. Because the extinction of a single species is irreversible, activities made to avoid extinction should be viewed as insurance against the loss of resources that may be important in the future—either on their own or as raw materials in pharmacological, agricultural, and industrial operations.

The rate at which water resources are being consumed and deteriorated raises similar issues. Water withdrawals and contamination of water bodies have increased as a result of human activities. While freshwater resources are still plentiful globally, they are dispersed unevenly across and within countries.

One out of every five people on the planet lacks access to safe and inexpensive drinking water, and half lack appropriate sanitation. Around one-third of the world's population is forecast to live in nations with medium-to-high water stress, with the number expected to rise by 2025.

Many of these tendencies jeopardize nature's ability to sustain future wellbeing. They also place a significant burden on the wellbeing of today's generation due to their negative effects on human health. Environmental harm may already account for 2% to 6% of overall disease burden in OECD countries, and 8% to 13% in non-OECD countries (OECD, 2001c).

Environmental degradation's health implications are an important part of the social-environmental interface. A better knowledge and measurement of the impact that environmental threats place on today's wellbeing may be necessary for long-term environmental policy adoption.

4.4. THE SOCIAL DIMENSION OF SUSTAINABLE DEVELOPMENT

To handle these environmental challenges in a way that is consistent with diverse countries' development and social agendas, a coordinated approach is required. It is especially critical given the global nature of many of the concerns mentioned above.

In some circumstances, such as climate change, governments cannot reverse negative trends on their own. In some cases, such as biodiversity and water scarcity, the repercussions of ongoing degradation extend beyond national boundaries. Globalization of economic activity, as well as changes in countries' relative economic weights, have altered policy priorities from local to regional to global levels.

As a result, national policies have become less effective on their own in many sectors, leading to calls for new multilateral approaches. International cooperation, on the other hand, necessitates agreed action priorities and cost-sharing standards. When there are huge discrepancies in economic situations among countries, reaching an agreement on these objectives is challenging.

This outcome is all the more likely when a huge number of people—mostly in developing nations—are unable to meet their basic needs due to poverty, starvation, illiteracy, and a lack of essential services. Poverty has long-term implications that spread across countries in the form of conflicts, migration, and disease.

As a result, poverty reduction is critical to achieving global sustainable development. To achieve this goal, governments, businesses, civic society, and the donor community must all put in more effort. There are also significant overlaps between poverty reduction and environmental conservation agendas.

Donor countries have decided to focus on seven worldwide development goals that, if completed over the next 15 years, will improve the lives of millions of impoverished people in developing countries, based on agreements from a number of UN conferences in the 1990s.

For food, fuel, shelter, fodder, and medical plants, rural inhabitants, for example, rely directly on their surrounding ecosystems—grasslands, woodlands, wetlands, and coastal fisheries. Environmental variables, such malnutrition and other preventable risk factors, are important for the health of persons living in poor countries in both rural and urban regions (World Bank, 2000).

Environmental sustainability, in general, can only be realized as part of a comprehensive development strategy that includes sustained economic growth, financial soundness, institutional development, enhanced governance, effective education and health investment, and poverty reduction.

OECD countries can play a critical role in assisting developing countries in achieving these objectives by increasing access to critical investment flows and domestic markets. International trade and investment liberalization aids developing countries' economic progress and has the ability to raise millions of people out of poverty.

It can also help developing countries safeguard the environment by spreading and implementing cleaner technology, cooperating to establish good governance systems, and assisting producers in developing countries to meet consumer demand for goods produced in a sustainable manner.

Globalization, on the other hand, will not offer its full potential benefits if new technologies, finance, and export markets benefit only those countries that have the circumstances to effectively exploit these opportunities, while marginalizing those that do not.

Development cooperation helps developing nations, particularly the poorest, increase their capacity to fully exploit globalization's potential for poverty reduction.

In OECD countries, social factors are equally crucial in the goal of sustainable development. Most OECD nations have made tremendous progress in developing comprehensive social safety nets, education, and health systems, as well as well-developed administrative, legal, and institutional infrastructure to offer these services to their inhabitants.

Concerns about equality and the social externalities of poverty, unemployment, poor skills, and bad health have long inspired social policy in OECD countries. Policies in these areas must adapt to changing conditions and are constantly reviewed, but a framework for addressing a wide range of social needs already exists.

Even if this concern is not always expressed in terms of sustainable development, such measures demonstrate an ongoing concern about current demands and future opportunities. However, social protection systems may need to change in order to help create the conditions for more determined action to protect long-term "environmental commons" and to address the structural changes that policy reforms require.

4.5. A FRAMEWORK FOR SUSTAINABLE DEVELOPMENT POLICIES: KEY POLICY RESPONSES

To close these knowledge and implementation gaps, a thorough plan is required. Governments in the OECD must take the lead. They must make their policy toolkit more market-oriented, integrative, and inclusive of developing-country concerns in particular.

Progress also necessitates a defined agenda, with a particular focus on areas where non-sustainable development patterns pose the most risk, such as climate change and natural resource management. Below are some recommendations for improving the effectiveness of policy interventions, which are expanded upon in the complete policy report.

Not all of the recommendations apply to every OECD country or in every situation. When assessing their effective implementation, different priorities and institutional conditions must be considered. Nonetheless, when fully implemented, these ideas provide a practical foundation for progress toward long-term sustainability.

Member countries are obviously responsible for implementation. The OECD, on the other hand, can play a significant role in assisting these initiatives. Outside of negotiation fora, the OECD provides a space for "without prejudice" conversations, where Members can create shared viewpoints.

It can also help track progress toward sustainable development, collect comparable data in key areas such as subsidy indicators and effects, develop recommendations on the characteristics of sustainable development policies, analyze the socio-economic and environmental effects of various policies, and review progress in the implementation of domestic policies on a regular basis through its peer-review system (Figure 4.5).

Figure 4.5. Logos on different aspects of sustainability.

Source: Image by pixabay.com.

4.5.1. Making Markets Work for Sustainable Development

Expanding the use of market-based instruments and reforming assistance programs to make price signals more coherent with the goal of decoupling environmental concerns from economic growth have tremendous potential across the OECD area.

Using market-based instruments, certain environmental goals could be addressed more cost-effectively. Externalities and market failures would be addressed by increasing the use of environment-related taxes and tradable permit systems, as well as policy failures by reducing environmentally detrimental subsidies.

Improved international coordination, targeted interventions, such as compensating those most affected by reforms in a way that does not jeopardize the environmental effectiveness of market-based instruments, and general measures, such as phasing in reforms and programs to build public acceptance, can all help overcome obstacles to these reforms.

Market-based instruments will need to be used in conjunction with other interventions such as rules, voluntary agreements, and information in practice. All of these tools have the potential to be more effective.

Increase the use of environment-related fees and tradable permits to account for externalities and market failures. While the instrument's choice and design will vary depending on country circumstances and the problem being addressed, this indicates that:

- Setting environmental tax rates, for example, by imposing new taxes on some items and processes (especially those that are now tax-exempt) and better targeting existing taxes.
- Using tradable permit systems to solve global (e.g., climate change), regional (e.g., eutrophication), and domestic (e.g., local air pollution) issues.
- Exemptions from environmental charges and limits on tradable permit systems that undermine their efficacy should be reduced.
- Using the proceeds from these instruments to support national goals.
- This could include initiatives to ease transition and garner public support for these tools, with other more distortive levies being reduced first. If these funds are used to fund specific environmental programs, make sure to examine them on a regular basis to ensure that they don't distort expenditure priorities. Limit the grandfathering of marketable permits in time to reduce competition distortions.

Correct policy failures through reforms of environmentally damaging support programs that include:

- Eliminating environmentally harmful subsidies and making the remaining ones conditional on specific improvements in environmental performance.
- Ensuring that benefits from environmental service support payments cover the cost of providing, and making the cost-benefit analysis clear.
- Considering all economic, environmental, and social advantages and costs projected from proposed regulations to improve the effectiveness of other policies.

Improving the environmental efficacy of voluntary agreements by incorporating procedures for monitoring, verification, and control. Educating and enlightening producers and consumers on the environmental and social consequences of their decisions while avoiding unforeseen trade outcomes.

Address the potential effects of more ambitious environmental policies on employment and income distribution, as well as the redeployment of workers affected by these policy reforms, through labor market measures (e.g., income support, job-search assistance, and retraining) and other interventions that increase labor market flexibility and function.

4.5.2. Strengthening Decision-Making

Governments must also "set an example" when it comes to supporting sustainable development. Governments should concentrate their internal policy development and implementation efforts on better integrating the three dimensions of sustainable development (economic, environmental, and social); improving their own capacity to support sustainable development; and developing transparent and productive mechanisms for interacting with civil society (Figure 4.6).

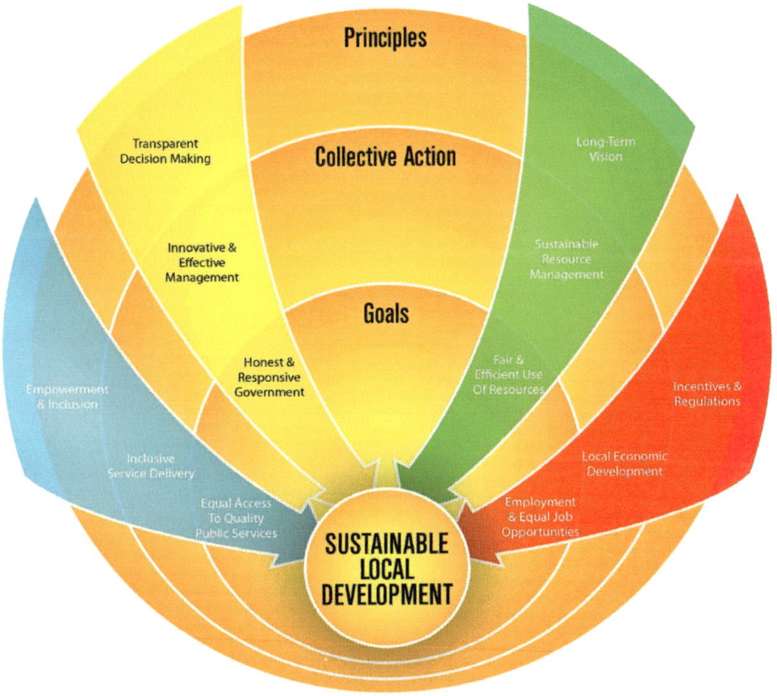

Figure 4.6. Sustainable local development.

Source: Image by flickr.com.

Improve policy integration capacity at all levels of government by:

- Using methods such as environmental, social, and regulatory impact assessments, as well as cost-benefit analysis, ensuring that essential economic, environmental, and social issues are integrated into sectoral policy analysis, design, and implementation before choices are made.
- Ensuring that the finest scientific advice on environmental concerns is coordinated at the highest levels of government and delivered to decision-makers in a timely way.
- International collaboration to establish common approaches to making economic, environmental, and social policies supportive of one another.
- Evaluating the coherence of their international engagements in order to improve international policymaking.

- Clearly outlining policy aims and deadlines for sustainable development and performing regular progress reviews (including through peer review).
- Build government capacity to use information and communication technology to effectively coordinate across departments.
- Giving the public access to information and robust challenge mechanisms (e.g., judicial processes).

At all levels of government, increase transparency and public participation by enabling the transition to sustainable development by allowing enterprises, workers, consumers, and nongovernmental organizations to participate effectively in policy discussions on production and consumption patterns.

4.5.3. Harnessing Science and Technology

Scientific advancement and technical advancement are significant drivers of increased production and living standards. New technologies hold great promise for decoupling long-term economic progress from environmental damage.

However, there is no guarantee that innovations will arise when and where they are most needed, or at a cost that accounts for all environmental and social costs involved with their implementation. Governments must develop a legislative climate that sends the correct signals to technology inventors and users both domestically and abroad, fund basic research, and appropriately support private ventures.

Expand the use of market-based techniques in environmental policy to provide persistent incentives to innovate and distribute technology that promote sustainable development goals (SDGs). Use performance criteria instead of metrics that prescribe and support specific technologies when market-based instruments aren't appropriate.

Support long-term basic research with finance and capacity-building efforts (e.g., development of centers of excellence). Increase study into ecosystems, the value of the services they give, the long-term implications of human activity on the environment, and the effects of new technology on employment.

Separate technological promotion responsibilities from those for health, safety, and environmental protection within governments to address unexpected environmental and social implications of technology (Figure 4.7).

Figure 4.7. The helix of sustainability.

Source: Image by commons.wikimedia.com.

Support applied research efforts that are obviously in the public interest (e.g., public health and environmental protection) and are unlikely to be performed by the private sector by:

1. Collaborating with industry to create and disseminate innovative technology.
2. Enabling public-private and inter-firm collaboration with cleaner technology and practice pioneers.
3. Seeking for potential for increased international research collaboration, particularly on themes vital to long-term growth.
4. Allowing competition among technologies that can achieve the same policy goal, as well as equitable access by foreign and domestic investors to "learning opportunities" (e.g., protected niche markets and similar programs).

4.5.4. Managing Linkages with the Global Economy

International trade and financial movements support long-term economic growth and development, as well as the achievement of environmental and social objectives. When trade and investment policies, as well as environmental and social policies, work together, each contributes more to long-term growth.

This coherence should be reinforced by OECD countries in both local and international debates. Developing countries require improved access to OECD markets as well as active support from OECD countries for capacity building activities in order to prosper in an environmentally and socially sustainable manner.

Improve trade, investment, environmental, and social policy coherence by:

- Reforming trade-distorting and environmentally destructive domestic policies.
- Evaluating the environmental and social consequences of trade and investment liberalization, as well as incentive policies aimed at recruiting foreign direct investment, and establishing or refining appropriate methodology to do so.
- Developing practical measures to ensure that trade and investment disciplines, as well as environmental and social policy instruments, continue to be mutually complementary.
- Promoting awareness and effective implementation of OECD instruments dealing with multinational enterprises, corporate governance, and bribery in the private sector; providing a supportive regulatory and institutional framework for private sector activity; and encouraging the use of environmental and social codes of conduct in the private sector.
- Support developing countries' capabilities and capacities to expand in ways that strengthen environmental protection and social development by:
- Expanding market access for developing nations, particularly in sectors where economic liberalization is most likely to support sustainable development.
- Examining economic and environmental policies with the objective of poverty alleviation in mind.
- Promoting the achievement of the worldwide development goals outlined in the deferred acquisition cost (DAC) report "Shaping the Twenty-First Century: Development Cooperation's Contribution." Most OECD nations are directed in achieving

these objectives by the widely accepted threshold of 0.7% of gross national product (GNP) as a suitable level of official development assistance (ODA).

- Continuing to assist the world's poorest countries in strengthening their ability to participate in the global economy's long-term development. This entails developing the legal and institutional frameworks required to attract private capital flows to those countries while minimizing negative environmental and social consequences, as well as providing suitable support for technology cooperation.
- When development cooperation funds are utilized to promote the provision of global public goods (e.g., climate change), they should be focused on initiatives that have demonstrable local advantages as well as regional and global benefits.

4.5.5. Responding to Climate Change

Climate change is a pressing issue that requires strong international cooperation and leadership from OECD countries to accomplish the Kyoto Protocol's mitigation targets. Climate change goals must be better aligned in OECD countries' domestic policies (Figure 4.8).

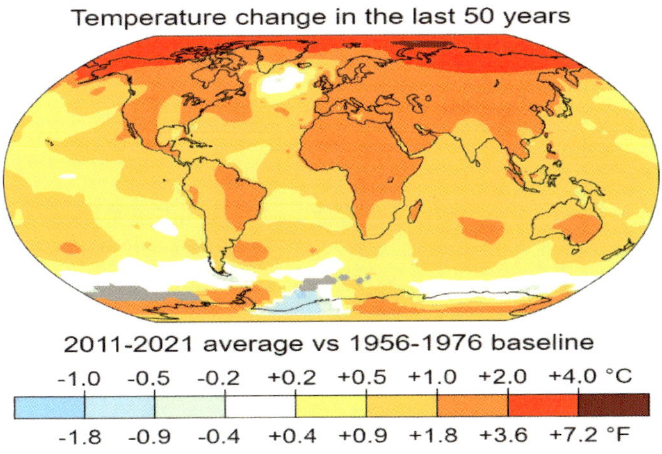

Figure 4.8. Climate change increasing global temperature.

Source: Image by commons.wikimedia.com.

They must also implement market-based measures such as pollution trading systems, carbon levies, and subsidy reforms, as well as combine these policies with targeted technology development and diffusion programs (e.g., low carbon emissions energy sources).

Finally, in order to stabilize concentrations at levels that avoid catastrophic interference with the climate system, they must create long-term mitigation strategies and improve their cooperation with developing countries.

Take a comprehensive strategy to climate mitigation by: Mitigating all sources of greenhouse gases and removing carbon from the atmosphere through sinks. Including both the ancillary benefits of mitigation programs and the climate advantages of other policies in climate policies (e.g., energy efficiency and diversification).

- Reforming subsidies that boost emissions or restrict sink absorption, particularly in transportation, energy, and agriculture, and considering steps to make the transition easier.
- Evaluating and reporting on the consequences of Export Credit Agency assistance for greenhouse gas emissions.
- Funding research and technology projects that reduce barriers to the adoption of more energy-efficient technologies and lower-carbon energy sources, as well as study into the social impacts of policy changes.
- Creating standardized methods for monitoring and tracking emissions in order to facilitate transparent reporting, verification, and review, as well as improve compliance.
- Developing adaptation techniques to limit exposure to climate change risks and facilitate the transition to climate-resilient lifestyles.
- Raising knowledge of climate change, its effects, costs, and advantages of policy actions, through information and engagement with the communities and sectors most affected, in order to make the transition to new forms of labor and consumption easier.

Develop policies to guide long-term mitigation for stabilizing concentrations at levels that do not endanger the climate system by:

- Identifying and reviewing emission limits that are consistent with the Framework Convention on Climate Change's objectives.

- Encouraging developing countries to participate in mitigation policies
- An important step toward reducing long-term climate change.
- Providing financial and technical assistance to underdeveloped nations to help them improve their ability to execute climate mitigation and adaptation programs.

4.5.6. Managing Natural Resources

Natural resources are both the raw ingredients for economic activity and the foundations for life itself. Many of the ecosystem services offered by natural resources, on the other hand, are difficult to reflect in market prices. Natural resource management that is sustainable requires accurate pricing that takes into account both use and non-use values.

Governments should review present legislation in order to better align markets with conservation goals and to improve research, monitoring, and enforcement capacities. They should also step up their efforts to assist developing countries in building their capacity to manage their natural resources sustainably.

Improve the decision-making knowledge base by:

- Supporting research on environmental thresholds for renewable resources, techniques for calculating non-market values of natural resources, and technologies that use or recycle natural resources more efficiently.
- Developing indicators and techniques for assessing the state of natural resources; their use and the variables that influence it (e.g., prices, and subsidies); threats to ecosystems, such as invasive species; the relationships between natural resources and the people who directly rely on them; and the socio-economic impacts of policy reform. Make markets more conservation-friendly by:
- Increasing the use of environmental taxes, tradable permits, and other market-based methods to natural resource management.
- Improving approaches for considering ecosystem services when making policy decisions that influence natural resources. By clarifying property rights, disseminating information, and establishing institutions to enforce contracts, encouraging

the creation of markets for goods and services produced in a sustainable way (e.g., eco-tourism).

- Reforming and making cross-subsidies apparent in subsidies that encourage over-exploitation of natural resources. Clarify the public benefit and make the foundation for this assistance obvious when contemplating support for environment-related services from natural resources.
- Use cost-benefit analysis for project assessment when planning investments in natural resource infrastructure (e.g., irrigation works and public water supplies), taking into account the most important consequences, and make complete cost recovery of private benefits a long-term aim.
- Addressing adverse social impacts from changes in resource management policies.

For example, the effects on income distribution and employment in specific industries

In a way that allows for systemic change. Provide direct income support to poorer users rather than cross-subsidies or lower fees when pricing natural resources to meet social goals.

4.6. POLICIES AND STRATEGIES FOR SUSTAINABLE DEVELOPMENT

The sustainable livelihoods framework underlines the relevance of policies, procedures, and structures in enabling individuals to generate diverse types of capital, as well as in facilitating the development of alternative livelihood options. Policy processes can be thought of as a bridge between diverse capitals, such as human capacities and natural resources, and what poor and vulnerable people can really do and achieve.

Governments, private businesses, and civic society, for example, work together to establish how markets operate. They all adopt policies and strategies of various types in order to make their programs more effective, efficient, and closely connected with stated aims and policies, such as environmental protection.

Of course, the three domains of government, business, and civil society all interact and intersect. Governments may own or control businesses; numerous interest groups are represented in government and may participate in state administration and policymaking; and businesses may provide government-related services or fund political parties and charities.

Furthermore, how they interact is heavily influenced by the political structure and ties inside any given country. The distinction between development policies and strategies is not always evident. Typically, policies state both the goals (what to achieve) and the means (how the goals are expected to be attained), but only in broad terms.

Governments at all levels formulate public policy, which includes legislative plans as well as a variety of activities and services. Strategies (for the government, enterprises, or charities) are more realistic than policies; they take into account the various parties' capacities, as well as their relative shortcomings and strengths (the stakeholders).

Nonetheless, plans only provide a general outline for a path of action, not specific instructions on what to do and how to attain objectives.

4.7. PLANNING FOR SUSTAINABLE DEVELOPMENT

This section outlines some broad policy goals as well as strategic tools and methodologies that governments, NGOs, and others can use to develop medium- to long-term strategies. Although it is impossible to delve into depth on particular governments' environmental policies, including how policies are agreed upon and implemented, some general strategy making processes are described. This section also goes through several indicators that illustrate how far we've come in terms of achieving policy goals in the area of sustainable development.

4.8. ENVIRONMENTAL POLICIES AND STRATEGIES OF GOVERNMENTS

4.8.1. Policy Instruments

The following are some of the policy instruments that governments can use to achieve some level of sustainable development:

- Regulation, such as through laws and bylaws that prohibit the use of particular substances and establish environmental standards and pollution limitations. Certain procedures, such as EIA in the event of significant and potentially damaging projects, can also be mandated by law.

- Market-based mechanisms, such as taxation and subsidies. Subsidies for the development of environmentally friendly technology like sustainable agriculture, tariffs to limit the importation and use of specific chemicals, and taxes on pollution, deforestation, mining, and other environmental externalities are just a few examples.

Tariffs and resource taxes thus serve as disincentives: they discourage undesirable behavior and signal to markets to seek alternatives, especially when they become the government's primary source of revenue. They are, in reality, an alternative to income taxes or taxes on the trade of locally grown food goods, which impede the growth of livelihoods and employment prospects and provide no incentive for local people to protect the environment.

- Public awareness initiatives that educate citizens and businesses about the environmental consequences of their actions.
- Governments can also invest in mangrove forest regeneration, toxic water and soil cleanup, infrastructure to safeguard human populations from landslides, and the protection of steep mountain slopes, for example.
- Many governments are considering filing claims based on the idea that the polluter pays in cases of industrial pollution, even if the pollution occurred before anti-pollution legislation or when standards were different. This is obviously less appealing to governments if they were formerly the owners of the industries, as many developing countries are.

4.8.2. National Environmental Policy Documents

National Environmental Management Action Plans (NEAPs or NEMAPs), National Conservation Strategies (NCSs), and/or National Strategies for Sustainable Development (NSSDs) have been produced in most developing and industrialized countries (Figure 4.9).

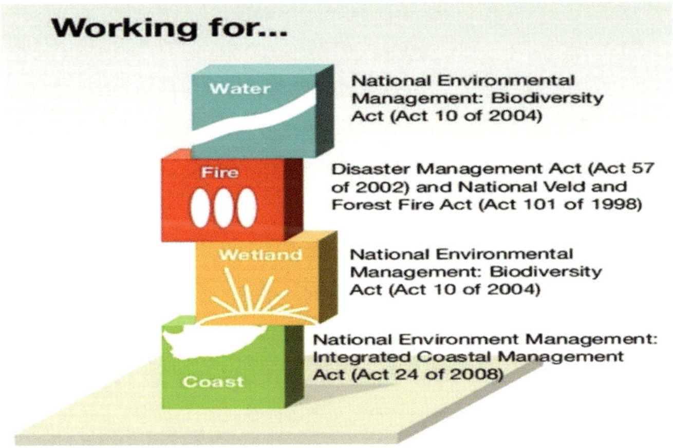

Figure 4.9. National environment policy acts.

Source: Image by flickr.com.

This is frequently accomplished with the financial and technical assistance of bilateral and multilateral organizations such as the World Bank and regional development banks, UNEP, UNDP, bilateral funders, and environmental organizations like as the International Union for Conservation of Nature (IUCN) and world wide fund for nature (WWF). The IUCN promotes the NCSs, which aim to investigate the feasibility of incorporating pro-conservation conditions into the economic development process.

The World Bank advocates NEMAPs and has helped several low-income nations build them; many examples can be seen on the Bank's publications and website. Environmental issues and mitigation policies are formulated in NEMAPs in order to integrate environmental management into national decision-making.

4.8.3. Strategic Environmental Assessment

Strategic Environmental Assessment (SEA) is a method for incorporating environmental factors into specific (sector) policies, laws, plans, and programs, on par with economic and social concerns. SEA does not work at the project level; hence it should produce more concrete results than the many national strategies or general policies can.

Nonetheless, it appears to have evolved from decades of experience with EIA, a project management technique. SEA is a relatively new development, and many developing-country governments have yet to adopt it.

However, SEA appears to be useful, and a number of industrialized countries have adopted legislation and institutional arrangements to support it, as well as development agencies such as the World Bank launching sectoral and regional (strategic) environmental assessments. There are some guidelines presently, and the literature is growing.

4.8.4. Environmental Policies and Strategic Plans of Development Organizations

Few development NGOs, whether local or worldwide, have explicit policies on environmental sustainability, however, most agree to some interpretation of sustainable (human) development. One reason for this is a lack of internal capacity for dealing with issues that aren't often considered as core to the organization's goal, such as "to eliminate poverty" or "to alleviate human suffering."

The relationship between social and environmental development is frequently underappreciated. Following the positive dialogues at the UN Conference on Environment and Development (UNCED) in 1992 (where a Global Forum was organized, dominated by NGOs—UNCED was about environment and development), development NGOs have fewer links to the world of environmental campaigners than some might have expected.

Even so, many in development circles recognize the value of such connections, if only for the 'opportunity' that serious environmental degradation 'offers' for tackling poverty issues. Sustainable development and the environment are frequently included in development organizations' core policies and medium-term strategic plans.

'Achieving sustainable livelihoods' is one of Oxfam's general strategy goals. Several strategic goals are developed under this broad 'roof,' the most important of which is to boost income, employment prospects, and food security while increasing or maintaining social fairness and environmental sustainability. These goals are then translated into strategies and a practical approach to development that employs a variety of analytical and participative techniques, as seen in multiple CARE programs as well as UNDP and Department for International Development (DFID).

NGOs' strategies include initiatives and campaigns to promote or oppose policies that affect people's livelihoods and the environment. Many development NGOs, for example, support poor subsistence farmers and commercial smallholders by promoting sustainable, low-input agriculture.

Oxfam's research on the causes of global poverty and the links between (mainly Northern) consumption and (primarily Southern) poverty in preparation for a large-scale international campaign is another example. The Ox/am Poverty Report, the campaign's main document, includes a chapter on ecological footprints.

The idea is that affluent people's consumption demands drive global environmental change such as climate change and the utilization of rainforests by foreign logging firms. Thus, the 'ecological footprint' of high-consumers can be considered as the primary cause of rising sea levels, increasing river floods, and the loss of fish species.

International economic policies, particularly trade rules, preserve, and stimulate these spending patterns. Because impoverished countries and vulnerable groups of people are the first to be affected by environmental changes, a poverty-reduction strategy must naturally include a campaign against unsustainable resource usage by the wealthy.

4.9. NATIONAL POLICIES AND CAMPAIGNS FOR SUSTAINABLE DEVELOPMENT

Many national policies and regulations have an environmental component. Campaigns by civil society organizations for more or better environmental protection, on the other hand, are rarely solely environmental. They are more likely to be efforts for local, excluded people to get access to economic development processes on their own terms and in their own interests.

Environmental degradation is sometimes one of numerous grounds for demonstrations and ideas for alternate (local) development trajectories. 'The environment' can thus be considered as one 'entry point' into poverty-related activism, which necessitates strong ties between development NGOs and local environmental activists and NGOs, as well as sector ministries and government services with an interest in improving environmental conditions (Figure 4.10).

Figure 4.10. UN Environment conference.

Source: Image by flickr.com.

4.9.1. Land and Livelihoods

Campaigns to ensure access to agricultural land, "ancestral domain," forests, and pastures are common, and they are one of the most essential measures to protect the livelihoods of poor and vulnerable women and men.

Campaigners primarily target national governments because they draught and administer laws governing land ownership, tenure, and usage rights, however, this is frequently done informally with traditional leaders.

The World Bank, bilateral funders, and other international development agencies frequently play a key role in research and legislative formulation. Land supports livelihoods and civilizations in as many different ways as there are people on the planet. However, there are parallels and lessons to be learnt from the experiences of others.

One learning from Vietnam is that assistance with land-reform legislation implementation at the local level, along with national dialogue, can result in revised and improved implementation techniques. In many other cases, however, land is hotly contested, ownership patterns result in acute poverty and misery, and land disputes can escalate to civil war.

4.10. THE EMPLOYMENT EFFECTS OF POLICIES DESIGNED TO ACHIEVE SUSTAINABLE DEVELOPMENT

Government regulations to protect critical natural capital, combined with the market-based instruments favored by ecological economists-cap and trade pollution permit schemes (see OECD, 2004a) and ecological tax reform (ETR) (Lawn, 2000; Brown, 2001; and Repetto et al., 1992), or ecological fiscal reform (EFR), which combines ETR with reductions or elimination of environmentally harmful subsidies—will almost certainly raise the costs of raw materials.

Business managers will look for ways to cut costs by making better use of these resources. If denied access to a resource, some resource extraction companies may be forced to shut or drastically reduce their activities. The fossil-fueled energy sector is in the same boat.

Meanwhile, other firms in the affected firms' supply chain would see a drop in demand for their services. The multiplier impacts of these cuts can be particularly severe in regions where the local economy is heavily reliant on the shrunken industry.

These settlements are generally located in rural areas where alternative types of employment are few, and retrenched people' only options may be retraining or relocation. Such a scenario could well capture the regional consequences of Tasmania's moratorium on harvesting old growth trees.

The policies necessary to mitigate the effects of localized social dislocation are well-known. Indeed, explicit strategic policy initiatives have been made in the past to support regions and enterprises afflicted by adverse market dynamics (albeit for reasons other than sustainable development).

In Australia, one example that comes to mind is the occasion in 1997 when the federal and state governments each gave $10 million to help mitigate job losses in the Newcastle region following the closing of the BHP steel works. However, when looking at the economy as a whole, the issue remains as to what impact sustainable development policies will have in the long run, once the initial effects have passed.

Will such policies inevitably damage the economy and, as a result, future job opportunities? Or can such measures be prescribed with confidence to alleviate concerns about economic restructuring based on sustainable development?

In this regard, there are two sets of literature to consult. The first is a large and expanding body of research that attempts to model and anticipate the impacts of ETR on employment. ETR, often known as 'green taxes,' is an attempt to move a country's tax base away from resources it wants to utilize more of, such as labor, and toward resources it wants to conserve, such as natural capital and the services or flows of commodities it produces.

ETR may also focus on pollution or other forms of environmental degradation that threaten the availability of these services or flows. The 'Porter hypothesis' is the second body of literature that gives insight on the employment conundrum. This is the idea that well-designed environmental requirements can spur innovation inside businesses, increasing resource productivity and partially or completely offsetting the costs of complying with the new rules. In a nutshell, tough environmental regulations may boost innovation and competition (Porter and van der Linde, 1995).

Later refinements of the Porter hypothesis clarify that 'environmental regulation' must be interpreted broadly to include not just 'command and control' type regulations, but the entire suite of policies available to governments, or what we refer to here as 'sustainable development policies' (that is, EFR, and market-based instruments that artificially create markets, voluntary agreements with firms, government support for technology development, and so on) (see, for example, Norberg-Bohm, 2000 and OECD, 2002). If the Porter hypothesis is correct, it is reasonable to believe that employment levels will improve, or at the very least not deteriorate, especially given most innovation takes the form of resource productivity increases.

4.11. CONCLUSION

In the conclusion of the chapter, it discussed about the important elements of sustainable development policies. It also discussed about the various policies and strategies for the sustainable development, planning, and a framework for sustainable development. This chapter discussed provide highlights on the social dimensions of sustainable development.

Towards the end of the chapter, it discussed about the various environmental policies and strategies of governments such as policy instruments, national environmental policy, strategic environmental assessments. In this chapter, the employment effects of the policies design in order to achieve sustainable development have also been discussed.

REFERENCES

1. (n.d). *Policies and Strategies for Sustainable Development*, 160–216 [e-Book]. Available at: https://oxfamilibrary.openrepository.com/bitstream/handle/10546/122750/bk-environments-livelihoods-ch-v-010100-en.pdf;jsessionid=B0130E8600CAC01C7F2FDCCDAA628D6C?sequence=29 (accessed on 21 June 2022).
2. Dempsey, N., Bramley, G., Power, S., & Brown, C., (2009). The social dimension of sustainable development: Defining urban social sustainability. *Sustainable Development, 19*(5), 289–300. [online] Available at: https://www.researchgate.net/publication/229889535_The_Social_Dimension_of_Sustainable_Development_Defining_Urban_Social_Sustainability (accessed on 21 June 2022).
3. Jens, M., (2018). *Redefining Policies for Sustainable Development.* [online] 2030 Spotlight. Available at: https://www.2030spotlight.org/en/book/1730/chapter/redefining-policies-sustainable-development (accessed on 21 June 2022).
4. OECD, (2001). *Policies to Enhance Sustainable Development* (pp. 1–32). [e-Book] Organization For Economic Cooperation and Development,. Available at: https://www.oecd.org/greengrowth/1869800.pdf (accessed on 21 June 2022).
5. Pooja, M., (n.d). *7 Policies for Sustainable Development–Explained*!. [online] Economics Discussion. Available at: https://www.economicsdiscussion.net/economics-2/7-policies-for-sustainable-development-explained/2123 (accessed on 21 June 2022).

CHAPTER 5

ECONOMIC GROWTH AND ENVIRONMENTAL DEGRADATION

CONTENTS

The chapter can be seen as an earnest attempt to facilitate the understanding between economic growth and environmental degradation while briefly touching upon the various factors that determine economic growth such as the GDP, etc. Difference between developing and developed economies in terms of the harm that they cause to the environment is highlighted by mentioning that the relationship between economic activity and degradation of environment in developing countries is more detrimental.

This sets the stage to discuss the various stages of economic growth and their impact on the environment through the Environmental Kuznets curve (EKC) hypothesis. Shortcomings of this hypothesis also find a mention. Not just economic but other natural factors such as deforestation, overpopulation, to name a few are also mentioned along with socioeconomic factors that lead to pollution and subsequent damage along with their impact. Lastly, ways to combat the growing concern of environmental degradation is addressed with emphasis on education, awareness, and individual contribution towards a better world.

5.1. INTRODUCTION

In the recent years, climate change and global warming have had an increasing impact on people's quality of life. Growing economic activity and the resultant environmental degradation are regarded to be one of the primary drivers of this problem. Due to the production structures, the correlation between economic activity and environmental deterioration in developing countries may be more detrimental to the environment.

Ecuador, for instance, is a country with a low level of manufacturing participation in gross domestic product (GDP); the majority of national income and state budget originate from primary exports aimed at foreign markets, particularly petroleum exports (Central Bank of Ecuador [BCE], 2015).

Environmental contamination induced by private sector agricultural operations has piqued Ecuador's interest in recent years, particularly due to deforestation coupled with agricultural frontier growth. Furthermore, this country spends nearly a sixth of its national budget on energy subsidies (Ministry of Finance of Ecuador (MFE) 2015).

The subject of how to lower this spending has spurred a wide scholarly debate with significant policy implications. The primary argument for cutting or abolishing this spending is because it contributes to environmental pollution while not necessarily benefiting low-income people (Whitley, 2013). Nonetheless, Ecuadorean policymakers are likely to sustain spending on these subsidies due to institutional weakness and social pressure.

Without exhausting resources or depleting the environment beyond repair will the world be able to sustain economic growth indefinitely? What is the relationship between rising incomes and improved environmental quality? Are there trade-offs between achieving high and sustainable rates of economic growth and maintaining high environmental standards?

Growing economic activity (production and consumption), according to some social and physical scientists such as Georgescu Roegen and Meadows et al., necessitates greater inputs of energy and materials and generates greater quantities of waste by-products.

Increased extraction of natural resources, waste accumulation, and pollutant concentration will thus overwhelm the biosphere's carrying capacity, resulting in environmental degradation and a decline in human welfare despite rising incomes. Furthermore, an argument prevails that degradation of the resource base will eventually put economic activity itself at risk.

In order to save the environment and even economic activity from itself, the world must make a transition to a steady-state economy and economic growth ought to cease. At the other extreme, are those who argue that the fastest road to environmental improvement is along the path of economic growth: with higher incomes comes increased demand for goods and services that are less material intensive, as well as demand for improved environmental quality that leads to the adoption of environmental protection measures.

As Beckerman puts it, "The strong correlation between incomes, and the extent to which environmental protection measures are adopted, demonstrates that in the longer run, the surest way to improve your environment is to become rich." Some went as far as claiming that environmental regulation, by reducing economic growth, may actually reduce environmental quality.

Yet, others have hypothesized that the relationship between economic growth and environmental quality, whether positive or negative, is not fixed along a country's development path; indeed it may change sign from positive to negative as a country reaches a level of income at which people demand and afford more efficient infrastructure and a cleaner environment.

The implied inverted-U relationship between environmental degradation and economic growth came to be known as the "EKC," by analogy with the income in equality relationship postulated by Kuznets. At low levels of development, both the quantity and the intensity of environmental degradation are limited to the impacts of subsistence economic activity on the resource base and to limited quantities of biodegradable wastes.

As agriculture and resource extraction intensify and industrialization takes off, both resource depletion and waste generation accelerate. At higher levels of development, structural change towards information-based industries and services, more efficient technologies, and increased demand for environmental quality result in leveling-off and a steady decline of environmental degradation (Figure 5.1).

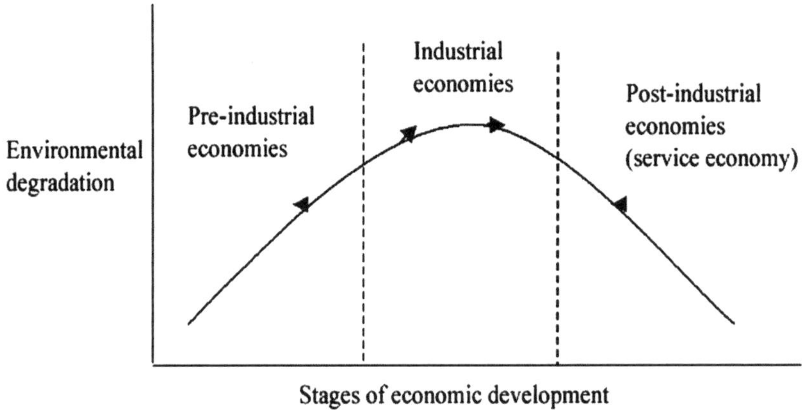

Figure 5.1. Stages of economic development.

Source: Image by Wikimedia Commons.

The issue of whether environmental degradation i) increases monotonically, ii) decreases monotonically, or iii) first increases and then declines along a country's development path, has critical implications for policy. A monotonic increase of environmental degradation with economic growth calls for strict environmental regulations and even limits on economic growth to ensure a sustainable scale of economic activity within the ecological life-support system.

A monotonic decrease of environmental degradation along a country's development path suggests that policies that accelerate economic growth lead also to rapid environmental improvements and no explicit environmental policies are needed; indeed, they may be counterproductive if they slow down economic growth and thereby delay environmental improvement.

Finally, if the EKC hypothesis is supported by evidence, development policies have the potential of being environmentally benign over the long run (at high incomes), but they are also capable of significant environmental damage in the short-to-medium run (at low-to-medium-level incomes). In this case, several issues arise:

- At what level of per capita income is the turning point?
- How much damage would have taken place, and how can it be avoided?
- Would any ecological thresholds be violated and irreversible damage take place before environmental degradation turns down, and how can they be avoided?
- Is environmental improvement at higher income levels automatic, or does it require conscious institutional and policy reforms? and
- how to accelerate the development process so that developing and transition economies can attain the same improved economic and environmental conditions enjoyed by developed market economies?

The empirical relationship between economic growth and the environment at different stages of economic development and explore how economic growth might be decoupled from environmental pressures. Particular attention is paid to the role of structural change, technological change and economic and environmental policies in the process of decoupling and the reconciliation of economic and environmental objectives.

The environmental degradation is the deterioration of the environment through depletion of resources which includes all the biotic and abiotic element that form our surrounding that is air, water, soil, pant animals, and all other living and non-living element of the planet of earth. The major factor of environmental degradation is human (modern urbanization, industrialization, overpopulation growth, deforestation, etc.) and natural (flood, typhoons, droughts, rising temperatures, fires, etc.) cause.

Today, different kinds of human activities are the main reasons for environmental degradation. The automobile and industries increase the number of poisonous gases like SOx, NOx, CO, and smoke in the atmosphere. Therefore, the government must enhance filling the gap in the legal system to avoid illegal activities.

The impact of environmental degradation with its future impacts, city planners, industry, and resource managers plans to be considered to mitigate the long term effects of developmental environmental degradation. The environmental degradation is deterioration of the environmental through depletion of resources which includes all the biotic and abiotic elements that form our surrounding that is air, water, soil, plant, animals, and all other living and non-living element of the planet of earth (Bourque et al., 2005; Malcolm and Pitelka, 2000).

The environment is something we are very familiar with. It's everything that makes up our surroundings and affects our ability to live on the earth. Environmental degradation is a very serious problem worldwide which covers a variety of issues including pollution, biodiversity loss, and animal extinction, deforestation, and desertification, global warming, and a lot more

Environmental degradation is also having a useful aspect, more new genes have been created, and some species have grown as someone's have declined. For natural selection, species are constantly regenerating as the environment changes, and human activity is the main driver's power. Human is also a product of nature; this shift is to natural replacement.

5.2. CAUSES OF ENVIRONMENTAL DEGRADATION

Modern urbanization, industrialization, overpopulation, deforestation, etc. and natural calamities such as flood, typhoons, droughts, rising temperatures, fires, etc. are human caused. Environmental pollution refers to the degradation of the quality and quantity of natural resources. Different kinds of human activities are the main reasons for environmental degradation.

Unplanned urbanization and industrialization have caused water, air, soil, and sound pollution. Industrialization, urbanization, and sewage waste help to increase pollution of the sources of water (Olorode et al., 2015).

Similarly, the smoke emitted by vehicles and industries like Chlorofluorocarbon, nitrogen oxide, carbon monoxide, and other dust particles pollutes the air. Since man began to use tools and gradually formed a society, he began to play an important role in the evolution of the natural environment.

5.2.1. Land Degradation

Land degradation is a worldwide problem: land degradation may occur naturally as well as man made activities. The climate change majorly combined with human activities for continuous soil degradation. Wilcox et al., (2003), Vanacker et al., (2014), Maurya, and Malik (2016a), noted that surface soil disturbances can modify surface topographical features and the vegetation patch structure (Mohr et al., 2013; Malik and Maurya, 2015).

The deforestation, desalination, waterlogging desertification, wasteland, and soil erosion are major causes of land degradation. FAO estimated that about 2 billion people (or ¾ of the population of developing countries at that time) depended on biomass for their daily energy consumption (Kumar et al., 2020) (Figure 5.2).

Figure 5.2. A picture of degraded land.

Source: Image by Pixabay.

5.2.2. Pollution

Air pollution refers to the release of harmful contaminants (chemicals, toxic gases, particulates, biological molecules, etc.) into the earth's atmosphere. These contaminants are quite detrimental, and in some cases, pose serious health issues. Water pollution is said to occur when toxic pollutants and particulate matter are introduced into water bodies such as lakes, rivers, and seas.

These contaminants are generally introduced by human activities like improper sewage treatment and oil spills. Pollution is a very serious worldwide problem, pollution resulted in the deterioration of the quality of natural biotic and abiotic factors (Rahman et al., 2017; Cheng et al., 2016). Water pollution is a very big problem especially in developing countries in the world.

The water covered about 71% of the total earth's surface and groundwater. The groundwater scarcity is especially in the developing countries of the worldwide (Karikari and Ansa, 2006). Water is one of the more demandable of all urban and rural amenities and indispensable for human activities including water for drinking and irrigation, recreational opportunities and habitat for economically important fisheries.

Pollution poses a serious risk to life, especially when the water is a source of drinking and for domestic purposes for humans, polluted waters are potent agents of diseases such as cholera, typhoid, and tuberculosis. Olaniran (1995) defined water pollution to be the presence of excessive amounts of a hazard (pollutants) in water in such a way that it is no longer suitable for drinking, bathing, cooking or other uses.

> Pollution is the introduction of contamination into the environment. Water pollution is generally induced by humans. It results from the actions of humans carried on to a better self. These could be treated under the various activities that man engages in, which leads to pollution. The growth of the human population, industrial, and agricultural practices is the major cause of pollution (Maurya and Malik, 2016a).

As they respire, the decomposers use up dissolved oxygen (O_2) and the Biological Oxygen Demand (BOD) reduces. The flora and fauna of the rivers experience change and reduction in number due to death by suffocation (Maurya and Malik, 2016b; Maurya et al., 2019). The growing problem of pollution of the river ecosystem has necessitated the monitoring of water quality.

Freshwater is a finite resource, essential for agriculture, industry, and even human existence, without freshwater of adequate quantity and quality, sustainable development will not be possible. Industry and automobiles are the primary and secondary contributors to air pollution worldwide (Kay, 1999); the automobiles are used every gallon of gasoline manufactured, distributed, and then burned in a vehicle, produced along with carbon dioxide

(CO_2), carbon monoxides, sulfur dioxide, nitrogen dioxide, and particulate matter; these emissions contribute to increased global warming (Alexander and Kanner, 1995; Mark, 1997).

The environmental protection agency (EPA) estimates that industrial workers suffer up to 300,000 pesticide-related acute illnesses and injuries per year, mostly cholinergic symptoms from anticholinesterases and lung disease from airborne exposure (Hansen and Donohoe, 2002; Mellon et al., 1995). These are toxic, remain in the environment long-term, resist degradation, and can travel long distances (Figure 5.3).

Figure 5.3. A firm polluting the air.

Source: Image by Max Pixel.

5.2.3. Global Warming

Global warming which is also referred to as climate change is the observed rise in the average temperature of the Earth's climate system the global surface temperature is likely to rise a further 0.3 to 1.7 °C in the lowest emissions scenario, and 2.6 to 4.8 °C in the highest emissions scenario. These readings have been recorded by the "national science academies of the major industrialized nations."

Future climate change and impacts will differ from region to region. Expected effects include an increase in global temperatures, rising sea levels, deforestation, imbalance climatic condition, changing precipitation, and expansion of deserts (Cunningham et al., 1999). Global warming has several adverse effects on human health, and agricultural production.

It leads to an increase in heat-related diseases, civil conflict, decreases economic sources shown in Figure 5.4. Besides, it also indirectly affects human health due to the higher incidence of malaria, dengue, yellow fever and viral encephalitis caused by the expansion of mosquitoes and other disease carriers to warm areas. The adverse effect on agricultural production is due to the increased frequency of droughts, floods, and hurricanes and increased incidence of pests, causing a shortage of food.

Figure 5.4. Climate change is the main cause behind global warming.

Source: Image by Pixabay.

5.2.4. Overpopulation

It is very likely that population growth as a missing scientific agenda accounts in part for the reduced public knowledge and interest in this issue. The extent of environmental degradation varies across countries and regions of the world. Rapid population growth puts a strain on natural resources which results in degradation of our environment.

The mortality rate has gone down due to better medical facilities which have resulted in increased lifespan. More population simply means more demand for food, clothes, and shelter. You need more space to grow food and provide homes to millions of people. This results in deforestation loss of biodiversity, destruction of the ecosystem which is another factor of environmental degradation.

5.2.5. Landfills

Landfills pollute the environment and destroy the beauty of the city. Landfills come within the city due to the large amount of waste that gets generated by households, industries, factories, and hospitals. Landfills pose a great risk to the health of the environment and the people who live there. Landfills produce a foul smell when burned and cause huge environmental degradation (Figure 5.5).

Figure 5.5. A picture of landfill waste garbage.

Source: Image by Pixabay.

5.2.6. Deforestation

Forests are invaluable property of a nation because they provide raw materials to modern industries, timber for building purposes, habitats for numerous types of animals and micro-organisms. Good fertile and nutrient-rich soils having a high content of organic matter offer protection to soils by binding the soils through the network of their roots and by protecting the soils from the direct impact of falling raindrops.

They encourage and increase the infiltration of rainwater and thus allow maximum recharge of groundwater resources, minimize surface run-off and hence reduce the frequency, intensity, and dimension of floods. Deforestation is the cutting down of trees to make way for more homes and industries.

Rapid growth in population and urban sprawl are two of the major causes of deforestation. Apart from that, the use of forest land for agriculture, animal grazing, harvests for fuelwood and logging are some of the other causes of deforestation. Deforestation contributes to global warming as decreased forest size puts carbon back into the environment.

Deforestation gives birth to several problems encompassing environmental degradation through accelerated rate of soil erosion, increase in the sediment load of the rivers, siltation or reservoirs and river beds, increase in the frequency and dimension of Hoods and droughts, changes in the pattern of distribution of precipitation, intensification of greenhouse effects increase in the destructive force of the atmospheric storms, etc. (Figure 5.6).

Figure 5.6. Nature forestry deforestation.

Source: Image by Public Domain Picture.

5.2.7. Natural Causes

Things like avalanches, quakes, tidal waves, storms, and fires can totally crush nearby animal and plant groups to the point where they can no longer survive in those areas. This can either come to fruition through physical demolition as the result of a specific disaster or by the long-term degradation of assets by the presentation of an obtrusive foreign species to the environment.

The latter frequently happens after tidal waves, when reptiles and bugs are washed ashore, of course, humans aren't totally to blame for this whole thing. Earth itself causes ecological issues, as well. While environmental degradation is most normally connected with the things that people do, the truth of the matter is that the environment is always changing. With or without the effect of human exercises, a few biological systems degrade to the point where they can't help the life that is supposed to live there.

5.2.8. The Economic Logic

Environmental change is one of the myriads of pressures or demands made upon state resources and attention. Many of the responses to environmental stress that occur involve uncoordinated human responses greatly affected by markets. Accordingly, producers, and consumers respond to changes in prices, relative incomes, and external constraints.

But frequently market 'signals' do not reflect social values, as in the case of intergenerational equity, for example, or the deleterious effects of environmental degradation are not internalized in market prices and remain as 'externalities.' As a result, states often choose to intervene with collective actions aimed at managing environmental change and reducing the associated adverse social and economic effects.

5.3. FACTORS RESPONSIBLE FOR ENVIRONMENTAL DEGRADATION

5.3.1. Socio-Economic Factors

Besides the pure economic logic, there are several other socio-economic factors such as population pressure, poverty, unemployment, ignorance, and lack of incentives for using the environment in a socially optimum manner on sustainable basis. So long as the human and animal population was within the carrying capacity of locally available natural resources and local environment, there was no environmental degradation due to human actions.

But as the population increased and local economies got integrated with external economies through trade, the process of degradation of natural resources and the environment started. The need to meet the increasing demand of rapidly increasing human population for food, fiber, and other agricultural commodities has necessitated the intensification and chemicalization of agriculture, leading to degradation of land and decline in its productivity.

Further, the fact that many communities who depend directly on natural resources for their livelihood are very poor, ignorant, and have no alternative employment opportunities means that they are compelled by their circumstances to over-exploit and degrade the natural resources accessible to them. Illicit felling of trees from forests, hunting, encroachment of forest land, and poaching are some of the activities resorted to by the communities, partly driven by their basic needs and partly by greed. This might happen even if it is to the longer-term detriment of the communities' own wellbeing.

Another important economic reason for environmental degradation is the fact that protection and conservation of environment has a high opportunity cost, especially in developing countries like India. For instance, in the case of forests, the opportunity cost is the value that could be derived by clear-cutting the timber and using the forest land for agricultural purpose, or as a site for a hydropower project.

Likewise, the opportunity cost of conservation of a marine ecosystem is the value that could be derived from depleting the entire fish stock to extinction. In view of this, the local resource users do not have any incentive to protect and conserve the environment.

5.3.2. Technological Factors

Another major reason of environmental degradation in India is the fact that beginning the mid-1960s, there have been many technological breakthroughs in the agricultural sector, which ushered in the so-called "Green Revolution."

For example, there has been widespread adoption of high yielding varieties of crops for few major food grain crops such as rice and wheat in conjunction with increased use of water, chemical fertilizers and plant protection chemicals. This has led to the increasing uniformity within those species and varieties of crops and hence the loss of biodiversity and increased levels of degradation of land due to excessive irrigation and pollution of water bodies due to leaching of harmful residues of chemical fertilizers and pesticides.

Increasing use of tractors and other farm machinery in agriculture is causing air pollution. Besides, development, and widespread use of water extracting devices such as drilling machines and power-operated submersible pump sets has led to the over-exploitation of groundwater basins and development of mechanized trawlers to over-fishing of marine fisheries and pollution of sea water.

5.4. EXTENTS OF ENVIRONMENTAL DEGRADATION

5.4.1. Land Degradation

Trash and garbage are a common sight in urban and rural areas of India. It is a major source of pollution. Indian cities alone generate more than 100 million tons of solid waste a year. Street corners are piled with trash. Public places and sidewalks are despoiled with filth and litter, rivers, and canals act as garbage dumps.

Soils are a key element in the climate change equation and perhaps the least well understood. Although models of soil organic matter decomposition predict increasing rates with increasing temperature, field measurements seem to contradict model results (Sax et al., 2002). In addition to increases in CO_2 emissions, industrialization has increased the amount of nitrogen deposition.

Nitrogen deposition from human activities may help forests that are nitrogen-limited, but excess nitrogen deposition can lead to soil acidification and reduced nutrient availability to plants (Aber et al., 2001; Magnani et al., 2007).

5.4.2. Degradation of Water Resources

Microbe contamination of groundwater due to sewage outfalls and high concentration of nutrients in marine and coastal waters due to agricultural runoff are among the most serious threats (Kumar et al., 2019a). Contact with unsafe drinking or bathing water can impose serious risks (both acute and delayed) on human health.

While tap water is subject to treatment and is required to meet detailed testing and purity standards, it is not always disinfected of diarrhea inducing microorganisms, as illustrated by waterborne disease outbreaks such as that caused by Cryptosporidium in Milwaukie in 1993, which affected over 400,000 people.

Furthermore, fecal coliforms are not prohibited in bottled water (Nation Staff, 1996), and water bottled and sold within the same state is not subject to Food and Drug Administration standards (Hammitt et al., 2006).

Today 40% of waters are unfit for fishing or swimming, and levels of mercury in fish in 40 states. Clean Water Act of 1972 states to publish a list of all water bodies that fail to meet water quality standards, and for the states to set pollution limits and scale back pollution in watersheds until standards are met, compliance is negligible and enforcement weak.

Discharge of untreated sewage is the single most important cause for pollution of surface and groundwater in India (Kumar et al., 2019b). There is a large gap between the generation and treatment of domestic wastewater in India. The problem is not only that India lacks sufficient treatment capacity but also that the sewage treatment plants that exist do not operate and are not maintained.

In a National Resources Defense Council study of the quality of bottled water (Nation Staff, 1996), approximately one-fifth of samples exceeded bacterial purity guidelines and/or safe levels of arsenic or other synthetic organic chemicals (AJS, 1999). Between 25% and 40% of bottled water was merely repackaged municipal tap water.

The cost of illness approach and Shuval calculates the disability-adjusted life years (DALY), to estimate the health costs of illnesses linked to recreational coastal water pollution. India is known for having serious water pollution problems, primarily due to untreated sewage. Rivers like the Ganges, Yamuna, and Mithi are contaminated because they flow through densely inhabited areas.

Effluents are another by-product of industries that poses threat to the environment, leather, and tanning businesses, petroleum companies, and chemical manufacturing sectors all produce substantial waste products that are dumped directly into neighboring streams without treatment, polluting rivers and harming aquatic life.

Due to bad design, poor maintenance, and a lack of stable electricity to operate the facilities, as well as absentee personnel and poor management, the majority of government-owned sewage treatment plants remain closed the bulk of the time. Only 209 of India's 3,119 towns and cities have partial sewage treatment facilities, according to a World Health Organization survey, and only 8 have full wastewater treatment facilities.

Over 100 Indian cities discharge untreated sewage into the Ganges River. Investment is required to close the gap between India's sewage production of 29000 million liters per day and its treatment capacity of just 6000 million liters per day (Figure 5.7).

Figure 5.7. River with garbage dump.

Source: Image by Wikimedia Commons.

5.4.3. Drought, Desertification, and Water Scarcity

Drought and scarcity of water are the third major climate change impact that may have a considerable impact on climate-related migration. Droughts, desertification, and water scarcity are all predicted to become more common as the consequence of global warming. Around one-third of the world's current population is expected to be affected by these events.

Droughts are expected to displace millions of people around the world, causing food instability and threatening human livelihoods. As sea levels rise, salinization of groundwater and estuaries will expand, reducing the amount of freshwater available to humans and ecosystems in coastal locations. Furthermore, shifting precipitation patterns put a strain on the availability of access to clean water supplies (Figure 5.8).

Figure 5.8. Effects of water scarcity in desert.

Source: Image by Flickr.

5.4.4. Degradation of Fisheries

Fish is an essential component of the human diet in many places of the world. As a result, the number of fish collected in natural water bodies has increased dramatically. This finding highlights the importance of studying fish stocks in natural water bodies, particularly commercial fish, in order to manage them effectively.

Natural and fishing-related losses in fisheries include spoilage, breakage, size, discarding bycatch, and operational losses. Although the severity of the problem varies from a particular location to another, the country as a whole loses massive amounts of fish after capture before reaching consumers.

Depicted trade work and GDP production economic scale structure technique and conservation of environmental policies structure as a first step toward overcoming losses and defining remedies to the present problem.

The fishing method, inadequate handling facilities, and delays between catch, collection, and distribution were the main causes of losses, as were the lack of regulations governing the quality and standards of fish sold for human consumption, lack of regular government supervision, poor extension service, and fragmentation of duties and responsibilities in different institutions.

However, the protection of marine and coastal areas, as well as habitat restoration, should not be viewed as a replacement for traditional management measures, but rather as part of a comprehensive coastal zone and fisheries management program.

5.5. EFFECTS OF ENVIRONMENTAL DEGRADATION

5.5.1. Impact on Human Health

Human health might be jeopardized as it is at the receiving end of the harm caused by environmental degradation. Respiratory problems like pneumonia and asthma are potentially arise in areas exposed to toxic air pollutants. The death count is said to have reached millions when it comes to people who have died off due to the indirect effects of air pollution (Adakole and Oladimeji, 2006).

5.5.2. Loss of Biodiversity

For the maintenance of the balance of the ecosystem in the face of combating pollution, restoring nutrients, protecting water sources and stabilizing climate, biodiversity is essential. Under the heading of major causes of loss of biodiversity deforestation, global warming, overpopulation, and pollution find a decisive place.

5.5.3. Ozone Layer Depletion

The goal of protecting the earth from harmful ultraviolet rays is achieved by the ozone layer which is responsible for its protection. The presence of chlorofluorocarbons, hydro chlorofluorocarbons in the atmosphere is causing the ozone layer to deplete. As it will deplete, it will emit harmful radiation back to the earth (Buhaug et al., 2010).

5.5.4. Loss for the Tourism Industry

The degradation of the ecosystem could be a major setback for the tourism industry, which depends on tourists for its daily income. Most tourists will be put off by environmental degradation such as loss of green cover, biodiversity loss, massive landfills, increasing air and water pollution.

5.5.5. Economic Impact

The enormous price that a country may have to bear as a result of environmental degradation can have a significant economic impact in terms of green cover restoration, landfill cleanup, and endangered species protection. The economic impact can also be measured in terms of lost tourism revenue. As you can see, there are numerous factors that might impact the environment. If we are not careful, we may contribute to the global environmental deterioration that is unfolding.

We can, however, take action to stop it and care for the world we live in by providing environmental education (EE) to people, which will help them gain a better understanding of their surroundings, allowing them to address environmental concerns and make the environment more useful and protected for our children and future generations.

5.6. THE BASIC ENVIRONMENTAL KUZNETS CURVE

The EKC is a proposed link between various indicators of environmental degradation and the per capita income. Pollution emissions rise and environmental quality falls in the early stages of economic expansion, but after per capita income reaches a certain threshold (which varies depending on the indicator), the pattern reverses, and economic growth leads to environmental improvement.

This means that environmental damages or emissions per capita are inversely proportional or U-shaped function of per capita income. This means that environmental damages or emissions per capita are inversely proportional U-shaped function of per capita income.

According to the EKC, economic expansion initially causes environmental degradation, but at a certain degree of economic growth, a society's interaction with the environment improves and levels of environmental degradation decrease. From a basic perspective, it appears that economic growth is beneficial to the environment.

However, experts counter that economic progress does not always imply a better environment; in fact, the opposite is often true. At the absolute least, it necessitates very targeted policies and mindsets to ensure that economic expansion is compatible with environmental improvement. The EKC concept gained popularity in the 1990s, prompting a flood of studies to test it for a range of contaminants (Figure 5.9).

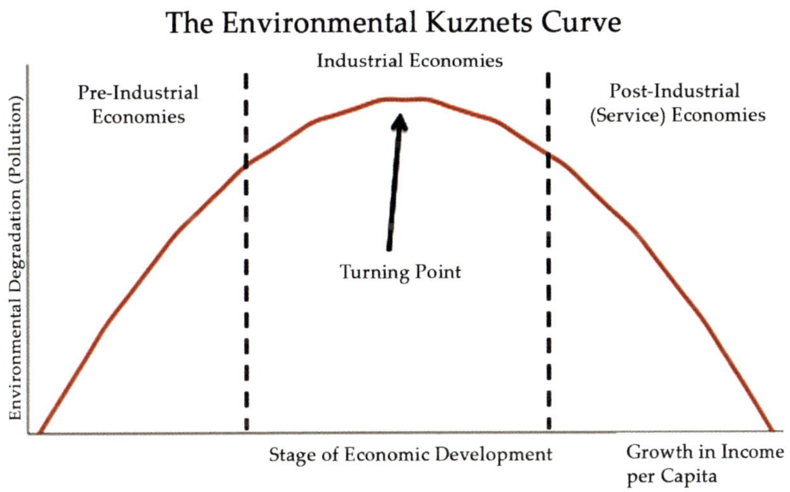

Figure 5.9. Environmental Kuznets curve.

Source: Image by Wikimedia Commons.

5.7. CAUSES OF ENVIRONMENTAL KUZNETS CURVE

5.7.1. Empirical Evidence of Declining Pollution Levels with Economic Growth

According to studies, rising economic expansion in the United States led to increased car use, but lower levels of air pollution due to regulation (in particular sulfur dioxide levels declined).

5.7.2. Spare Income with Growth

More discretionary income is availed by people after making the payment for their basic necessities in the condition of economic growth that has high rates; therefore, they are more amenable to paying higher prices in return for better environmental standards.

5.7.3. Focus on Living Standards as Opposed to Real GDP

Increasing the real GDP and rates of economic growth is a concern of traditional economic theory that concentrates on the same. However, there is a growing awareness that the link between economic growth and living standards can be weak. Thus, focusing on living standards potentially has chances of becoming politically popular.

5.7.4. Improved Technology

Long-term economic growth is primarily driven by the conditions of improved technology and higher productivity. With a higher productivity, a higher output can be witnessed, as fewer raw materials used. For example, since the 1950s, the technology of car use has drastically made fuel efficiency better. In the 1950s, various cars had a significantly low mile per gallon. In recent years, car manufacturers have made earnest attempts to reduce fuel consumption and have started to develop hybrid technology.

5.7.5. Solar and Renewable Energy

The progress in solar technology is an excellent example of how improved technology has reduced the potential for environmental damage. With the cost of solar energy significantly falling in recent years, it has given rise to the prospect of clean technology.

5.7.6. De-Industrialization

In its earlier stages, economic developments lead to a shift from farming to manufacturing. This further resulted in greater environmental degradation. However, increased productivity and rising real incomes see a third shift from industrial to the service sector. An economy like the UK has seen industrialization shrink as a share of the economy. Generally, the service sector has a lower environmental impact than the manufacturing sector.

5.7.7. Role of Government Regulation

Generally economic growth and development see a growth in the size of government as a share of GDP. Enabling the government to implement taxes and regulations in an attempt to solve environmental externalities which harm health and living standards.

5.7.8. Diminishing Marginal Utility of Income

The marginal utility of rising income diminishes. The benefit from your first £10,000 annual income is very high. But, if income rises from £90,000-£100,000 the gain is very limited in comparison. Having a very high salary is of little consolation if you live with environmental degradation (e.g., congestion, pollution, and ill health). Therefore, a rational person who is seeing rising incomes will begin to place greater stress on improving other aspects of living standards.

5.8. CRITICISMS OF KUZNETS ENVIRONMENTAL CURVE

5.8.1. Empirical Evidence is Mixed

There is no certainty that as the economy grows, pollution levels will decrease. Pollution is not simply a function of income, but various other factors. For example, the effectiveness of government regulation, the development of the economy, population levels.

5.8.2. Global Pollution

A reduction in industry and growth in the service sector has been witnessed by various developed economies however; they still import goods from the developing countries. In that sense, they are exporting environmental degradation. Pollution may be decreasing in the United Kingdom and the United States, but environmental deterioration in countries that export to these countries is increasing.

In the case of deforestation, for example. Higher-income countries tend to halt deforestation, but they continue to import beef and furniture from countries that are converting forests into cropland.

5.8.3. Growth Leads to Increased Resource Use

Some economists think that with industrialization, there is less environmental deterioration. However, as the economy continues to grow, some resources will unavoidably be utilized in bigger quantities. There is no certainty that environmental degradation will continue to decline over time.

Countries with the highest GDP have highest levels of CO_2 emission. For example, US has CO_2 emissions of 17.564 tons per capita. Ethiopia has by comparison 0.075 tons per capita. China's CO_2 emissions have increased from 1,500 million tons in 1981 to 8,000 million tons in 2009.

5.9. EMPIRICAL MODELS OF ENVIRONMENT AND GROWTH

The environment-growth debate in the empirical literature has centered on the following five questions. First, is the often-hypothesized inverted-U-shaped relationship between income and environmental deterioration, referred to as the EKC, exist, and if so, how robust and universal is it?

Second, what effect does population growth, income distribution, international commerce, and time-and-space dependent (rather than income-dependent) variables play?

Third, how relevant is a statistical link calculated from cross-country or panel data to an individual country's environmental trajectory, as well as the expected trajectory of today's developing and transition economies?

Fourth, how can ecological thresholds and irreversible damages impact the inverted-U relationship between environmental degradation and economic growth? Is it possible to understand a static statistical relationship in terms of carrying capacity, ecological resilience, and sustainability? Lastly, what is the role of environmental policy both in explaining the shape of the income-environment relationship, and in lowering the environmental price of economic growth and ensuring more sustainable outcomes?

Empirical models of environment and growth generally consist of reduced form single-equation specifications relating an environmental impact indicator to a measure of income per capita. Few models use emissions of a particular pollutant (e.g., SO_2, CO_2 or particulates) as dependent variables, whereas the others use ambient concentrations of various pollutants as recorded by monitoring stations; yet other studies employ composite indexes of environmental degradation.

The common independent variable of most models is income per capita, but some studies use income data converted into purchasing power parity (PPP), while others use incomes at market exchange rates. Different studies control for different variables, such as population density, openness to trade, income distribution and geographical and institutional variables.

The functional specification is usually quadratic, log quadratic or cubic in income and environmental degradation. They are estimated econometrically using cross-section or panel data and many test for country and time-fixed effects. The ad hoc specifications and reduced form of these models turn them into a "black box" that shrouds the underlying determinants of environmental quality and circumscribes their usefulness in policy formulation.

Some recent efforts have been made to investigate the theoretical foundations of the environment-income link, as well as some modest attempts to dissect the income-environment relationship into its constituent scale, composition, and abatement effects. However, as Stern points out, the theoretical models have not been explicitly empirically tested, and we still lack a rigorous and systematic decomposition study.

5.9.1. Theoretical Underpinnings of Empirical Models

The structure of the income environment interaction is determined by the peculiarities of production and abatement technologies, as well as preferences and their evolution with income increase. Some authors concentrate on changes in production technology as a result of structural changes that accompany economic expansion.

Others have focused on the features of abatement technology. Others have concentrated on choice qualities, including income elasticity for environmental quality. A few writers have developed comprehensive growth models based on realistic assumptions about technological and preference features, from which they construct EKCs.

The model by López consists of two production sectors, with weak separability between pollution and other factors of production (labor and capital), constant returns to scale and technical change and prices that are exogenously determined. When producers get a free pass on the environment or pay set pollution fees, pollution levels always rise.

The pollution-income relationship is determined by the features of technology and preferences when producers pay the full marginal social cost of the pollution they produce. With homothetic preferences, pollution levels rise in lockstep with income; with non-homothetic preferences, the faster marginal utility falls with consumption levels, and the higher the elasticity of substitution between pollution and other inputs, the less pollution rises in lockstep with output growth.

Empirically plausible values for these two parameters result in an inverted-U-shaped relationship between pollution and income. This tends to explain why in the case of pollutants such as SO_2 and particulates, where the damage is more evident to consumers and, hence, pollution prices are near their marginal social costs, turning points have been identified at relatively low income levels.

In contrast, turning points are found at much higher income levels, or not at all, for pollutants such as CO_2, from which damage is less immediate and less evident to consumers, and hence underpriced, if priced at all.

Selden and Song, using Forster's growth and pollution model with a utility function that is additively separable between consumption and pollution, derive an inverted-U path for pollution and a J-curve for abatement that starts when a given capital stock is achieved; that is, expenditure on pollution abatement is zero until "development has created enough consumption and enough environmental damage to merit expenditures on abatement."

Two sets of factors contribute to an early and rapid increase in abatement:

i) on the technology side, large direct effects of growth on pollution and high marginal effectiveness of abatement, and ii) on the demand side (preferences), rapidly declining marginal utility of consumption and rapidly rising marginal concern over mounting pollution levels. To the extent that development reduces the carrying capacity of the environment, the abatement effort must increase at an increasing rate to offset the effects of growth on pollution.

The income elasticity of demand for environmental quality has been stressed in a number of empirical EKC models as the theoretical underpinning of the inverted-U-shaped link between pollution and income.

According to Arrow et al., the inverted-U-shaped curve "is consistent with the notion that people spend proportionately more on environmental quality as their income rises, economists have conjectured that the curve applies to environmental quality generally." A number of earlier studies found income elasticities for environmental improvements greater than one.

Kriström reviewed the evidence from contingent valuation method (CVM) studies that found income elasticities for environmental quality much less than one.

By adapting a static model of an endlessly lived home in which pollution is generated through consumption and reduced by abatement, the role of income elasticity of demand for environmental quality in EKC models is investigated. He finds that the higher the income elasticity of demand for environmental quality, the slower the growth of pollution when positive, and the faster the decline when negative, but there is no special role assigned to income elasticity equal to or greater than one.

It was found that when preferences are non-additive or pollution affects output, pollution can actually decrease even with a zero or negative income elasticity of demand (e.g., reduced labor productivity because of damage to health, material damage due to acid rain or loss of crop output due to agricultural externalities).

While preferences compatible with a positive income elasticity of demand for environmental quality are beneficial, they are neither required nor sufficient for an inverted-Ushaped relationship between pollution and income, according to him. In non-valuation research, McConnell found little microeconomic evidence that supports the responsiveness of preferences to income changes in macroeconomic EKC models.

In overlapping generation models pollution is generated by consumption activities and is only partially internalized as the current generation considers the impact of pollution on its own welfare but not on the welfare of future generations. In these models, the economy is characterized by declining environmental quality when consumption levels are low, but given sufficient returns to environmental maintenance, environmental quality recovers and may even improve absolutely with economic growth.

Andreoni and Levinson derived inverted-Ushaped pollution-income curves from a simple model with two commodities, one good and one bad, which are bundled together. Increased income leads to increased consumption of the good, which leads to an increase in the bad. This forces consumers to make a choice: they can spend some of their income on abatement to mitigate the negative consequences of the bad by foregoing some consumption of the good.

When increasing returns characterize abatement technologies, high-income individuals (or countries) can more readily accomplish higher consumption while emitting less pollution than low-income individuals (or nations), resulting in an inverted-U-shaped optimal pollution-income path.

When a lumpy investment is required or when a lower marginal cost technology (e.g., scrubbers or treatment plants) is required, the abatement technology is characterized by growing returns; poor economies are not large enough or polluted enough to earn a worthwhile return on investment and end up using low fixed-cost, high marginal-cost technologies, while rich economies are large enough and polluted enough to make effective use of high fixed-cost, low marginal-cost technologies.

Because different pollutants require different abatement solutions, the income-environment link may or may not be inverted. According to the authors, similar results can be obtained from other "good-bad" combinations, such as driving a vehicle associated with a mortality risk that can be mitigated by investments in safety equipment: "both the poor who drive very little and the rich who invest in safe cars face lower risk from driving than middle-income people."

Khan discovered an inverted-U-shaped association between hydrocarbon emissions and household income in California, and Chaudhuri and Pfaff discovered an inverted-U-shaped relationship between indoor pollution and household income in Pakistan.

Even though many of the models used in econometric estimations of the EKC have been ad hoc formulations, there has been no scarcity of theoretical micro-foundations of an inverted-U-shape relationship between income and pollution, ranging to the abatement technology and consumer preferences, from production structure.

5.10. SOLUTIONS TO ENVIRONMENTAL DEGRADATION

5.10.1. Stop Deforestation

Stopping deforestation is critical for our environmental system to prevent the negative effects of environmental degradation. We cannot afford to chop or burn down trees because they store greenhouse gases, create oxygen, and provide a natural habitat for a variety of animals and plants that may become endangered if these forests are destroyed.

In the sake of environmental protection, a massive afforestation campaign should be initiated. Reforestation or afforestation can help us make an even bigger difference (Figure 5.10).

Figure 5.10. A logo of stop deforestation.

Source: Image by Wikimedia Commons.

5.10.2. Government Regulations

When problems arise that result in serious environmental deterioration, governments must intervene and provide a framework. Governments impose high levies on activities that affect the environment and provide financial incentives for ecologically favorable conduct. These will also compel businesses and individuals to refrain from behaviors that harm the environment.

5.10.3. Fines and Punishment for Illegal dumping

It is no longer a rarity to see or come across huge piles of wastes, old house items, construction waste or used products dumped by the roadside, in the forests, or non-designated dumping sites. The emergence of this trend and its spreading is becoming a problem because it hinders the objective of keeping the environment clean and can have serious impacts on wildlife and habitat.

This malpractice is termed as illegal dumping, according to environmental protection agencies and departments, it is considered unlawful on account of the harm it causes to the environment. To mitigate the negative environmental repercussions, there should be stiff penalties for un-authorized dumping. People and businesses will continue to dump rubbish illegally since they know the consequences are minimal even if they are caught.

As a result, increasing the sanctions for unlawful dumping would encourage people to dispose of their rubbish at official waste disposal locations (Figure 5.11).

Figure 5.11. No dumping sign board.

Source: Image by public domain picture.

5.10.4. Reduce Consumption Levels

It has become imperative that we minimize our consumption. Our sophisticated civilization is always on the lookout for the latest technologies, smartphones, and fashionable clothing, among other things.

However, this behavior results in significant resource depletion and waste production. To avoid negative environmental implications, we must drastically reduce our consumption levels.

5.10.5. Reuse and Reduce Waste Generation

You may cut down on waste by making better use of your things and food. If you want to get rid of outdated but still functional items, be creative in giving them a new look or repurposing them.

Your material assets will be better utilized as a result. If they can no longer be used, separate them and donate them to recycling.

5.10.6. Avoid Plastic

Plastic waste is a major environmental issue that contributes to enormous plastic pollution and environmental deterioration. To reduce plastic waste, avoid purchasing things with plastic wrappers or packaging, and avoid using throwaway plastic bags, plates, containers, silverware, and other items. Instead, bring your own reusable items that you can reuse multiple times.

5.10.7. Education

Environmental Education (EE) is a methodology wherein familiarity is picked up by people with their surroundings and secure learning, abilities, values, experiences, and passion, all of which lead to empowerment that enables them to act—separately and aggregately—to take care of present and future environmental issues.

It is the study of relationships and interactions between natural and human systems. To put it briefly, EE is provided in order to create a better understanding of the world around people so that they know how to take care of it in a proper manner, making the world a better place.

It is absolutely essential that children should know about the adverse environmental consequences of our behavior during our daily routine and the ways in which our ecological footprint can be improved.

This learning should begin in elementary school. In comparison to adults, children are usually more ready to learn new things and adjust their behavior.

When these youngsters grow up, they are more likely to act in an environmentally good manner, and they may even persuade their parents to act in an environmentally favorable manner.

5.10.8. Convince Others

You can increase your positive influence even more by persuading others of the importance of ecologically friendly behavior. Tell them what environmental deterioration implies for future generations and how minor changes in our daily lives can help to mitigate these negative consequences.

We can, however, take action in order to halt it and take care of the world that we live in through providing EE to the people who will help them pick familiarity with their surroundings and lead to them taking care of environmental concerns thus making it more useful and protected for our children and other generations to come.

5.11. CONCLUSION

After reading the chapter it can be concluded that the degradation of the environment is a major concern that is intertwined with the economic activity. We have seen the correlation between the two through the presentation of instances like the impact of environment on tourism and fisheries. These are essential activities that add to the livelihood of many people.

The chapter suggests the need to treat this as a personal and immediate concern which is why the various solutions to environmental degradation are centered in the differences that can be made by individuals themselves. There is a need for conviction or the impact will be graver than it already is.

REFERENCES

1. Alvarado, R., & Toledo, E., (2016). Environmental degradation and economic growth: Evidence for a developing country. *Environment, Development and Sustainability, 19*(4), 1205–1218. [online] Available at: https://www.researchgate.net/publication/301313579_Environmental_degradation_and_economic_growth_evidence_for_a_developing_country (accessed on 21 June 2022).
2. Conserve Energy Future, (2022). *Causes, Effects and Solutions to Environmental Degradation-Conserve Energy Future.* [online] Conserve Energy Future. Available at: https://www.conserve-energy-future.com/causes-and-effects-of-environmental-degradation.php (accessed on 21 June 2022).
3. Maurya, P., Ali, S., Ahmad, A., Zhou, Q., Da Silva, C. J., Khane, E., & Ali, A., (2020). An introduction to environmental degradation: Causes, consequence and mitigation. *Environmental Degradation: Causes and Remediation Strategies*, 1–20. [online] Available at: https://www.aesacademy.org/books/edcrs-vol-1/01.pdf (accessed on 21 June 2022).
4. Theodore, P., (2003). Economic growth and the environment. [e-Book] *Economic Survey of Europe,* 25–72. Available at: https://unece.org/fileadmin/DAM/ead/pub/032/032_c2.pdf (accessed on 21 June 2022).
5. Tim, E., Mallika, I., Gian, P. A., & Alex, R., (2010). *Economic Growth and the Environment.* [e-Book] DEFRA. Available at: https://assets.publishing.service.gov.uk/government/uploads/system/uploads/attachment_data/file/69195/pb13390-economic-growth-100305.pdf (accessed on 21 June 2022).

CHAPTER 6

ROLE OF AGRICULTURAL ECONOMICS FOR SUSTAINABLE DEVELOPMENT

CONTENTS

The following chapter introduces the concept of agro-economics and its various characteristics. Few definitions by researchers and scholars are enclosed. The history of the development of the concept of Agricultural economics in the 19th century is traced. Further, the importance of agriculture in the developing, developed, and underdeveloped nations is spoken about.

Characteristics of agricultural economics that include land distribution system, supply of consumer's good, industrial inputs, labor employment etc. are highlighted. Next section speaks about the cruciality of agriculture and its role in economic development especially in the Indian economy.

Lastly, current issues in agricultural economics such as the MSP, rebuilding of economies, and budgetary policies are discussed.

6.1. INTRODUCTION

Agroeconomics is an applied social science that examines how producers, consumers, and societies use scarce resources when producing, marketing, and consuming food and fiber products. Market forces govern agricultural markets. There is no doubt that agriculture is one of the most important economic sectors. Agriculture economics is a relatively new field of study.

A separate discipline of agricultural economics does not have enough literature on many aspects. Following the depression of the 1890's, which resulted in serious effects on agriculture, economists became interested in conducting farm management studies in a systematic manner.

In the 1920s, renowned economists like Henry Moore of Columbia University and Henry Schultz of Chicago University contributed to Agricultural Economics by applying quantitative methods, and initiated a number of demand and supply studies which were influenced by Walras and Pareto. A major work on agricultural production economics was also published by Black in 1926 (Figure 6.1).

Figure 6.1. Policy seminar: transforming food systems to deliver healthy, sustainable diets: the view from the world's science academies.

Source: Image by flickr.

In the past quarter of this century, Taylor has done more than any other writer to shape the development of Agricultural Economics. As early as 1961, G.E. Braundow integrated the earlier work on supply and demand functions into an integrated model of agricultural commodities demand and supply in the U.S.A. over the past forty years.

Agriculture Economics is an economics that deals with agriculture and consists of the words i.e., Agriculture and Economics. Agriculture comes from the Latin word "age"r, which refers to the soil, and "culture", which refers to its cultivation. Agricultural production in its broadest sense includes the cultivation of crops and raising of livestock.

. Agriculture economics is an applied area of science wherein the standards of decision are applied in the utilization of scant assets like land, work, capital, and the board in cultivating and partnered exercises.

Agriculture economics, is a science where the standards and strategies for financial aspects are applied to the extraordinary states of agrarian industry (Prof. Grey). Agriculture Economics is the investigation of connections emerging from the wealth getting and wealth using action of man in agribusiness. (Hibbard).

Agriculture economics is an applied social science managing how human decide to utilize specialized information and the scarce production assets, for example, land, work, capital, and the executives to deliver food and fiber and to disseminate it for utilization to different individuals from the general public throughout a period (Cramer and Jensen).

The underlying foundations of Agriculture economics can be followed back to ancient Egypt, seemingly to the first agriculture economist Joseph. Joseph deciphered the fantasies of the Pharaoh of Egypt and accurately anticipated seven years of gala and seven years of starvation & famine. What is agriculture economics?

If you were to say "Agricultural economics is the application of economic principles to agriculture," you would be technically correct-but in a narrow context. This definition doesn't recognize the monetary, social, and ecological issues tended to by the agriculture economic context. To see agroeconomics as being restricted exclusively to the financial matters of cultivating and farming activities would be erroneous.

These activities represent simply 2% to 4% of the country's result. In reality, the extent of rural financial matters works out in a good way past the farm gate to incorporate a more extensive scope of food-and fiber-related activities. When seen according to this more extensive point of view, the agrarian area represents around 12% to 15% of the country's output.

Development in agriculture production is important not exclusively to increment food accessibility and raise nourishment levels of the populace; it is fundamental for the development process. Without a doubt it is acknowledged that an essential for fast monetary development is the diverting of agrarian excess (creation in overabundance of own utilization) to the non- farm sector.

It will not however, be our purpose to analyze the way in which the agricultural sector can make a contribution to development.1 Rather the importance of agricultural production will be taken as given and we will focus instead on the determinants of agricultural output.1 In this and the accompanying two chapters specific consideration will be given to

- the variables which impact the supply of agriculture products;
- the elements which administer the use of useful productive inputs (labor, fertilizer, machinery etc.);
- the productivity of asset use; and
- the effect of mechanical change.

These points are fundamental to the investigation of horticultural business sectors and specifically to the plan of powerful improvement arrangements pointed toward rousing agrarian makers, preparing assets in the area and spreading new advancements and technologies. The main elements of the theory of production economics which have proved useful in the study of agricultural markets.

Likewise, all branches of economics, production economics is concerned with the allocation of scarce resources to alternative uses. In production theory the main choices center upon what to produce (which product or combination of products), how much to produce (the level of output) and how to produce (the combination of inputs to use).

The decision making unit is the firm which is defined as a 'distinct agent specialized in the conversion of inputs into desired goods as outputs' (Hirshleifer (1976)). (The aggregate of all the firms in a given market is termed industry) Whilst not mirroring the full intricacies of productive activity in an economy, this definition is a helpful disentanglement for financial examination and economic analysis.

In the agriculture sectors of developing and developed nations, there are farms, producing cash crops for the domestic and foreign market, which fall inside the meaning of a firm. In the agricultural nations there may likewise be various subsistence farms in which all creation is consumed and none goes through the market.

Notwithstanding, pure subsistence farming is rare (Wharton (1970)) and it is more considered normal that marketable produce some measure of surplus. We would subsequently contend that the theory introduced in this part has direct pertinence to the investigation of farming business sectors in both developed and developing nations.

For sure the primary disadvantage of the theory when applied to the developing nations isn't its emphasis on commercial aspects of production yet rather on the differentiation among firms and consumers. As we probably are aware, agriculture is a significant industry in many nations, as a result of its capacity to give the most fundamental need to human life—food. Because of sheer developing masses of individuals, particularly in developing nations, interest for food would increment (Figure 6.2).

Figure 6.2. Image showing agricultural land.

Source: Image by pxhere.com.

Related with this would be an adjustment of structure of diet coming about because of higher pay levels in many nations. Accordingly, even as of now, in many non-industrial nations, horticultural business overwhelms, despite the way that many farm laborers are moving to the non-farming sector looking for a superior life.

Notwithstanding, as a nation grows financially, the overall significance of agriculture declines. The essential justification for that is the Engel's Law (suggested in 19th century), which depends on the way that as customers' buying power (wages) builds, the extent of pay spent on food declines. This has been seen in many created countries throughout recent years.

In any case, one ought to remember that albeit direct work in agriculture in these nations is low, agriculture is as yet a significant industry. This is on the grounds that a considerable lot of them had accomplished their advancement objectives through moving work and capital from agriculture, making it a wellspring of monetary development.

Moreover, its significance is additionally characteristic of current food and nourishment issues confronting a large number of the nations. As clear from the title—agriculture economics, the discipline outgrew two significant parent disciplines—agriculture (or agronomy) and economics (investigation of shortage prompting decision making by people through utilization of assets).

It emerged in the late nineteenth century, consolidating the hypothesis of the firm with advertising and association hypothesis, and created all through the 20th century to a great extent as an observational part of general economics.

Its prominence in the U.S.A. may likewise be credited to the foundation of the United States Department of Agriculture (USDA), which emerged because of significance of agriculture as well as by rich information gathered by the USDA, starting during the nineteenth century.

The main expert note of farming economics was in 1907 where the American Economic Association (AEA), in its yearly gathering, devoted a session to "What is agrarian economics?," which turned into an ordinary point at these gatherings. This maybe brought about the production of the American Farm Economics Association in 1919, which held its name until 1968 when it turned into the American Agricultural Economics Association (AAEA).

Comparative improvements occurred in different areas of the planet, despite the fact that subtleties on them are either not accessible or exceptionally difficult to gather. At the micro level, there is a need to comprehend the applicable production functions and the connection among labor and capital. When is it beneficial to utilize labor saving, 'lumpy' capital?

Furthermore, most courses will likewise take a gander at the results (externalities) of certain kinds of agrarian creation, for example, the impact of increased nitrogen fertilizer use. Similarly, we can utilize consumer theory to comprehend how customers settle on decisions about the food they purchase (including diets and fads).

Many courses will likewise take a gander at the food sectors all the more for the most part, and find out if there is unreasonable market power in the possession of supermarkets. At the macro level, the subject investigates the manner in which states choose how to help farmers.

In developed economies, strategy would in general be devised in order to help and safeguard farmers subsidies at costs and farming import levies under the European Union's Common Agricultural Policy for instance—frequently with tremendous impacts on trade flows and trade relations.

Interestingly, developing countries look for ways of guaranteeing sufficient supply of nourishment for their kin and to get sufficiently close to world business sectors to procure trade income. Both are troublesome assignments and both can be educated by the farming market analyst. Horticultural financial matters research has tended to consistent losses in rural creation, as well as ranchers' expenses and supply reactions.

Much research has applied economic theory to cultivate level choices. Investigations of hazard and decision-production under vulnerability have true applications to trim insurance contracts and to understanding how farms in agricultural nations go with decisions about innovation reception.

These themes are significant for understanding possibilities for creating adequate nourishment for a developing total populace, dependent upon new asset and ecological difficulties, for example, water shortage and worldwide environmental change.

6.2. CHARACTERISTICS OF AGRICULTURE ECONOMICS

6.2.1. Land Distribution System

Agriculture development relies upon proper land management. The ideal size of land and prolific and plain terrains are worked with for agrarian creation. To guarantee the advanced development of land in the developing and underdeveloped nations, the agriculture economist proposed removing the unequal and unexpected land distribution system.

6.2.2. Supply of Consumer's Goods

Supply and demand are the two major parts of a market. Supply describes how producers and manufacturers, enormous or little, respond or act in the market place, while creating and selling an item. A comprehension of what variables meant for supply circumstances in the past will assist with cultivating supervisors comprehend conceivable inventory possibilities later on.

Agriculture production is considered as the essential period of consumer's goods supply in the society. The creation exercises of buyer's merchandise are talked about in agriculture economics.

6.2.3. Supply of Industrial Inputs

Agriculture supplies raw materials to industry. Production, distribution, and marketing of industrial inputs are all aspects of agricultural economics.

6.2.4. Labor Employment

The economy of the emerging nations is fundamentally founded on agriculture. Farming areas have a colossal chance to ingest the uneducated and wasteful work. For this situation, the more work can be utilized by utilizing little capital, that implies work—capital ratio is extremely low.

6.2.5. Primary Stage of Economic Development

Monetary advancement implies a positive change in quantitative and subjective way of life being. Agriculture is considered as a primary sector to make the economy healthy in its owned. Any other way, the foundation of industry can't be of strength.

6.2.6. Capital Formation

Agriculture is considered an essential underpinning of financial improvement in farming financial matters. So the unfamiliar a money is procured by trading agrarian items, which is useful for capital development and urges the investors to the huge scope of speculation.

6.2.7. Risk and Uncertainty

Normal calamity and natural degradation influence the farming creation adversely. Lack of adequate data of agrarian items and insanely impractical to arrange among organic market because of the presence of time duration. Risk and uncertainty are existed in both production and marketing and uncertainty is the prominent feature of agricultural economics.

6.2.8. Existence of Middlemen

Existence of different middlemen and broker is found in the marketing of agricultural commodities. Farmers are deprived to have fair price for their commodities.

6.2.9. Subsistence Farming

The subsistence farming is the main feature in the developing countries. In this case, the land is not cultivated commercially. Most of the farmer are operated their land for subsistence purpose.

6.3. IMPORTANCE OF AGRICULTURE AND ITS ROLE IN ECONOMIC DEVELOPMENT

Agriculture sector forms the backbone of the Indian economy. India is agricultural country, endowed with abundant natural resources. So prosperity of the nation is largely dependent on agriculture. The role of agriculture in national economy is of vital importance (Figure 6.3).

Figure 6.3. Panoramic view of farmer's field under conservation agriculture in Malawi.

Source: Image by flickr.

6.3.1. Share of Agriculture in the National Income

Between 1950–51 to 1960–61 the portion of agriculture was more noteworthy than 50% of absolute GDP. The portion of agriculture is diminishing constantly and it has declined to 14% in 2011–12. Notwithstanding, the portion of assembling administrations and administration areas are expanding. The agriculture assumes on significant part in the country's economy which is as yet reliant upon agriculture.

6.3.2. Agriculture As a Source of Livelihood

Agriculture gives work to around 52% of all out work force in the country. Agriculture overwhelms the economy so much that an extremely high extent of working populace in India is taken part in agriculture.

6.3.3. Importance of Agriculture for Industrial Development

Indian agriculture has been the cause of supply of natural substance to driving businesses, for example, cotton, jute, and sugar and so forth. There are numerous enterprises that rely upon agriculture in an aberrant way like handloom winding around, oil squashing, rice husking and so on.

Since 10th long-term plan onwards the significance of food handling businesses is by and large progressively perceived and given due weightage in monetary turn of events.

6.3.4. Role of Agriculture in the Field of International Trade

Significance of agriculture additionally emerges from the job it plays in India's exchange. Agriculture items like tea, sugar, oilseed, tobacco, comprise the principal things of products.

6.3.5. Support of Transport and Trade

Agriculture offers fundamental help for India's vehicle framework since railroads and streets secure majority of business from the development of agriculture transports. Inner exchange is for the most part in horticultural items. Accordingly farming exchange gives more chances to support area.

6.3.6. Prosperity of Farmers is Prosperity of Industry

Great harvests and high items improve the buying force of ranchers accordingly expanding the interest for other made merchandise. It will assist with invigorating the development of the non-horticultural area and furthermore help to diminish and stress on unfamiliar to trade profit.

Agriculture development straightforwardly affects destitution destruction. Agriculture development is a significant variable impacting expansion, farming wages and business age. Obviously agriculture is the foundation of Indian economy and flourishing in agriculture can impact the success of Indian economy.

6.4. NATURE OF AGRICULTURE ECONOMICS

The idea of agriculture financial matters is with the end goal that it acquires the vast majority of the standards from general financial matters, hence there is no essential distinction between broad financial matters and horticultural economics.

Thus, the need to isolate these two is that rural financial matters doesn't suggest direct utilization of the principles but before application they are changed. These alterations are so huge and different that there is a finished avocation for studying it as a different part of information.

6.4.1. Micro As Well As Macro

Both micro and macro tools for studying agriculture economics are used. When the subject of study is individual farmers then it is micro-economics and when we study agricultural economy as a whole then it is called macroeconomics.

6.4.2. Static As Well As Dynamic

The basic difference between the two is that in former, time variable is not taken into account while the latter analysis deals with a period of time.

6.4.3. Applied Science or Pure Science

Agricultural economics such as Frosten and Leoger have classified it as an applied science as it is concerned with the identification, description, and classification of economic problems of agriculture. Thus, agriculture economics is concerned with the evolving of appropriate principles that govern the amount of land, labor, and capital that the farmer should use to maximize his profit and using the factors efficiently.

6.4.4. Science or Art

Agriculture is the science and craft of development of yields and raising the domesticated animals and isn't just a method of occupation yet in addition a lifestyle. Agriculture financial aspects is a science since it depends on the standards and confirmation of information. It is a workmanship since it manages the different methods of use of the standards and to suit the circumstances.

The previous definitions show the extent of rural financial matters as given in the presentation segment. A typical topic of shortage of assets and selection of purposes runs practically through these definitions. Like that, farming financial aspects isn't unique in relation to the overall financial aspects.

6.5. SCOPE OF AGRICULTURE ECONOMICS

Every one of the devices of investigation utilized overall financial aspects are utilized in agriculture economics aspects also. As if there should arise an occurrence of general financial aspects, we have similar parts of horticultural financial aspects for example, financial matters of creation, utilization, dissemination, showcasing, funding, arranging, and strategy making.

Agricultural economics analyzes how a farmer chooses different endeavors, how he picks different exercises in a similar venture: how the expenses are to be limited: what mix of contributions for an action are to chosen: however, measure of each yield is to be delivered yet kind of business connection the rancher must have with individuals from whom they buy their feedback or to whom they sail their item.

Agriculture economics doesn't concentrate on just the way of behaving of a farmer at the farm level. That is, as it were, the micro analysis. Agricultural issues have a macro viewpoint also. Insecurity of agriculture and agrarian joblessness are the issues that must be managed, essentially at the large scale level (Figure 6.4).

Figure 6.4. Climate-smart soils: testing soil health in Western Kenya.

Source: Image by flickr.

And afterward, the overall issues of agriculture development and the issues like those unsettling tenurial frameworks and tenurial arrangements, research, and extension services which are again predominantly macro in character. Such problems and their origin and impacts are the subject matter of agricultural economics.

The extent of agriculture economics is bigger than 'mere economizing of resources.' Agriculture is a significant area, of the general economy. The shared reliance of the different areas of the economy on one another is deeply grounded. Development of one area is essential for the development of the other area.

In that capacity, in agriculture financial matters, we likewise concentrate on how advancement of agriculture helps the improvement of different areas of the economy.

6.5.1. Changing Scope of Agricultural Economics

Agriculture economics matters is an applied region as well as a hybrid discipline. The field of agricultural economics aspects incorporates utilization of monetary science apparatuses to the agrarian area. Truth be told, a part of applied financial aspects takes the instruments of both miniature and macroeconomics and utilizations them to tackle issues in a particular region.

Monitoring recommends that agriculture economics aspects outgrew a consolidation between rural economy and homestead the board in the early piece of the 20th century. Utilization of financial standards to farming pursuits isn't new. Truth be told, before the investigation of ranch the board was extremely old, it started to utilize standards, hypothesis, and data from financial aspects.

A portion of these included neoclassical political economy and the hypothesis of the firm applied to the homestead creation, credited to Marshall. Farming financial aspects discipline included large numbers of these applications and further advanced throughout some undefined time frame.

The significance of agribusiness in financial advancement has prompted squeezing requests on the job in which agrarian business analysts are expected to play. Truth be told, Gardner and Rausser propose that the topic of rural financial matters has both widened and extended lately.

For instance, since the farming area has gone through steady changes under the effect of new innovation, moving requests, and developing foundations, one of the significant areas of action in agricultural economics matters is the investigation of strategy issues.

Appraisal of effect of a given arrangement on the government assistance of different individuals from the general public is a significant distraction of farming financial analysts. Notwithstanding the advancement of strategy examination, different regions were additionally added to the extent of agricultural economics aspects. Remembered for this setting was the investigation of country economies.

Farming was credited for supporting the rural economy straightforwardly or by implication, which brought the investigation of country improvement inside the domain of agrarian financial aspects. Notwithstanding the over two regions (throughout some stretch of time), one has seen a few different augmentations to the discipline.

Among these are regions connected with regular assets and financial turn of events (especially in the agricultural nations). Concentrates on connected with regular assets will quite often check out at the job of such assets in the development of monetary products, including food. Natural issues confronting the general public drove farming financial experts to participate in ecological arrangements connected with agricultural production (Figure 6.5).

In the field of monetary turn of events, assessment of new tasks for financial turn of events, utilizing instruments, for example, financial effect examination or advantage cost investigation, is currently remembered for the discipline. Accordingly, agrarian business analysts concentrate on the occasionally clashing necessities of ranchers, untamed life species, foresters, and open air recreationalists.

However, the expression "agribusiness" had not been utilized until all the more as of late, agricultural economists had been making huge commitments on issues connected with agribusiness for a long time. This region underscores a coordinated perspective on the food framework that reaches out from exploration and info supply however, creation, handling, and appropriation to retail outlets and the buyer.

The investigation of coordination among vertical and even members inside the well-established pecking order, known as agribusiness economics, and the study of decision-production inside the elective pecking order administration structures, known as agribusiness the executives. Connected with these are the issues managing trade and development.

As a matter of fact, trade, and development have overwhelmed agricultural economics research especially after the 1980s, with a later expansion of food utilization and inventory network investigation in the food business utilizing a modern hierarchical methodology.

There are numerous different regions that have been brought inside the extent of agricultural economics, as proven by arranging of a few equal meetings in a commonplace agricultural economics gathering.

For instance, the 2018 Annual Conference of the AAEA included: finance, risk examination, ecological, and asset economics, conduct, and exploratory economics, rural development and local economics, value investigation and econometrics, food and agriculture promoting, strategy examination, store network the board, institutional economics, worldwide exchange and global turn of events, normal asset economics (counting area and water economics), creation economics, and in addition to numerous others, as meetings for show of flow research.

A lot more regions can be recorded notwithstanding these recorded above to do full equity to what agricultural economists do.

6.6. AGRICULTURE FOR SUSTAINABLE DEVELOPMENT

To be sustainable, agriculture must meet the needs of present and future generations for its products and services, while ensuring profitability, environmental health and social and economic equity. Sustainable agriculture requires a system of global governance that promotes food security concerns in trade regimes and trade policies, and revisits agricultural policies to promote local and regional agricultural markets.

6.7. AGRICULTURE AS A BACKBONE AND HEART OF AN ECONOMY

Most likely agriculture is at the core of the economies of the nations of the Global South. The area is fundamental for monetary turn of events, ecological obligation and social advancement. With 60% individuals in the Global South relying upon agriculture (FAO, 2015), it still today gives jobs to the larger part, specifically in emerging nations, and holds the work and assets for the advancement of the ventures and administrations areas.

For example, agriculture supplies nourishment for individuals as well as unrefined components as significant hotspots for the business, for example, fiber crops for the manufacturing of ropes and strings. Nonetheless, in spite of its significance to the economy, agriculture is customarily politically disregarded and has stayed in most non-industrial nations, particularly the most underdeveloped nations, to a great extent immature (FAO, 2002).

Agricultural creation in the low pay nations are as a rule described by sluggish creation because of interior troubles, for example, a restricted ability base and outer hardships, for example, the high weakness to insecurities of the frequently essential wares they send out, high vacillations underway, and high state reliance.

Also, agricultural land is in non-industrial nations frequently described by debased normal assets and land-use clashes (IPBES, 2019). Also, neediness rates among farmers are disproportionally high (FAO, 2015). The issues are firmly interlinked with the frequently ongoing issues of destitution, particularly food frailty.

In any case, the majority of these nations have huge unexploited agricultural potential—to be specific for manageable turn of events and in this manner agriculture could generally add to better the monetary, social, and environmental circumstance of a nation.

6.8. A BRIEF HISTORY OF AGRICULTURE FOR DEVELOPMENT

Looking back in development history, agriculture has been in the global debate in and out of fashion since the 1950s, the beginnings of global development cooperation. Whereas during the 1950s and early 1960s manufacturing industries have been pushed as a first priority in development efforts and agriculture came second, soon after agriculture was center-staged in considering the concerns of population growth and a global food crisis (De Janvry, 2010).

In the 1960s and 1970s under the classical paradigm of development economics, agriculture was conceptualized as an instrument for industrialization. The paradigm was grounded in success stories from the "Western Experience" to the then-recent "Asian miracles." It was also when the Green Revolution started and saved millions of lives from a mass famine.

The other side of the coin would only manifest itself later. Pingali et al., (2019) argue that the Green Revolution was so successful, e.g., in India, because the technologies were scale-neutral and smallholder farmers could take advantage of the higher productivity of family labor.

The technological and biological inputs were complemented by institutional support, for instance the direct procurement of food grains, minimum support prices (MSPs) and input subsidies. However, the focus was clearly on staple grains and regions with access to irrigation benefited more than others.

To that time—not only in India—agricultural growth was held to be the key pillar for industrial growth. The Green Revolution was initiated externally. However, the history of agricultural cooperation between Western development actors and developing countries is a complex story to tell and not yet fully understood nor sufficiently researched (de Janvry, 2010).

6.8.1. Economic Development

What exactly is the contribution of agriculture for economic growth? What role does it play in the economic development of a country? Surely, this is a complex field—links and relationships are intertwined, which does not always allow for clear attributions to a certain sector, but there are also some pretty straightforward impact mechanisms.

The debate on the role of agriculture in economic growth is as old as development economics itself, however, the idea that agriculture is central to the growth process in poor countries is relatively recent (Block & Timmer, 1994).

At first agriculture was regarded by development economists as an ancillary to industrialization only, concretely as a mere source of labor and transferable capital surplus (Lewis, 1954; Rosenstein-Rodan, 1943; Hirschman, 1958; Jorgenson, 1961; Ranis & Fei, 1961).

Only when Schultz's "efficient farmer" hypothesis was published in 1964 and also its following literature showed how agriculture is capable of stimulating growth—namely how growth in the agriculture sector can have significant multiplier and spillover effects to other sectors, academics started to change their thinking. The fact alone that agriculture growth improves the food security in the country illustrates its enormous leverage power.

Because this in turn has a positive impact on social stability and health, and in turn again productivity and the overall economy (Meijrink & Roza, 2007). Looking at economic theory, economic growth requires an increase in total factor productivity, which in turn needs technological progress and public expenditures for infrastructure, research, health, and human capital developments etc. (Sarris 2003, Solow, 1956).

Structural economists like Lewis (1954) or Kuznets (1966), etc., have empirically demonstrated that growth is brought about by structural transitions. Thus one basic idea is that economic development of a developing country goes through a structural transition from an agriculture-dominated to an industry- and services-dominated economy.

This demonstrates also the basis of the following impact considerations of economic development in this thesis. One can break down and classify agriculture's potential contribution to economic development into a few categories.

6.8.2. Environmental Responsibilities

The need for action to reverse damage to the climate is of the utmost urgency and people are required to accelerate their efforts to reduce environmental impacts in response. They also know that environmental issues are likely to become increasingly commercially important and a potential differentiator.

Figure 6.5. Climate protection.

Source: Image by piqsels.com.

6.9. AGRICULTURE AS AN ENGINE OF ECONOMIC GROWTH

An economy needs an engine of growth for its sustained development like industry, tourism or export agriculture. The incomes and saving from this initial stimulus can be further invested.

Whereas so called developed countries were mostly stimulated by industrial innovations (e.g., the steam engine for the industrial revolution) and were only accompanied by agricultural progress, some developing countries like India, China, and Taiwan, reached high growth rates with agriculture-led productivity changes (ibid.).

The increased production of food was mainly used domestically due to the existing demand. Thus the domestic terms of trade for the agricultural products did not deteriorate (Pingali et al., 2019). However, a substantial part of the costs for achieving this improvement was funded by external donors, including the major international agricultural research centers (Sarris, 2003).

In that regard international cooperation played an important role for initiating agriculture-led growth. However, the cost per agricultural producer of improving agricultural productivity was relatively low due to the high population densities (ibid.).

For agricultural growth, the framework has to be right too: According to Gérard (2014) there is a set of broad principles needed for a thriving agricultural sector boosting national economic growth: for instance macroeconomic and political stability, access to markets, information, technology, and banking facilities especially a credit system.

6.10. CONTRIBUTION OF AGRICULTURAL ECONOMICS TO DEVELOPMENT

This rapid expansion coupled with the essential role of food in our society has generated a field of economics solely dedicated to observing and predicting trends within the agriculture market landscape. Basic macro and micro-economic principles apply to farming, as do the existence of externalities such as climate change and nutritional health.

Agricultural economics is defined as the economic system that produces, distributes, and consumes agricultural products and services. This represents a large interconnected supply chain on a global scale. Interesting trends in the agricultural market pertain to the decrease in cost for the actual farming aspects and an increase in costs for the distribution and sales system (particularly in the U.S.).

This is largely a result of technological progress greatly reducing the need for human labor in the production of agricultural goods, weighting the costs more heavily on the human resources side of the equation. The politics and economics of agriculture are also relevant issues on the global scale. US agricultural subsidies have had a large impact on international trade flows.

The subsidies make US agricultural products artificially cheap, too cheap for developing nations to compete with. Developing nations, which may rely more heavily on agriculture in their economy than developed nations, argue that the US should reduce its agriculture subsidies.

This tension is perhaps the biggest cause of the failure of the Doha Round, a World Trade Organization (WTO) push for more open global trade, to make any progress since its initiation in 2001.

6.11. SUBSIDIES AND INCOME SUPPORT

An agricultural subsidy is an administration award paid to officeholders in the business to diminish expenses and impact the inventory of products. At the point when states need to guarantee their residents approach quality food sources at sensible costs, an assortment of administrative backings are given to the business to guarantee it keeps up with low expenses of creation and high result.

This is by and large as subsidy and pay upholds, which mitigate a few cutthroat elements and working costs to keep up with sensible price tags in the market financially.

6.11.1. Subsidies

An agricultural subsidy is defined as a government grant paid to farmers to supplement income and influence the overall cost and supply of certain commodities. In this industry, subsidized goods generally include wheat, corn, barley, oats, sorghum, milk, rice, peanuts, tobacco, soybean, cotton, lamb, beef, chicken, and pork.

Illustrates the governmental priorities, based upon subsidies provided, for specific agricultural goods in the United States. These subsidies play a large role in enabling higher supply at lower price points, supporting the domestic agricultural industry. Another, less direct, form of subsidy is in the taxing system for consumers.

Consumers are not charged tax on food goods and clothes, which are considered necessities and thus should be provided at the lowest costs possible. These consumer-based subsidies are another governmental attempt to enable citizens in the country to purchase basic food stuffs required to survive.

Food stamps are a similar concept, used to empower low income individuals and ensure they have access to these basic foods as well (food stamps are often limited to milk, eggs, bread, and other core foods).

6.11.2. Impact of Subsidies

Global Effect: While domestic subsidies are really great for driving up creation locally, it smothers rivalry with regards to global trade. Government help with an industry is contended to give an unreasonable upper hand to those organizations, falsely bringing down their expenses of creation, now and again beneath the practical level for nations (particularly developing countries) not getting these backings.

Developing Nations: A supplement to the above conversation is the impact on neediness and developing countries without the foundation to give sponsorships to their own farmers. The International Food Policy Research Institute has assessed a complete loss of financial development in developing countries at $24 billion of every 2003, all of which mean lost pay for people who frantically need it.

Nutrition: Another interesting side effect of subsidies and the artificially reduced price of food is obesity and overeating. Some argue that these low prices provide the incentive to buy more food than is necessary, and this over consumption has resulted in a highly unhealthy culture (particularly in the U.S.).

Environmental Implications: As food prices reduce distribution increases, thus driving an environmental externality that already existed even further. The cost, environmentally, of transporting a high quantity of agricultural goods across the globe has resulted in high degrees of pollution and waste.

Overall, while subsidies are largely a good thing and enable individuals to buy the necessities, there are clear cut downsides to subsidies as well. Politics must find a way to mitigate the negative consequences while increasing the positive effects, allowing for balanced and healthy consumption across all demographics.

6.11.3. Price Supports

Price supports are subsidies or cost controls utilized by the public authority to misleadingly increment or reduction costs in the agriculture market. The agriculture business is a basic part of any public economy since it addresses both a significant piece of GDP and it is a center need for residents inside the framework.

Because of the way these products are necessities, it is likewise critical to remember the manner by which organic market would work assuming there was a restricted stock (expected for endurance, and accordingly potential interest potential gains could be limitless). Because of these variables, states establish an assortment of cost controls on the agriculture business, both in the U.S. furthermore, abroad.

6.11.4. Applying Price Support to Agricultural Economics

The United States right now pays out around $20 billion every year to farmers and makers in agriculture as subsidies by means of farm bills to falsely lessen costs and shift the stock bend outward to guarantee the general stockpile in the market is sufficiently high to fulfill every single planned shopper.

It means a lot to take note of how emphatically the beneficiaries of cultivating subsidies have changed over the long run in the United States. In 1925, there were around 6,000,000 little homesteads of which 25% of the country lived. By 1997, 72% of homestead deals come from 157,000 enormous ranches and just 2% of the U.S. populace dwells there.

This is an intriguing monetary element with regards to cultivate subsidies, as these subsidies are generally going to companies of significant size, instead of little farmers. The subsidies give a cost floor (or a minimum cost where farmers can be repaid for specific items).

This is a critical monetary arrangement of value control to guarantee farmers have legitimate impetus and incomes to keep on delivering at the degree of merchandise wanted by the U.S. government. Agricultural economics is a profoundly muddled market because of these value supports and controls, especially according to the viewpoint of sponsorship and cost control.

6.11.5. Supply Reduction

Agricultural total stock can be diminished through outer limit potential or administrative interventions. Agricultural economics is generally limited by ideas of environment and by and large world food delivering limit (e.g., farmlands and foundation), while at the same time being empowered by government strategy, innovative advances, and the proceeded with development of emerging countries.

Figuring out the decreases in total inventory in this industry, because of legislative strategy or monetary cutoff points, is a basic part in grasping agricultural economics. We will take a gander at both the administrative parts and the climatic/total interest parts adding to in general inventory in this industry.

6.11.6. Governmental Policy

Government strategy to a great extent affects the agriculture market. The two appropriations and price ceilings are normal and influence the general organic market harmony focuses on the lookout. Administrative strategy to decrease supply likewise exists and is executed frequently from a worldwide trade viewpoint.

Perhaps the biggest gamble in this industry, because of the serious level of appropriation, is 'dumping.' Dumping is the most common way of selling underestimated merchandise in another market, disturbing price tags and balance. In this situation, government approaches might set quantities, or import limits, to lessen supply.

A subsequent decrease in supply that is very normal in developing countries. Many non-industrial countries come up short on requirements to produce the suitable stock of agriculture to take care of the populace. In this situation, the utilizing of the excess in one nation can help the other country by means of help, and thus right the stock/request balance in the giving country to the ideal level.

6.11.7. Climate Change

Environmental worries have additionally been generally referred to as a reductive impact on the agriculture market. A dangerous atmospheric deviation has been gradually expanding temperatures as the ozone layer dissolves because of an assortment of poisons, changing the biological system midpoints beyond the developmental climate wherein numerous agricultural items generally developed.

Environment changes implies an alternate developing climate for plants, which are not accustomed to it. delineates the decrease in yield because of modifying climatic conditions. Changes in environment radically diminish total inventory.

Different worries rotate around emotional soil harm because of momentary yield expanding systems, developing invulnerability to pesticides, loss of rural space for cultivating (because of urbanization), and accessibility of clean water for water system.

These elements might lessen the total inventory and in this manner drive up costs. shows rising food costs, maybe from some of the stock decrease factors talked about in this iota (or possibly unidentified elements). Controlling supply is a basic part of guaranteeing everybody approaches reasonable food, and keeping up with our environment will plainly assume a basic part in the years to come.

Economic growth is constantly joined by a declining portion of agriculture in complete result, pay, and business. At cutting edge progressive phases, the workforce in agriculture begins to totally decline. Two fundamental powers, which together produce the major underlying changes, are at the core of the improvement cycle.

In the first place, the speed of agricultural development is restricted by the development of interest for its result, 90% of which is food in everything except a small bunch of nations. Thusly, the development of interest is restricted by the propensity for the extent of family spending on food to decline as earnings rise.

In India, with a for each capita pay of $240, for instance, families burn through 60 to 70% of their pay on food; in a $10,000 per capita economy, for example, Canada, they spend under 20% on food and can appreciate assortment and quality undeniably. This propensity, known as Engel's Law, is seen in all economies as they develop.

The cutoff points to agricultural development forced by the development in homegrown interest can, in any case, be raised assuming pay development is extensively diffused in the economy and nations trade their excess production. (This choice is accessible just partially, on the grounds that Engel's Law works on a worldwide scale, as well with respect to individual nations.)

On account of nonfood agriculture, contest from modern substitutes develops as venture and advancement bring down the cost of modern labor and products comparative with agricultural unrefined components. Normal models are the utilization of artificial materials rather than regular strands (cotton, fleece, jute) for dress, the replacement of oil or coal for wood, and the change from lumber to steel and concrete in development.

Replacement is only from time to time absolute, nonetheless, so interest for normal items ordinarily keeps on developing. To benefit, makers need to focus on promoting as well as on effective production. With development, farmers become progressively taken out from purchasers. As means cultivating gives approach to promoted creation, the degree for specific showcasing, transport, handling, and bundling is developed.

In the industrialized economies, these exercises produce considerably more worth added and work than does agriculture itself; the homestead entryway worth of food is presently only 33% of the cost shoppers pay for it.

The subsequent fundamental power representing the underlying change in agriculture is expanded agricultural efficiency, made conceivable by mechanical advancements and collected public and confidential speculation. Business expands and broadens as an outcome of the overall decrease in the agricultural work force.

In the beginning phases of development, nearly everyone works in agriculture. A large portion of the exercises later named "modern" and "administration" are at first done, while possibly not inside agriculture, in rustic are as the production of dress, furnishings, and apparatuses; development of lodging and different structures; transport, handling, and showcasing; training, medication, social, and social exercises.

As development advances, these exercises become separated and isolated from agriculture, until just center agricultural creation capacities remain. While some nonagricultural exercises are as yet done in rustic regions, current industry and administrations open up new and subjectively various open doors, a large number of which require moderately high abilities and instruction.

Albeit this interaction is one of the best advantages of development, it is additionally the most challenging to deal with in human terms.

6.12. AGRICULTURAL ECONOMIC POLICY AND DEVELOPMENT

Price policy for agricultural items comprises a significant component of generally agricultural monetary policy. MSPs for significant grains, heartbeats, oilseeds, and other business crops, specifically, cotton, jute, and sugarcane, are fixed by the Government consistently based on the proposals made by the Commission for Agricultural Costs and Prices (CACP).

The main element considered by the CACP in making its suggestions on MSPs for various yields is the expense of development/creation for which the information base is given by the DES through its arrangement plot for concentrate on cost of development.

Examination of different price policy issues in the arising financial climate requires advance data on the creation of various harvests, supply-request situation, as well as customary observing of price developments in both the homegrown and global business sectors.

The viability of price policy in helping creation and efficiency of agriculture on top of homegrown too as outside request can't be evaluated in that frame of mind of standard information on region, creation, and yield of various harvests.

Additionally, information on homegrown and global prices for different agricultural wares, patterns in acquirement, off-take, and supplies of food grains, utilization of various agricultural items, their commodities and imports, and so on accept huge importance in the arising outer financial climate, which is progressively impacted by the WTO.

The significance of a sound information/database on various features of agriculture can't hence be overemphasized. The Plan Schemes of DES look to fill this need. With regards to the need to take on an all-encompassing way to deal with the execution of individual plans with between related targets, it has been proposed/chose to combine the on-going arrangement plans into three wide umbrella plans.

6.13. CURRENT ISSUES IN AGRICULTURAL ECONOMICS

The post-war time of the 1950s and 1960s was a nearly steady one concerning agricultural policy. It was a period of remaking in light of the agricultural price support estimates set up by the created nations during the 1930s during the Great Depression.

Global trade in agriculture was affected by the provincial designs still set up over a significant part of the third world, the first and second universes were gotten by the virus battle into shared trade confinement, and the USA's mind-boggling financial power prompted approaches by which it really balanced out worldwide grain and numerous different business sectors other than.

Cycles of progress beginning during the 1960s started to sabotage the circumstances for security. The fruitful modifying of the economies of Western Europe and Japan gave them more independence of activity, and the development of their agricultural areas behind defensive boundaries started to change the example of agricultural trade.

The monetary expenses of the USA's agricultural approaches, by which it as a result held the liberated world's grain stocks, turned out to be excessively difficult, with the goal that in 1970, in the administration of Richard Nixon, choices were taken to decrease stocks by accentuating grounds redirection and advancing oat sends out.

Numerous nations in Asia and Africa became free, and with their quickly developing populaces put new expectations upon the exchanging request, not least due to their requirements for extra food imports. The arrangement of swapping scale strength, which had been made following the Bretton Woods Conference of 1944, reached a conclusion in 1971.

The resultant liberating of trade rates added altogether to different wellsprings of vulnerability introduced by the 1970s which were escalated by the super inflationary states of 1973 to 1975. Large numbers of the issues which are viewed as in this book should be visible as agricultural policy commitments to a continuous interaction important to for the most part reestablish security to world trade and the financial framework.

6.14. CONCLUSION

In the conclusion of the chapter, this chapter discussed about the several characteristics of agricultural economics such as land distribution system, supply of consumer's goods, labor employment and so on. In this chapter, the importance of agriculture and its role in economic development has also been covered. This chapter discussed about the nature of agriculture economics such as micro economics, macro-economics, static as well as dynamic, applied science or pure science.

Towards the end of the chapter, it discussed about the scope of agriculture economics, role, and contribution of agriculture in sustainable development, history of agriculture for development. In this chapter, agricultural economic policy and development strategies have been discussed.

REFERENCES

1. (n.d). *Agricultural Economics.* 1–52. [e-Book] Available at: http://sdeuoc.ac.in/sites/default/files/sde_videos/agri%20economics%20teaching%20note%20MA%20ECO-.pdf (accessed on 21 June 2022).
2. (n.d). *Directorate of Economics & Statistics,* 1–14. [e-Book] Available at: http://eands.dacnet.nic.in/pdf/abbout_us.pdf (accessed on 21 June 2022).
3. Henry, B., Allan, B., Ian, C., Johnathan, K., Ian, L., David, C., & Trevor, Y., (1989). *Principles of Agricultural Economics: Markets and Prices in Less Developed Countries.* [e-Book] Cambridge University Press. Available at: http://www.rvskvv.net/images/Principles-of-Agricultural-Economics_17.04.2020.pdf (accessed on 21 June 2022).
4. Michael, H., (2020). *What is the Role of Agriculture for Sustainable Development? Lessons from India.* [e-Book] NADEL, ETH Zürich: MAS in Development and Cooperation. Available at: https://ethz.ch/content/dam/ethz/special-interest/gess/nadel-dam/teaching/MAS/MASPapers2018-2020/Michael_Herger.pdf (accessed on 21 June 2022).

CHAPTER 7

NEOCLASSICAL ECONOMICS AND SUSTAINABLE DEVELOPMENT

CONTENTS

7.1. INTRODUCTION

The phrase "neoclassical economics" is vague and is used in a variety of contexts. Most mainstream economists do not identify as belonging to the neoclassical school. Thorstein Veblen invented the phrase "neo-classical" in 1900. It describes Alfred Marshall's supply and demand diagram as a combination of the subjective and objective theories of value.

Marshall merged the classical notion that a commodity's value is determined by its production costs with the new findings of marginalism, claiming that value is determined by individual utility. The market diagram illustrating the confluence of (objective) supply and (subjective) demand has remained a major component of neoclassical economics to this day.

The general theory of neoclassical economics focuses on supply and demand as the driving factors behind the production, price, and consumption of commodities and services. It arose about 1900 to compete with prior classical economic ideas. Neoclassical economics theories, as well as Keynesian economics, underpin modern-day economics.

Although the neoclassical method is the most extensively taught economic theory, it is not without its sceptics. The fundamental core of neoclassical theory constitutes today's modern economic mainstream,' dominating economics teaching and research. According to the neoclassical viewpoint, the primary economic challenge is the organization and distribution of finite resources.

This implies that efficiency—defined as the best use of available resources to maximize individual utility and, as a result, a country's welfare—becomes the most significant assessment criteria. The key research topics of neoclassical economics are microeconomics, which also analyzes household and corporate behavior; macroeconomics, which examines economic aggregates and market interaction; and econometrics, which acts as an analytical tool.

In general, mathematical models are employed to analyze the economic system. According to neoclassical economists, these methods are best suited for determining causal relationships. Neoclassical economics, like any other school of thought, is subject to constant change and growth (Figure 7.1).

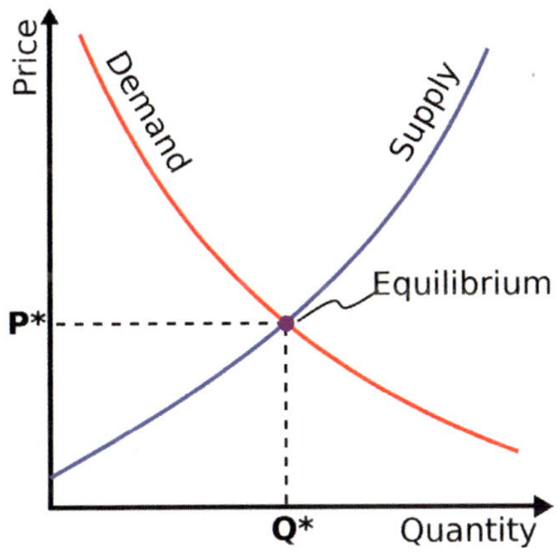

Figure 7.1. The intersection of supply and demand curves as the free market equilibrium.

Source: Image by Wikimedia commons.

Neoclassical economics has been increasingly varied over the last few decades, including a growing challenge to its ideas. The 'de-rationalization' of human actors in behavioral economics, a sub-school of neoclassical economics, is an example of this tendency. As a result, presenting a cohesive picture of the contemporary area of neoclassical economics is difficult.

Nonetheless, a distinction from other economic schools of thinking is attempted in the following by outlining the basic assumptions or axioms and the conventional methodologies of neoclassical economics. The basic economic challenge, according to neoclassical economics, is the scarcity of social resources. Because of this scarcity, economics should be studied as a discipline in order to establish welfare through the best allocation of resources.

Simply described, the economy is an exchange economy in which rational players engage in markets with exogenously determined resource allocations. Because the relationship provides mutual value, those actors trade with one another. Productivity is viewed as the source of an economy's functioning and an indicator of a nation's wealth.

Individuals can select between multiple options under the neoclassical economic model, and the goal of their decisions is to maximize their own utility. As a result, they operate in accordance with the rationality principle (also known as the 'economic principle,' according to which output is maximized for a given input or an input is reduced for a given output.

To achieve an optimal result, economic subjects base their judgements on a comparison of costs and benefits, with marginal units serving as essential elements according to the postulates of marginalism. The term marginal utility refers to the marginal gain in utility caused by an additional unit, while marginal expenses represent the marginal costs of this additional unit.

'Only a reasonable decision maker decides to do a certain activity if the marginal value of the action exceeds the marginal expenses' (Mankiw 2004, S.7, own translation). The abstract idea of the homo economics is frequently employed in this context. It portrays an ideal human who behaves logically, maximizing benefit while focusing on his or her personal utility.

Aggregate demand may be calculated by summing all of the various utility functions. The latter meets aggregate supply on the market. Supply and demand converge toward that equilibrium when supply equals demand and the market is cleared via the pricing mechanism, which is not further studied. Because of this characteristic, the pricing mechanism is an optimum allocation device.

Arne Heise (2007, 3) elaborates on the conditions of such a price mechanism in his description of neoclassical economics, highlighting the axiom of gross substitution, as per which all products (and services) are typically equally tradeable Only by applying this axiom can it be guaranteed that the pricing mechanism functions as an instrument of allocation and that market equilibria exist.

As long as there is no market failure—such as external impacts or the formation of monopoly or oligopoly structures—the market mechanism self-organizes to the economic optimum. This is referred to as a Pareto-efficient state since no party can better its own condition without harming the plight of others.

Nothing irritates neoclassical economists more than the idea that neoclassical economics is a fiction of their mind; that there is, simply, scientific economics and speculative hand-waving (by those who have never really grasped the finer points of mainstream economic theory).

In this way, neoclassicism is similar to racism in that, while it is ever present and dominating, no one professes to be governed by it. Critics must discover a precise definition of neoclassicism, if only to free neoclassical economists from the urge to hide behind immature arguments, such as the non-existence of their school of thought. The good argument may then commence.

The neoclassical synthesis (NCS), also known as the neoclassical—Keynesian synthesis or simply neo-Keynesianism, was a neoclassical economics academic movement and paradigm in economics that worked to reconcile John Maynard Keynes's macroeconomic thought in his book The General Theory of Employment, Interest, and Money (1936).

It was most notably developed by John Hicks (1937), Franco Modigliani (1944), and Paul Samuelson (1948) and dominated postwar economics, becoming the mainstream of macroeconomic theory throughout the 1950s, 1960s, and 1970s.

In the 1970s, a sequence of events upset the NCS, as stagflation and the work of monetarists like Milton Friedman placed doubt on neo-Keynesian notions of monetary theory. The period's conditions demonstrated the difficulties of maintaining sustainable development and a low level of inflation using the school's prescribed measures.

As a result, a slew of new concepts for macroeconomic research tools capable of describing the economic events of the 1970s would emerge. Following that, new Keynesian and new classical economists attempted to offer macroeconomic foundations for microeconomics by adding historically Keynesian and neoclassical traits, respectively.

These schools ultimately joined together to establish a "new NCS," similar to the one that today informs the mainstream of macroeconomic theory. Consumer perception is an important aspect of neoclassical economics since commodities or services derive economic value, free trade, and marginal utility.

The hypothesis has proved useful in cases where customer perception has been shown to have a role. For example, you want to buy designer clothing because of the associated brand name. Furthermore, the cost of producing garments may be small. In this case, the perceived value of the brand name outweighed its input cost, resulting in an 'economic surplus.'

At the same time, this theory appears incorrect when compared to the 2008 financial catastrophe, in which synthetic financial products with no ceiling were considered to be risk-free. Nonetheless, it was accountable for a memorable crisis (Figure 7.2).

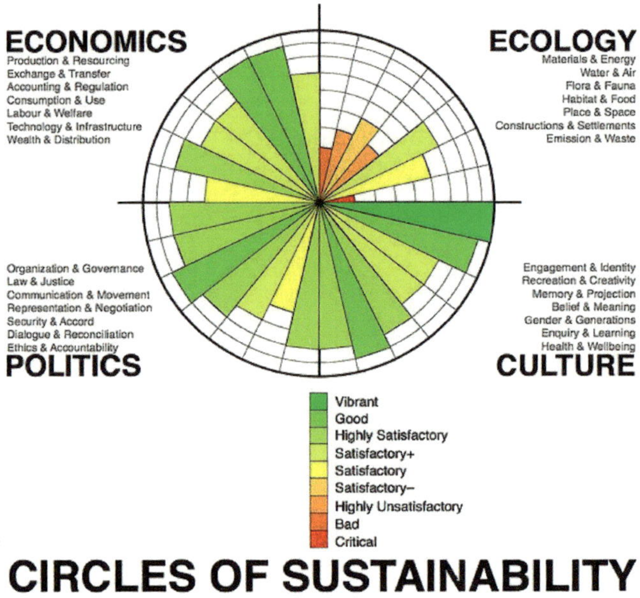

Figure 7.2. This image shows the sustainability of the metropolis of Melbourne across the four domains of sustainability—economics, ecology, politics, and culture—as developed by the UN global compact.

Source: Image by Wikimedia commons.

Neoclassical economics could also be determined by two positive and normative qualities: that the macroeconomy is extremely stable, i.e., that any deviations from potential GDP and full employment are temporary; and that government should take laissez-faire, or hands-off, approach, and not actively manage the macroeconomy.

The neoclassical school of thinking encompasses a variety of schools of thought. Traditional classical economics, monetarist economics, supply-side economics (or Reaganomics), and others are examples.

7.2. NEOCLASSICAL ECONOMICS HAS ENVIRONMENTAL CONSEQUENCES

Today's market systems are essentially governed by neoclassical economic ideas. These systems have provided unparalleled financial riches for our communities; however, four essential neoclassical economic assumptions frequently lead to environmental damage.

7.2.1. Replacing Resources

One underlying assumption is that natural resources and human resources (such as employees or technology) are generally interchangeable. This suggests that after a resource has been depleted, we will always be able to locate a substitute for it. As a result, there are no penalties for depleting resources in the market. Many resources can, in fact, be replaced.

However, the Earth's material resources are finite. Nonrenewable resources can be exhausted, while many renewable resources (such as soils, fish stocks, wood, and clean water) can be depleted if they are reduced faster than they are regenerated.

7.2.2. External Cost

A second neoclassical economics presumption would be that all expenses and gains connected with the trading of commodities or services are borne by those directly involved in the transaction. In other words, the costs and benefits are supposed to be "internal" to the transaction, experienced alone by the buyer and seller.

Many transactions, however, have an impact on other members of society. When a landowner clears a forest, the people who live nearby suffer from worse water quality, dirtier air, and fewer species. Pollution from a factory, power plant, or mining operation threatens the health of individuals who live nearby.

People who are not involved in environmental degradation end up bearing the price in such circumstances. Other people's costs associated with a transaction, external expenses are those incurred by the buyer or seller. Often, whole societies bear external expenses while specific people profit privately. The following are frequent external costs:

- People living downstream or downwind of a pollution source may have health issues, stress, or worry.
- Resource declines, such as fewer fish in a stream;
- Aesthetic harm, such as from air pollution, clear-cutting, or strip mining;
- Declining real estate prices, lost tourism revenue, greater health-care costs, and other factors.

If market pricing does not account for the social, ecological, or economic consequences of environmental degradation, taxpayers have the burden of covering them. When economists disregard external costs, we get a distorted picture of the implications of our decisions. One reason government establish environmental policies is to reduce external expenses.

7.2.3. Discounting

Third, neoclassical economics assigns less importance to future events than to existing events. Future consequences are "discounted" in economic terms. Discounting is intended to represent how people value items (we'd all prefer an ice cream cone today rather than being promised one next month).

Giving more weight to present costs and benefits than future costs and advantages, on the other hand, encourages us to neglect the long-term ramifications of our actions. Many environmental issues emerge gradually and discounting encourages us to minimize the effects of pollution and resource depletion on future generations.

In the argument over how to respond to climate change, discounting has emerged as a flashpoint. Economists believe that climate change will have significant societal consequences, although they disagree on how much to discount future effects—and so as far as how much we should invest now to combat climate change.

7.2.4. Growth

Economic growth is defined as a rise in the production and consumption of goods and services in an economy. Neoclassical economics holds that economic development is necessary for sustaining social order because it alleviates poor dissatisfaction by providing possibilities for poor people to become wealthy.

As the phrase goes, a rising tide lifts all boats; if we expand the general economic pie, each person's share will get greater (even if some people still have much smaller slices than others). Critics of the growth paradigm, on the other hand, argue that infinite growth cannot be sustained since resources to support expansion are eventually limited.

7.3. NEOCLASSICAL GROWTH MODEL

The Neoclassical Growth Theory is an economic growth model that describes how three economic factors, labor, capital, and technology, interact to produce a stable economic growth rate. The Solow-Swan Growth Model is the most basic and widely used variant of the Neoclassical Growth Model.

According to the idea, short-term economic equilibrium is the outcome of variable levels of labor and capital, both of which are important in the production process. According to the thesis, technological development has a substantial impact on the general functioning of an economy.

The three variables required for a developing economy are outlined in the Neoclassical growth theory. The theory, however, emphasizes the argument that temporary, or short-term, equilibrium differs from long-term equilibrium and does not need any of the three components.

The importance of international commerce as a replacement for low domestic aggregate demand has been stressed by neoclassical development theorists. They claim that governments should serve as facilitators of international commerce among economies. The government must remove commodity trade obstacles as part of the process of putting the economy on an autonomous, continuous growth path.

The Hecksher–Ohlin theorem, paired with comparative advantage, may then take care of the remainder. Subsequent amendments to this position call for the elimination of price distortions in domestic factors and commodity markets ("getting prices right"); this is in addition to the list of government actions needed to induce appropriate movements of factors of production across sectors, encourage the adoption of appropriate technology, and increase capital accumulation.

Domestic and foreign liberalization programs, in this opinion, are sufficient to achieve long-term economic development and structural transformation. Many economies have shown significant trust in this paradigm and have depended heavily on export-oriented growth. This has been a defining feature of Southeast Asian economies and modern China.

To some extent, growing economies like India and Brazil have bought into this line of thought. Surprisingly, export facilitation has resulted in fixed exchange rate regimes and unfettered international capital mobility in many Southeast Asian nations (Figure 7.3).

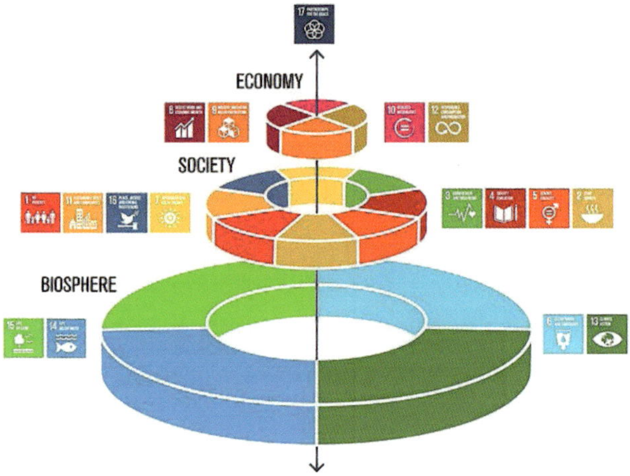

Figure 7.3. A new way of viewing the economic, social, and ecological aspects of the sustainable development goals (SDGs).

Source: Image by Wikimedia commons.

Despite the amazing economic expansion, there have frequently been concerns with capital flight induced by interest rate cuts when currencies were discounted to stimulate exports. As a result, in developing economies such as India, where complete capital account convertibility has long been considered and debated, words of warning have always been issued forward to go slowly on this front.

7.4. THE SOLOW MODEL

The Solow Growth Model is an endogenous economic expansion model which examines changes in an economy's production over time as a result of changes in the population growth rate, savings rate, and pace of technological advancement. The Nobel Prize-winning economist Robert Solow constructed the first neoclassical growth model, which was based on the Keynesian Harrod-Domar model.

The Solow model serves as the foundation for the current economic growth theory. The first model we'll talk about in this session is a model of economic growth produced by MIT's Robert Solow in the 1950s that is an excellent example of this broad approach.

Solow's goal in constructing the model was to intentionally overlook some crucial features of macroeconomics, such as short-run changes in employment and savings rates, in order to create a model that aimed to represent the economy's long-run history.

The resulting work (A Contribution to the Theory of Economic Growth, QJE, 1956) is still extremely important today and, despite its simplicity, contains a number of very helpful insights into the intricacies of the developmental process (Figure 7.4).

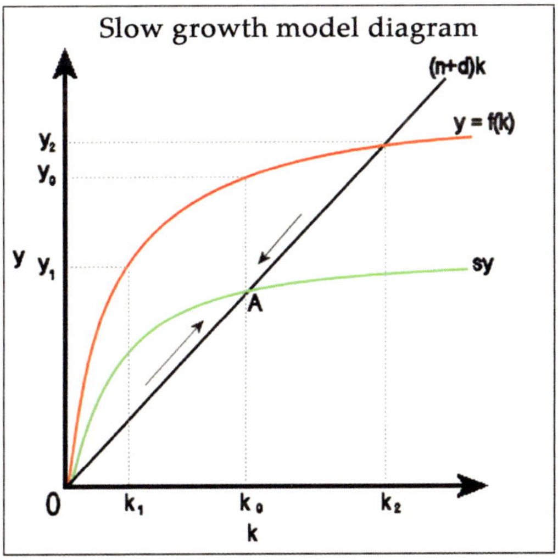

Figure 7.4. Solow growth model diagram.

Source: Image by Wikimedia commons.

From a methodological standpoint, the Solow model is particularly worth teaching since it gives a simple example of the sort of dynamic model that is often employed in today's more complex macroeconomic theory: Some of the methods and terminology taught here (such as the use of logs to determine growth rates, as well as the ideas of steady-state growth and convergent dynamics) are common in current macroeconomics.

7.4.1. Assumptions of the Solow Model

- The economy generates a single composite good that may be consumed or accumulated as a stock of capital. This is a skewed representation of reality. While we do not dispute that many products are generated in the economy, we consider just one 'composite' or 'aggregated' good for the sake of developing a model—after all, a model is a parable or a fable.

- The labor supply is uniform. In other words, we make no distinction between workers with various talents or, for example, blue-collar, and white-collar workers.
- There is a capital stock that has been accumulated in the past. This capital and labor are production elements or inputs into the manufacturing process.
- The production function has constant scale returns. This indicates that if labor and capital are raised by a particular percentage, say, production will grow by the same percentage. When labor and capital are both doubled, production doubles. As a result, there is a constant aggregation production function with constant returns to scale.
- The labor market expands at an exogenously determined pace of gL = n. Thus, the labor force at time t equals Lt = L0e nt.
- People save a certain percentage of their income. If S represents saving, then 7) S = sY. This is the same assumption as in the Harrod-Domar model. Some believe Solow did this on purpose to draw comparisons to the Harrod-Domar paradigm.
- There is no international trade.
- The government makes no economic interventions; there are no taxes or government purchases.

7.5. CAPITAL-GROWTH MODEL

Simple capital-growth models were used to create theoretical models of economic growth in the 1950s. Physical capital, like buildings, machinery, and equipment, is created to be utilized as inputs in the creation of finished goods and services. Physical capital is long-lasting in the sense that it may contribute to output for some time after it is created.

At each moment in time, production can be consumed for immediate pleasure or conserved and contributed to the capital stock to improve future consumption and production. In the fundamental neoclassical growth model, capital accumulation drives economic expansion. Labor productivity, consumption per capita, and welfare all rise when capital per unit of labor rises.

Capital accumulation will continue until the marginal productivity of capital—the rise in output from a unit of new capital input—equals the rate at which society is ready to trade off present consumption for future consumption, i.e., the social rate of time preference (Figure 7.5).

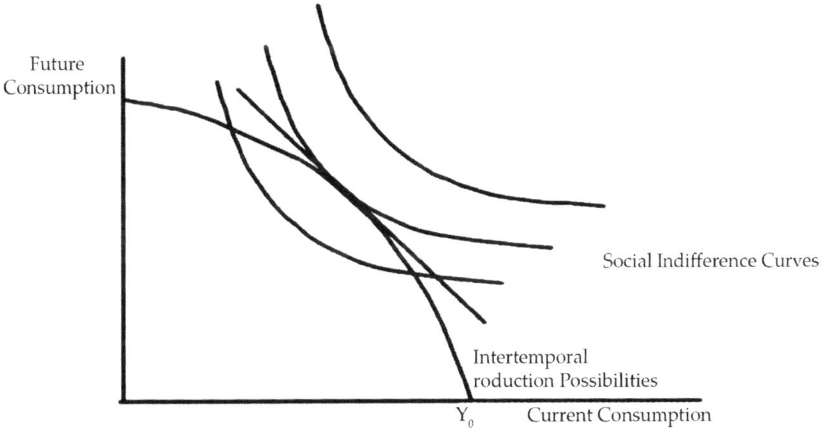

Figure 7.5. The social indifference curve.

Source: Image by Wikimedia commons.

Figure depicts the fundamental analysis, where the social indifference curves show society's preferences for various combinations of current and future consumption. Society is indifferent to present and future consumption combinations that are on the same indifference curve.

Combinations of consumption on one indifference curve are preferable over combinations on indifference curves below and to the left of that indifference curve. The slope of the indifference curve represents the pace at which society is ready to trade off current and future consumption, also known as the social rate of time preference.

The intertemporal factors of the production curve display the economic combinations of present and future consumption. Let Y0 represent the greatest amount of current consumption; it leaves no capital for future output, resulting in zero future consumption. If current consumption is smaller than Y0, the future capital stock is positive, implying that future consumption is conceivable.

The slope of the intertemporal production possibilities curve represents the rate at which output grows as the capital stock available for future production grows, i.e., the marginal product of capital. If the marginal product of capital declines as the capital stock grows, the production possibilities curve, as shown, is bowed away from the origin.

At the point where an indifference curve is just tangent to the intertemporal production possibilities curve, the best mix of present and future demand occurs. Given its manufacturing capabilities, society can achieve the greatest indifference curve. The marginal product of capital equals the societal rate of time preference at this moment because the slope of the production possibilities curve equals the slope of the indifference curve.

If the marginal product of capital is larger (less) than the willingness to sell present income for future income, saving more (less) would boost social welfare by adding more to future (current) consumption than is required to compensate for the drop in current (future) consumption. Basic neoclassical development was first supplemented with environmental and natural resources.

Models from the 1970s Population, the growth or depletion of natural resources, the cumulative environmental impact of waste emissions (as well as the impact on renewable resources), investments in the assimilative capacity of environmental resources, the impact of environmental quality on producers and consumers, investment in physical and human capital, and expenditures on pollution control are all important features of an ideal growth model that incorporates natural resources.

Furthermore, the model should contain natural-world constraints, such as the first and second principles of thermodynamics, and it should account for the uncertainty associated with the links between the economy and the environment. Obviously, it is a challenging task.

The inclusion of merely a capital stock, a natural resource, and an environmental quality variable necessitates the inclusion of at least three state variables. In general, characterizing the qualitative aspects of a model with more than two state variables without making limiting assumptions about functional forms or key linkages is technically challenging.

Because of the inherent complexity, most growth models must concentrate on the most conspicuous dynamic elements of economic-environmental interactions. The simplified models are not meant to be taken literally, but rather to identify crucial links and provide qualitative insights into the elements that influence the economy's direction.

Because results can be affected by certain assumptions, to establish the robustness of qualitative data, various formulations must be examined. One of the modeling process's assets is the capacity to investigate various situations.

7.6. SAY'S LAW AND THE NEOCLASSICAL PERSPECTIVE

This "new" view of how the macroeconomy works, as the name indicates, is a "new" view of the "old" classical model of the economy. The classical approach, which was the dominant economic thought until the Great Depression, held that short-term variations in economic activity would swiftly adapt back to full employment with flexible pricing.

Say's Law provides an excellent description of the reasoning underlying classical (and neoclassical) economics. Jean-Baptiste Say (1767–1832) was a French economist who lived in the early 1800s. According to Say's law, "supply creates its own demand."

Say's law is based on the idea that every time a thing or service is created and sold, it creates revenue for someone: a worker, a manager, an owner, or those who work, manage, and own enterprises that supply inputs along the production chain. Prices will rise and decrease according to supply and demand pressures in specific marketplaces.

The bottom line is that every sale generates revenue for someone, and therefore, according to Say's rule, a given value of supply must generate an equivalent value of demand someplace else in the economy. Because Jean-Baptiste Say, Adam Smith, and other economists writing around the turn of the nineteenth century who explored this viewpoint were regarded as "classical" economists, modern economists have adopted this viewpoint.

Neoclassical economists are those who typically agree with Say's law on the role of supply in determining the size of the macroeconomy. If supply always generates exactly enough demand at the macroeconomic level, it is difficult to comprehend why times of recession and severe unemployment could ever occur, as Say himself acknowledged.

To be clear, even if total supply always generates an equal amount of total demand, the economy may nonetheless face a situation in which some businesses win while others lose. Nonetheless, a recession is not a condition in which all company failures are exactly offset by an equal number of triumphs.

A recession occurs when the economy as a whole shrink in size, company failures outnumber remaining success stories, and many businesses incur losses and lay off people. Say's law, which states that supply creates its own demand, appears to be a decent approximation in the long term.

Over a period of years or decades, as an economy's production capacity to offer products and services expands, overall demand in the economy grows at nearly the same rate. However, recessions or even depressions can occur over shorter time frames of a few months or even years, in which enterprises as a group appear to experience a lack of demand for their products.

7.7. THE CURRENT CRISIS IN NEO-CLASSICAL ECONOMICS

Kuhn's views on paradigm function appear to be particularly pertinent to conventional economics. One can see how, for example, in the case of the firm theory in microeconomics or the theory that supports the IS-LM model in macroeconomics, economists have engaged in abstract and esoteric articulations of paradigms with little regard for their practical applicability.

The great irony is that these beliefs have endured the test of time long after their creators disavowed them. Joan Robinson, for example, authored a book on imperfect competition in the 1930s, which fostered the growth of study in this field and the proliferation of models of increasing depth and complexity. However, Robinson claimed that her early effort had been misplaced and that she intended to renounce it.

Despite her recantation, study into the theory of the business has proceeded along the lines she initiated. Similarly, John Hicks, who was responsible for developing IS-LM analysis as a tool for understanding Keynesian economics, recanted his prior beliefs, expressing surprise at how it had come to dominate economics instruction.

It is also obvious how certain sectors of the economics profession close ranks against new challenges by classifying them as "beyond the scope of economics." The discipline's main representatives, as well as the journals that publish their works, are frequently hesitant to extend the bounds of economics into issues bordering on politics, sociology, or environmental ethics.

As a result, critical economic concerns such as gender, racism, or environmental degradation are rarely covered in conventional economics courses, and are seen as fringe topics that are not truly scientific.' Kuhn's statements about the existing paradigm and its supporters' censoring function may also be considered pertinent to economics.

Articles or books that fundamentally question the prevailing paradigm have significant challenges in getting past the referees designated by publishers and journals because these referees are invariably major exponents of the incumbent paradigm. Similarly, candidates for positions as economists in government agencies or universities are less likely to succeed if they are regarded to hold unconventional ideas.

In this regard, Kuhn's theories echo the famous observation made by Keynes on the last two pages of the General Theory: Madmen in charge, hearing voices in the air, are distilling their hysteria from some intellectual scribbler from a few years ago. I am confident that the influence of vested interests is greatly overestimated in comparison to the slow invasion of ideas.

Not immediately, but after a certain interval; for in the field of economic and political philosophy, few people are influenced by new theories after the age of twenty-five or thirty, so the ideas that civil servants, politicians, and even agitators apply to current events are unlikely to be the most recent.

To put it another way, economists in universities influence students to study issues that appear to have little relevance to the real world, while economists in government departments devote their energies to convincing their superiors to implement policies that they studied in textbooks many years before.

7.8. THE ECOLOGICAL ECONOMICS CRITIQUE OF NEOCLASSICAL ECONOMICS

If one were to attempt to categorize the main criticisms currently leveled at neoclassical economics, one might identify first, the excessive formality and low priority accorded to the need to check theories for real world relevance (as in a 'No Reality, Please. We're Economists' musical, as Blaug has quipped);

Second, a fair amount of concern about the lack of 'plurality' in the views presented, there that only one 'brand' of economics is taught, and that this is done as though there were only one set of theories that a student has to understand; Third, a detailed criticism from ecological economists, especially Herman Daly.

The final complaint, of the three, may have the most far-reaching ramifications for business. Ecological economists see a "changed pattern of scarcity" in current economic systems. Economics, which is typically described as the study of how to manage scarcity, has long regarded man-made capital to be the resource most relevant to scarcity analysis.

This made sense at the time the idea was conceived when labor and natural resources were plentiful and the methods for collecting and utilizing these resources to satisfy fundamental human needs were extremely crude. As a result, human technological brilliance has focused on better and better machines, greatly increasing labor productivity by employing such tools.

In 1812, a single spinner could complete the job of two hundred employees in 1770. One can only speculate what order of Since 1812, modern technology has increased labor productivity by orders of magnitude. Natural capital—the natural resources such as rich soils, supplies of lumber, water, minerals, and fossil fuels, and the earth's and its atmosphere's capacity to absorb wastes—seemed so bountiful throughout this period that it barely received a mention in economic theory.

These natural contributions were certainly recognized during the early development of economic theory, but as theoretical refinement progressed and the focus remained on improving man-made capital, the production functions of the typical business began to be described as consisting of only two factors of production, labor (L) and man-made capital (M) (K).

Raw materials utilized as inputs in the manufacturing process, as well as any other services offered by the natural environment, were completely excluded from consideration. Meanwhile, ecological economists are emphasizing the importance of shifting the focus from man-made wealth to natural capital.

Natural capital is currently recognized as becoming increasingly rare in comparison to man-made capital. The capacity to catch fish is no longer the limiting issue; it is the fish themselves. The amount of water available is the constraint, not our knowledge and techniques of irrigating crops.

It is not the amount of pumping power, but the amount of groundwater in the aquifers; it is not the number of chainsaws, but the number of accessible trees, and so on. As a result, in the same manner, that labor productivity has increased dramatically over the previous 200 years, ecological productivity has increased significantly.

Economists say that it is time to redirect our efforts toward increasing natural resource productivity. This entails developing new technologies and reworking old procedures in order to attain current levels of productivity while using far fewer natural resources. It appears that human intellect is capable of accomplishing this.

So, if all of this is conceivable, why are neoclassical economists so hostile to the ecological economics critique? The answer requires some explanation and has a lot to do with how ecological economists understand the world in comparison to neoclassical economics. When the way a specific occurrence is seen alters fundamentally, a paradigm shift occurs in the physical sciences.

The same may be said for paradigm shifts in the social sciences. Ecological economists and neoclassical economists both study the economic system as it already exists. However, even before the study begins, the two schools of thought reach quite different conclusions about the desirability of economic development due to fundamental differences in their perceptions of the universe and how the circular flow fits into it.

The economy, according to ecological economists, is a subsystem of a limited, non-growing, materially closed (save for solar energy) environmental eco-system. The economy is inextricably linked to the environment. Alternatively, neoclassical economists see things a different way around with the ecosystem as a subset of the economy.

According to this worldview, the economy collects raw resources from the environment and then returns garbage to it. Economic development, on the other hand, can only occur within the confines given by the limited boundaries of the natural environment. Such constraints do not apply to an economy that includes the environment as a subsector.

This is particularly true when this is also expected, as neoclassical economists do, that man-made capital can compensate for any shortfalls in the natural resources sector. This final assumption requires a bit more explanation. Neoclassical economists created a concept known as the 'infinite growth' model in the 1970s.

The model claimed to demonstrate how and why output and consumption may continue to expand indefinitely. A crucial tenet of this model is that man-made capital will replace natural capital because 'fully functioning markets' will herald an imminent lack of natural capital, spurring technical advancement to find a substitute.

In almost the same manner with which we can understand how $10,000 in financial capital can sustain $1,000 in annual consumption at a 10% interest rate (ignoring taxes, etc.), the basic idea of the infinite growth model is that an economy can sustain an amount of production or consumption indefinitely as long as its productive capacity (which is a function of both man-made and natural capital) is not depleted.

Perhaps one should be glad that this model acknowledges the existence of raw materials and natural resources in manufacturing operations. The model's flaw is that its assumptions indicate that the composition of capital kept in the economy is unimportant.

Natural capital can be useful. Natural capital can be depleted, but man-made capital (by technological growth) can compensate. The economy may develop endlessly as long as the entire amount of capital (natural capital + man-made capital) is retained.

This paradigm lends itself to four quick observations. First, the model's production function implies that output can be maintained even if raw resources are reduced, as long as man-made capital and labor are raised sufficiently to compensate.

As Daly and Farley point out, the logic in this is equivalent to suggesting that if a cook bakes a five-pound cake, he or she can raise it to a 1000-pound cake by just stirring harder and baking it longer in a larger oven! In the real world, natural resources are required to keep man-made capital in excellent operating order. To put it bluntly, man-made capital is created from the flow of natural capital's resources and energy.

Second, the neoclassical economics theoretical framework was developed at a time when the 'limits to growth' discussions of the 1970s identified sources of raw resources as potential future constrictions on economic growth, while less attention was paid to (and may have been known about)' sinks'—the capacity of Earth's systems to accommodate wastes.

At the time, it was anticipated that scarcity of resources like oil, coal, copper, as well as other metals, would be the limiting forces to expansion. Nature's ecological services were not recognized by the model. In any event, they were not well appreciated at the time (Figure 7.6).

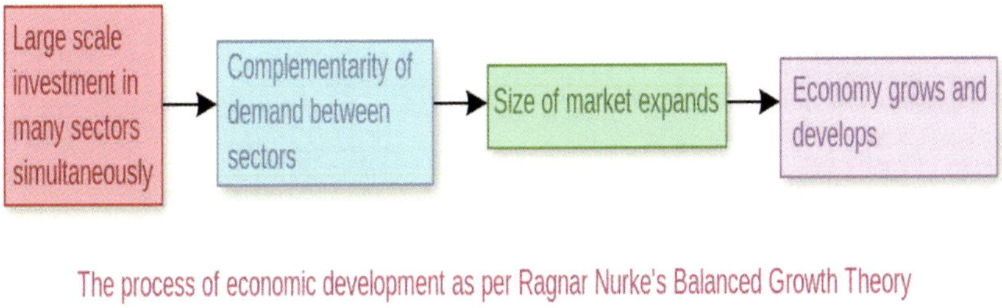

Figure 7.6. This diagram depicts the process of economic development as per Ragnar Nurkse's balanced growth theory.

Source: Image by Wikimedia commons.

Neither did the model predict that thirty to forty years later, the earth's ability to process manufacturing wastes into its atmosphere, groundwater, seas, and rivers is proving to be more instantly restrictive than future mineral supplies.

It's hard to understand how even "well-functioning markets" may communicate dangers to the earth's sinks, therefore, spurring technological advancement to discover solutions. Only more intense weather events in the sky, crop failures due to salt in groundwater, fish deaths in the ocean, and other such phenomena indicate dangers to the earth's sinks—not market pricing.

7.9. FROM ECONOMIC GROWTH TO ECONOMIC DEVELOPMENT

Capital formation has been a fundamental component of growth for ages and continues to be so today. However, its meaning has shifted throughout time. T.W. Schultz was the first to highlight the importance of human capital creation in addition to physical capital formation.

This resulted in a focus on education and training as requirements for progress, as well as the recognition of the problem of "brain drain" from the Third to the First World. Schultz's argument was further supported by Lewis (1965) and Singer (1965). Their thesis was centered on overall societal growth, which might be brought about through education, health, fertility, and so on.

Human capital development was therefore, recognized as an essential precondition for economic progress. According to this viewpoint, industrialization could never be self-sustaining if it came at the expense of social development. “Development is a growth plus change,” Singer (1965), and “change is not just economic but also social and cultural.”

He stated that growth has not solved the problem of poverty and advocated for “poverty-biased policies” to improve the quality of life of the underprivileged until now, all argumentations, including those in favor of progress, had been growth-centric.

When Seers (1969) released a crucial article in which development was viewed as a social phenomenon rather than just being described in the reductionist manner of per capita income increase, the growing preoccupation with development theory was jolted. According to Seers, development entailed progress toward the social goals of poverty reduction, employment, and equality.

With the introduction of the Human Progress Index (HDI) as a rather crude measure of development by academics and multilateral in the 1990s, the social perspectives of development became even more apparent. The HDI assesses nations’ life expectancy, literacy, education, and standard of living. This gives an idea of how economic policies affect people’s quality of life.

Amartya Sen and Mahbub Ul Haq created the index in 1990 with assistance from Yale University’s Gustav Ranis and the London School of Economics’ Meghnad Desai. Since its inception, the United Nations Development Program (UNDP) has its annual Human Progress Reports, the UNDP utilizes it as a standard indicator for classifying a country’s development.

Despite being a “vulgar measure,” as Sen describes, it brings forward larger dimensions of development than the per capita income measure it replaced and provides an avenue for scholars to dive into the wide array of specific metrics contained in the Human Development Reports (Figure 7.7).

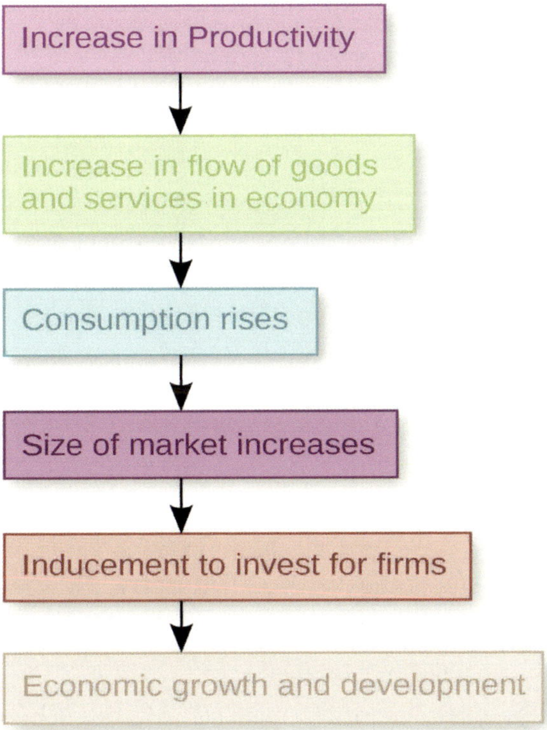

Figure 7.7. This diagram shows the process of how increased productivity leads to economic development and growth, as per Ragnar Nurkse.

Source: Image by Wikimedia commons.

Other international organizations, such as the World Bank, have begun to focus on social aspects such as poverty. As a result, whether in policymaking or academic research, social factors began to be included and eventually formed an essential component of economic growth..

7.10. NEOCLASSICAL ECONOMICS AND SUSTAINABILITY DEVELOPMENT

According to neoclassical economic theory, sustainability may be described as the maximizing of benefits over time. (This is supposed to also be human welfare; the claims of the non-human world will be included once we explore the ecological perspective.) Most economists simplify further by associating welfare maximization with utility maximization resulting from consumption.

Although this could be critiqued as oversimplification, it does contain many key aspects of human wellbeing (food, clothes, housing, transportation, health, and education services, and so on) and also has the logical benefit of reducing the issue to a quantifiable single-dimensional indicator.

A thorough economic study then asks if the idea of sustainability has had any economic value. Traditional economic theory holds that optimal allocation of resources should maximize benefit from consumption. If we accept time discounting as a technique of assessing the economic values of consumption over different periods of time, then sustainability looks to be nothing more than efficient resource allocation—a notion that is already well established in economics.

One point of contention with this reductionist approach to sustainability is the use of discounts. At a 10% discount rate, the value of $1 million one hundred years from now is the same as $72 today. As a result, it is fair to impose charges of spend up to $1 million on individuals in the year 2100 to enjoy $72 in consumption now.

According to this argument, substantial resource depletion and environmental harm may be regarded as acceptable, if not optimum, based on an economic efficiency criterion. The issue is that by agreeing to employ a discount rate, we have implicitly imposed a certain option on the relative wellbeing of present and future generations.

Howarth and Norgaard demonstrated that selecting a discount rate is similar to selecting allocations among generations. The use of a current market discount rate lends disproportionate weight to current consumer choices. When we analyze issues like soil erosion or greenhouse gas accumulation in the atmosphere, where the most harmful effects are perceived across decades or generations, we see a substantial bias against sustainability.

Thus, in order to achieve intergenerational justice, we must either apply a low discount rate or implement some sort of sustainability guideline governing resource consumption and environmental repercussions. A similar topic is the idea of natural capital. Soils and atmospheric functions are components of natural capital, which includes all of the planet's natural resources and environmental services.

Herman Daly has proposed that sustainable development might be operationalized in terms of natural capital conservation. This policy aim results in two decision rules, one for renewable energy resources and one for non-renewable sources.

The rule for renewables is to limit resource consumption to sustainable yield levels; the rule for non-renewable is to reinvest the earnings from non-renewable resource exploitation in renewable natural capital investment. Following these two guidelines will keep the stock of natural capital constant. Daly has also emphasized the relevance of the human population in maintaining a fixed per capita stock of natural capital.

There is really no compelling motive to maintain natural capital, according to neoclassical thinking.

The "Hartwick rule," developed from the work of Solow and Hartwick, asserts that consumption may remain constant or rise in the face of dwindling non-renewable resources if the rents from these resources are reinvested in reproducible capital. Unlike Daly's reinvestment rule, this does not necessitate the preservation of any specific stock of natural capital.

The Solow/Hartwick strategy is based on the idea that the two forms of capital are interchangeable. For instance, if we burn down trees but establish factories, for example, we will be better off if the economic value of the new industrial facility surpasses the economic worth of the lost woods.

Daly holds that "man-made and natural capital is inherently complemented and only slightly alternatives." If natural capital is of distinctive and unique value, neoclassical economic efficiency will not sufficient for long-term existence.

Markets, according to Neoclassical economics, should really be free of political interference; a market with minimum government intervention will self-adjust according to demand and supply principles. Furthermore, open markets provide customers with additional alternatives; customers are rational agents who buy products based on their utility (Figure 7.8).

Figure 7.8. Decent work & economic growth.

Source: Image by flickr.

Prior to actually buying a particular choice, consumers examine a variety of variables such as cost, usefulness, as well as satisfaction. According to neoclassical economists, the goal of sustainable development should reflect the need for societies to maintain their ability to produce economic wellbeing over time and, at the very least, to ensure that future generations have access to the same level of wellbeing as current generations.

In other words, in this context, sustainability is defined as the "non-decline" of individual wellbeing through time. To achieve this goal, neoclassical writers think that savings rates must be high enough to ensure that the capital stock accessible to society stays steady from generation to generation, allowing for a consistent flow of wealth across time.

An economy's productive capacity is comprised of its stock of facilities, knowledge, skills, the general level of education and training, and accessible natural resources. Nature is regarded as a specific type of capital, following in the footsteps of Harold Hoteling. Although it was only hinted at in literature in the 1970s, the idea of "natural capital" began to be more fully defined from the late 1990s onward, to the point that it is now widely used.

As a result, it has now formed part of the neoclassical theorists' school of thought on economic growth. However, these theorists' hypothesis concerns the substitutability of these various forms of capital: an increase in "capital generated by societies" should be able to compensate for a decrease in "natural capital" to ensure that individual productive capacity and wellbeing are maintained over time.

According to Robert Solow, an exchange occurs throughout time: the current generation consumes "natural capital" but passes on additional production capacity in the form of facilities, knowledge, and skill stock to future generations in exchange. Many theories are required to support this situation.

The first is about technological innovation, which must supply a mix of "contingency techniques" that allow for the replacement of diverse types of capital. The second is a definition of a certain investment regime: Hartwick requires that revenues from the exploitation of non-renewable natural resources be reinvested in technological capital through a taxation system or a dedicated investment fund.

Regarding the third point, while Solow's model does not include prices—it depicts a planned economy with only one agent deciding on resource allocation—the neoclassical proposed alternative theory that asserts that resource allocation should be decided by the "market."

The pricing system must identify the value of the various types of capital, as well as the rate of substitution that will be formed between them. As a result, there is a need to bring what was previously outside the market into it by assigning a monetary value to natural resources and pollutants. Economists refer to this strategy as the "internalization of externalities."

The constraints placed on the economic dynamic in this "weak" version of sustainability are not very restrictive: of note is the reaffirmation of the central importance of growth, confidence in technological progress and the pricing mechanism, and intervention of public powers in some areas considered strategic (information on the availability of reserves of natural resources and technical innovation)for the exchange of different types of capital This model is completed with other neoclassical analysis.

7.11. CONCLUSION

Present-day neoclassical economic theory and its applications to development policy extremely undervalue or overlook major ecological concerns. The economic values of environmental services, despite the fact very real, are systematically underestimated in cost-benefit analysis due to difficulties in measurement and valuation. 'Intangible' environmental benefits, such as those derived from the preservation of biological diversity, are even recognized less in economic analysis.

The irreversible environmental effects of projects or policies are typically regarded no differently from more reversible effects. The practice of discounting economic costs as well as benefits strongly favors policies with short-term benefits and long-term costs, often with highly negative environmental effects. Using Gross National Product as a measure of development progress inspires rapid overexploitation of a country's natural resource base.

Consumption of extravagant natural resource by industrialized nations may undermine long-term development prospects of developing countries. The emphasis of many developing countries on export crops rather than domestic food production often entails major environmental costs.

REFERENCES

1. (n.d). *The Neo-Classical Growth Model*, 38–60. [e-Book] Available at: https://www.egyankosh.ac.in/bitstream/123456789/23005/1/Unit-3.pdf (accessed on 21 June 2022).
2. Franck-Dominique, V., (2008). *Sustainable Development: An Overview of Economic Proposals*. [online] Open Edition Journal. Available at: https://journals.openedition.org/sapiens/227 (accessed on 21 June 2022).
3. Lara, B., (2016). *Neoclassical Economics* | Exploring Economics. [online] Exploring-economics.org. Available at: https://www.exploring-economics.org/en/orientation/neoclassical-economics/ (accessed on 21 June 2022).
4. Lumen learning, (n.d). *The Neoclassical Perspective* | Macroeconomics. [online] Courses.lumenlearning.com. Available at: https://courses.lumenlearning.com/wm-macroeconomics/chapter/introduction-to-the-neoclassical-perspective/ (accessed on 21 June 2022).
5. Williams, J., & McNeill, J., (2005). The current crisis in neoclassical economics and the case for an economic analysis based on sustainable development. *SSRN Electronic Journal.* [online] Available at: https://www.researchgate.net/publication/228320287_The_Current_Crisis_In_Neoclassical_Economics_and_the_Case_for_an_Economic_Analysis_Based_on_Sustainable_Development (accessed on 21 June 2022).

CHAPTER 8

GREEN ECONOMY AND SUSTAINABLE DEVELOPMENT

CONTENTS

8.1. INTRODUCTION

The concept of a green economy (GE) proposed by the United Nations Environment Program (UNEP) and promoted through its GE Initiative is one of the most widely recognized. A GE, according to UNEP, is one that "improves human wellbeing and social fairness while considerably lowering environmental dangers and ecological scarcity."

The term "GE" arose from discussions about the environment and development, which led to the discussion and promotion of the term "sustainable development" at the 1992 United Nations Conference on Environment and Development (UNCED) in Rio de Janeiro (also known as the Rio Summit or Earth Summit).

The term "GE" was coined by a group of top environmental economists in a ground breaking 1989 study for the Government of the United Kingdom titled Blueprint for a GE.

The study was commissioned to advise the UK Government on whether there was a common definition of "sustainable development," as well as the implications of sustainable development for measuring economic success and evaluating projects and policies.

Apart from the title of the paper, there is no further mention of the GE, and it appears that the writers used the word as an afterthought. Blueprint 2: Greening the World Economy, published in 1991 and 1994, was a follow-up to the previous study Blueprint 3 is about assessing sustainable development.

While the first Blueprint report's thesis was that economics can and should help environmental policy, the subsequent reports expanded this message to global issues such as climate change, ozone depletion, tropical deforestation, and resource loss in the developing world. All studies are based on decades of environmental economics study and experience.

The phrase was reintroduced in 2008 in the context of talks on governmental responses to various global crises. In the midst of the financial crisis and fears of a worldwide recession, UNEP advocated for "green stimulus packages" and highlighted specific sectors where largescale public investment could jumpstart a "GE" (Figure 8.1).

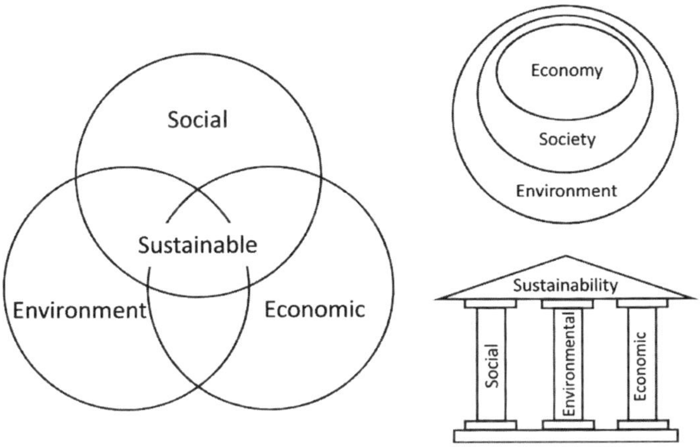

Figure 8.1. Three pillars of sustainability: in search of conceptual origins.

Source: Image by Wikimedia commons.

As part of their economic recovery efforts, numerous countries implemented major 'green stimulus' programs. UNEP started the GE Initiative in October 2008 to provide analytical and policy assistance for green sector investment and greening resource and/or pollution-intensive sectors. As part of this Initiative, UNEP commissioned one of the original writers of the Blueprint for a GE to write a study titled A Global Green Economy New Deal (GGND), which was launched in April 2009 and advocated a mix of policy steps to boost economic recovery while also improving global economic sustainability. The GGND urged governments to devote a significant portion of stimulus funds to green sectors and established three goals:

- economic recovery;
- poverty eradication; and
- reduced carbon emissions and ecosystem degradation.

It also proposed a framework for green stimulus programs as well as support for domestic and international policies. In the run-up to the United Nations Climate Change Conference in Copenhagen in June 2009, the UN issued an interagency statement endorsing the GE as a solution to solve various issues.

The declaration expressed hope that the economic recovery would serve as a watershed moment for an ambitious and successful worldwide response to humanity's various issues, on the basis of a global GE.

The UNEP Global Ministerial Environment Forum in Nusa Dua in February 2010 noted in their declaration that the GE idea "can considerably solve existing difficulties and bring economic development prospects and various benefits for all nations."

It also recognized UNEP's leadership role in further defining and promoting the idea and urged UNEP to contribute to this effort through the Rio+20 preparation process. The General Assembly determined in March 2010 that one of the two special themes for Rio+20 will be a GE in the framework of sustainable development and poverty eradication.

This drew a lot of international attention to the GE and related topics, as well as the publishing plethora of publications and other literature aimed at better defining and simplifying the idea. The flagship GE Report, issued by UNEP in November 2011 as part of its GE Initiative, was one of the main reports.

UNEP collaborated with think tanks and business players (including Deutsche Bank) to validate its economic analyzes. Importantly, the paper includes a working definition of the term "GE," which has subsequently been quoted in a variety of other publications.

Other publications from UNEP, UNCTAD, UNDESA, and the UNCSD Secretariat have sought to expand on the notion by outlining guiding principles, advantages, hazards, and developing international experience.

In December 2011, the UN Environment Management Group (a systemwide coordinating organization of over 40 United Nations specialized agencies, programs, and institutions) also presented their systemwide viewpoint on the green economy—Working Towards a Green Economy that is Balanced and Inclusive—recognizes and defines the usage of green economy (Figure 8.2).

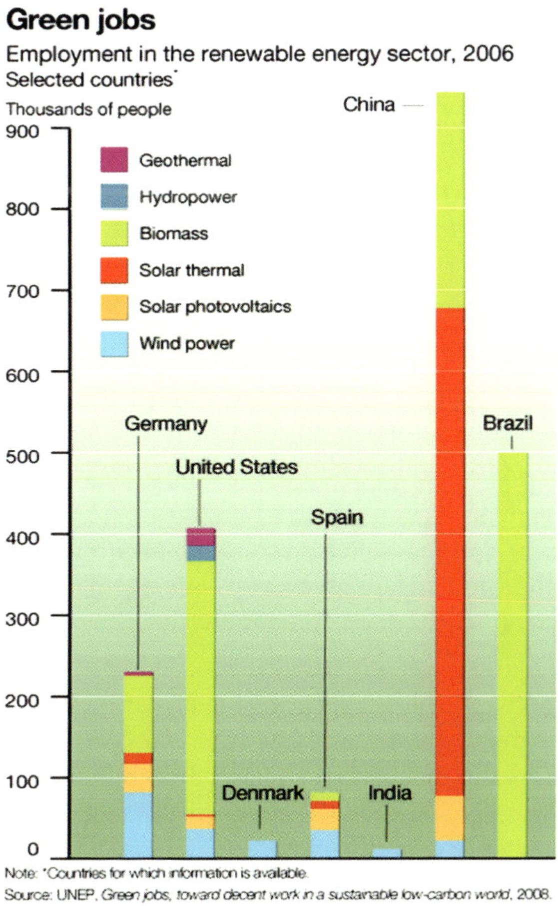

Figure 8.2. Green jobs.

Source: Image by flickr.

As well as other relevant terms the definition offered by UNEP in its 2011 GE Study is used in this report. In recent years, a number of non-governmental groups and collaborations have emerged with the goal of promoting a GE as a concept and doing research, analysis, and outreach.

There is no universally accepted definition of the GE, and at least eight distinct definitions have been discovered. The United Nations Environment Program, for example, defines the GE as "one that improves human wellbeing and social fairness while considerably lowering environmental dangers and ecological scarcity."

It has a minimal carbon footprint, is resource efficient, and is socially inclusive." This term has been mentioned in several recent studies, including those from the UNEMG and the OECD.

Another definition of the GE provided by GE can be defined briefly by the GE Coalition (a network of NGOs, trade union organizations, and others conducting grassroots work on a GE) as "a resilient economy that delivers a higher standard of living for everybody within in the natural boundaries of the earth."

There are several definitions of a GE, each emphasizing a particular feature. Some definitions (including the above-mentioned UNEP definition) are:

- A GE produces "increased human wellbeing and social equality while considerably lowering environmental dangers and ecological scarcity"
- A GE is defined as "an economy in which economic growth and environmental sustainability are mutually reinforcing while promoting social development progress."
- "Green growth (GG) implies promoting economic growth and development while ensuring that natural assets continue to deliver the resources and environmental services that we rely on for our wellbeing." It is concerned with the synergies and trade-offs that exist between the environmental and economic pillars of sustainable development.
- Very low Carbon development strategies are defined by the OECD as "forward-looking national economic development plans or strategies that include low-emission and/or climate-resilient economic growth." The idea of a GE supports—rather than replaces—sustainable development. However, this increased emphasis is in response to two recent developments:
  - Many governments, businesses, civil society, and the general public now recognize that we are approaching planetary limitations, not just in terms of greenhouse gas emissions, but also in our use of water, land, forests, and other natural resources.
  - The global crisis has caused a reassessment of major principles of the present economic model, as well as the adoption by a number of nations of programs to encourage

"green" energy sources and to establish new markets and businesses that may produce solid, long-term jobs (Figure 8.3).

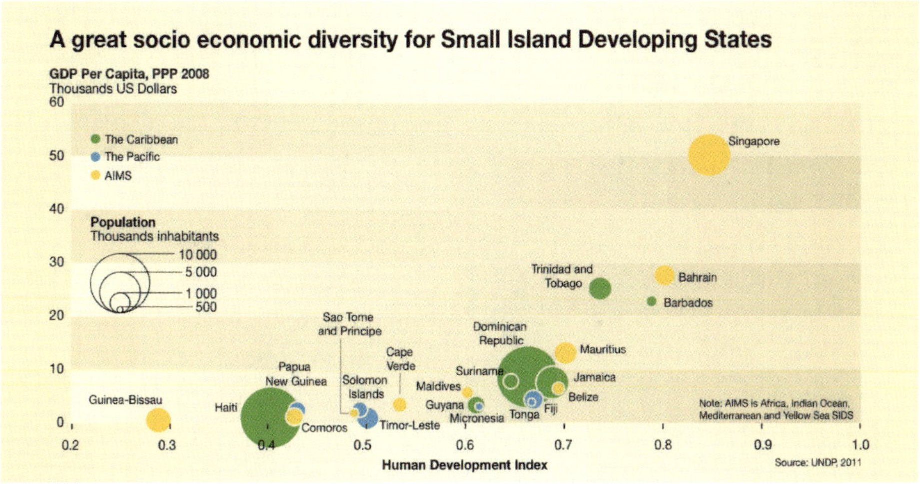

Figure 8.3. A great socio-economic diversity for small island developing states.

Source: Image by flickr.

The development of a GE was a major issue of the Rio+20 Conference, held in June 2012 to commemorate the Rio Summit's 20th anniversary. At Rio+20, governments resolved to position the GE as an important tool for sustainable development—one that is inclusive and capable of driving economic growth, employment, as well as poverty eradication while also protecting the health of the Earth's ecosystems.

8.2. IMPORTANCE OF GREEN ECONOMY

The GE is concerned with more than simply the environment; it is also concerned with the development and the economy. A GE may help both developed and developing countries in a variety of ways, according to development experts.

A GE should not only retain, but also increase, the value that the poor in developing nations obtain from agriculture, fisheries, and forest harvesting—all of which are essentially dependent on a healthy environment. It should contribute to the reduction of energy poverty by providing low-cost distributed renewable energy solutions.

And, if effective, it should help minimize the poor's susceptibility to the effects of unmanaged climate change, desertification, ocean degradation, and biodiversity loss, as well as the effects of local air, soil, and water pollution.

It should be a catalyst for new creative activities in both developed and developing nations, activities that produce more employment than conventional industries and improve energy security and industrial efficiency. There are more chances for investment in the construction, transportation, energy, and waste sectors, as well as industry, agricultural, and other industries.

Many of these industries will require services sector assistance, which will be an essential aspect of the GE. The environmental benefits of a GE are self-evident and do not require long elaboration. It should contribute to addressing global issues such as climate change, biodiversity loss, and desertification.

It should also contribute to national and regional initiatives to alleviate local pollution of air, water, and land. The transition to a GE would also lead to financial gains (clearly, any such shift involves risks and costs as well, and some of these are considered later in this paper). One clear potential benefit of a GE is the creation of new export markets.

Some of them are discussed more below, but well-known examples include large new markets for biofuels and renewable energy technology like solar panels and wind turbines. Opportunities in these markets may be driven solely by export demand, or by a mix of foreign demand and local capacity expansion in response to rigorous domestic environmental regulations.

A change to a GE may assist to preserve existing market share as well as open up new markets. Environmental-related product and process requirements (technical regulations), regulatory frameworks, and limitations are progressively increasing in most OECD markets, with serious consequences for developing-country exporters.

The increase in sustainable development-related norms and rules used by private customers is even more significant for some exporters. Furthermore, the emergence of climate change as a pressing policy issue threatens to give birth to new non-tariff obstacles, such as border carbon adjustment.

8.3. THE MACROECONOMIC DIMENSIONS OF GREEN ECONOMIC GROWTH

Ocampo identifies four distinct macroeconomic challenges that must be considered in the examination of the GE. The first is about inter-temporal welfare: how future generations' welfare is taken into account in current economic decisions, which is relevant for savings and investment decisions today but has broader implications because the social discount rate chosen should be used in cost-benefit analysis at the microeconomic and sectoral levels.

The second is concerned with the consequences of environmental deterioration on aggregate supply, as well as the implications of environmental investment and protection measures on both aggregate supply and demand.

The next point to consider is that economic expansion is always accompanied by the structural change that is emphasized by the considerable changes in production and consumption patterns that must be implemented in the transition to the GE, which may be described as nothing less than a new technological or industrial revolution.

The final one is about how worldwide projects in this field will be funded. The first two of these difficulties are addressed in this part, the third in the following one, while later sections examine technology and financing.

The first of these issues is the discount rate, which is used in current economic decisions to value future generations' consumption (welfare) and environmental damages that are being created today but will fully affect economic activity only in the future—for example, damages caused by climate change, biodiversity loss, or deterioration of water systems.

The significance of this problem is best appreciated in the context of the Stern Review on the economics of climate change. For example, $100 in environmental damage 50 years from now would be evaluated at $49.90 today using the Stern Review's 1.4% annual discount rate, but just $5.43 or $6.88 using the alternative rates favored by its detractors (6 and 5.5%, respectively).

As a result, having a large discount rate diminishes the social profitability of implementing mitigation activities now, preferring delayed action or perhaps no action at all. As a result, a high rate of discount diminishes the appeal of saving and investing now to benefit future generations.

This means that social discount rates, which are used to analyzes optimal economic development routes and related savings and investment decisions, are inextricably tied to ethical concerns over intergenerational equality. On these arguments, Ocampo defends Stern and proponents of aggressive environmental action using social discount rates that are lower (in fact, much lower) than market rates.

Indeed, he contends that true intergenerational fairness necessitates the application of a discount rate equal to the predicted pace of technological development (say on the order of 1.5 to 2%). This also indicates that current environmental savings and investments must be expanded in order to benefit future generations (Figure 8.4).

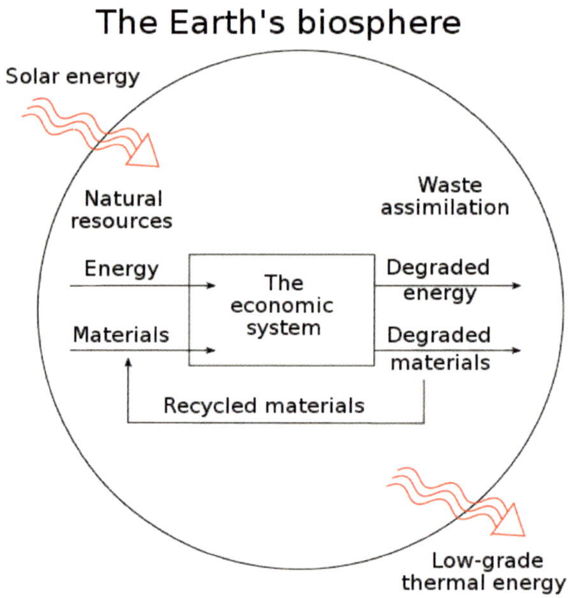

Figure 8.4. Diagram describing the flow of natural resources through the economy: Valuable resources are procured from nature by the input end of the economy; the resources flow through the economy, being transformed and manufactured into goods along the way; and invaluable waste and pollution eventually accumulate by the output end.

Source: Image by Wikimedia commons.

A counter-argument is that vigorous action now protects future generations against asymmetric and non-linear impacts that certain developments can have on the ecosystem (e.g., the fact that the risk of losses associated with climate change or species extinction, among other things, is greater than the probability of a more favorable outcome than those projected), including the increasing likelihood of extreme events (catastrophes).

As previously stated, this implies that appropriate environmental expenditures should be evaluated using low social discount rates in microeconomic and sectoral cost-benefit analyzes. Green investments have a twofold beneficial economic effect on aggregate supply and demand, according to macroeconomic considerations.

In the first case, according to UNEP's recent Green Economic report, reallocating investments to the GE may result in slower potential economic growth for a few years as renewable natural resources replenish (an effect that can be strong in some sectors, such as fisheries), but will result in faster economic growth in the long run.

Furthermore, investments in the GE lower the downside risks of unfavorable occurrences such as climate change, energy shocks, water scarcity, and ecosystem service loss. They will also result in additional employment in the long run, as green investments are often more labor demanding, and have a direct impact on poverty alleviation.

This is especially true in agriculture, where green technology will tend to increase the agricultural production of rural smallholders. When the fact that green investments today will raise aggregate demand is fully considered, the macroeconomic picture becomes even more favorable.

Indeed, such expenditures can assist boost economic activity and employment in the near run, which is a much-needed step for industrial economies still plagued by high unemployment rates. This beneficial effect may even offset any negative aggregate supply implications that such investments may have in the short run.

In turn, more investment stimulates productivity growth, supporting long-term growth, to the degree that it is embodied in new equipment or leads to learning-by-doing. To encourage sustainable growth, the composition of the demand stimulus must be carefully chosen: some forms of consumption and investment must be regulated to avoid excessive resource depletion and waste., but ecologically conscious investment and consumption should increase.

8.4. PRINCIPLES OF A GREEN ECONOMY

While definitions are helpful for interpreting the GE idea, there has been an attempt to create a set of guiding principles that go beyond mere definitions of the GE. These concepts aid practitioners in implementing the GE idea. In the run-up to Rio+20, a number of groups released sets of green economic principles.

That year, the United Nations Division for Sustainable Development performed a study of eight sets of principles. It discovered that there is a wide range of concepts recommended to improve the understanding and application of the GE.

However, there is significant overlap among the various sets of principles. The following is a list of the most prevalent green economy principles discovered in the review.

8.4.1. Common Green Economy Principles

- The GE is a strategy for attaining long-term development.
- It should generate good employment and green jobs.
- Conserves resources and energy.
- That it is mindful of planetary boundaries, ecological restrictions, and scarcity.
- Integrated decision making is used in the GE.
- The GE uses suitable indicators/metrics to track development beyond GDP.
- It is equal, fair, and just—across countries and generations.
- It should safeguard biodiversity and ecosystems.
- Provides poverty alleviation, wellbeing, livelihoods, social protection, and access to basic services.
- It enhances governance and the rule of law. It is open to everyone, democratic, participative, accountable, transparent, and stable.
- Externalities are internalized in the GE.

8.5. GREEN GROWTH

Nowadays, the world faces two major challenges: a rapidly rising global population and the resulting increased strain on the environment, both of which should be avoided as soon as possible, chiefly through proper internalization of external influences. Because of the magnitude of the present hazards, the most pressing concerns are those related to climate change (Figure 8.5).

Figure 8.5. Urban green growth.

Source: Image by flickr.

They necessitate taking the necessary preventive measures, but the lack of an agreed position in international negotiations concerning the division of burdens has caused respective countries to look independently for possible ways to balance their national paths of economic growth with potential problems, such as pollution and depletion of natural resources.

The aforementioned conditions resulted in the birth of the notion of GG, among other things. South Korea approved the National Strategy for GG and the 5-Year Plan for GG in 2009, largely in reaction to the global financial collapse.

Since then, South Korea has served as the concept's primary ambassador, spreading it across the world, mostly through the OECD platform. At the OECD Ministerial Council Meeting in June 2009, 30 members and five candidate nations (representing about 80% of global economic potential) approved a declaration asserting that environmental conservation and economic growth can coexist.

8.6. GREEN ECONOMY VERSUS GREEN GROWTH

GG is inextricably linked with the concept of a GE, which aims to promote overall social welfare and social justice while significantly lowering environmental hazards and ecological inadequacies. Although the notion of green development has lately gained prominence on the world stage, it has been the topic of discussions and analyzes in scientific communities for decades, particularly in the field of so-called environmental and ecological economics.

The phrase "GE" was first used in a study titled Blueprint for a GE in 1989, which was created for the government of the United Kingdom by a group of top environmental economists. However, other than the headline, there were no additional allusions to the GE, thus, it appears that the authors employed the phrase as a type of reflection.

The word was "refreshed" in 2008 in the context of measures implemented in reaction to the global financial crisis. In October 2008, UNEP launched the GE Initiative to provide analyzes and political support for investments in "green" sectors of the economy, as well as to turn conventional, material-consuming, and polluting industries "green."

The Global Green New Deal (GGND) study was released in April 2009. It included a suggestion for economic rebuilding and the strengthening of global economic stability. In turn, in February 2010, ministers, and heads of the Global Environment Forum delegation in Nusa Dua praised UNEP's leadership role in further defining and supporting the notion of a GE.

The UNEP published the GE Report in 2011, which included a working definition of the GE, which has been used multiple times in various publications. The United Nations Environment Program defines the GE as "one that improves human wellbeing and social fairness while considerably lowering environmental dangers and ecological scarcity."

The GE is defined by a significant increase in investment in sectors of the economy that create and reinforce the natural capital of the Earth or contribute to the reduction of ecological inadequacies and environmental dangers.

Renewable energy, low-emission transportation, energy-efficient housing, clean technology, waste management improvement, sustainable agriculture and forest management, and sustainable fisheries are among these areas.

Potential implementation directions will be discussed during the Rio+20 Conference. GE concepts were identified, with an emphasis on the importance of continuing to promote sustainable development by focusing on key problems, such as poverty elimination, ensuring intra-generational and inter-generational justice, improving economic effectiveness, and more equitable access to resources.

Without a doubt, the tendency toward a more integrated and comprehensive approach to incorporating the environment into economic operations is the driving force behind the inception and development of the concepts of GE and GG.

Both concepts seek to explore potential methods to improve the outcomes of economic activity while keeping in mind present climate issues and rising scarcity of natural resources, mostly through resource- and energy-efficient technical advancements. The fact that both conceptions strive in somewhat different directions may be perplexing.

The GE idea seeks for economic transformation to increase social welfare and justice while significantly lowering environmental dangers and ecological deficits. This change will be accomplished largely through "green" investment, the creation of "green" jobs, the development of a market for new goods (e.g., ecosystems service market), and the promotion of international commerce and the so-called circular economy (CE).

A clear purpose of the GE is to combat poverty and assist developing nations. In comparison, the major goal of the GG Strategy is to maintain economic growth while also recognizing the importance of natural capital in planning processes and national accounting.

The main measures to achieve this goal include adequate valuation of natural capital in light of its role as a production factor (that is, first, and foremost, ensuring proper measurement of pollution and resource utilization, but also preventing risks due to limited resources and eliminating harmful subsidies), as well as continued pressure on innovation and competition.

In turn, the notions of GG and GE are related by their promotion as a solution to financial and economic crises. Their goal is to stimulate the recovery of a weakened global economy aimed for investments in the market for environmental products and services, as well as the development of "natural" infrastructure, such as forests, waterbodies, or biological variety.

That is, forests, waterbodies, or biological variety. As according Allen and Clouth (2012), despite the fact that GE and GG are terms of various origins, that is, they are the result of different organizations' and target groups' efforts, the distinctions between these concepts have become blurred, and they are now used almost interchangeable terms. However, such an approach is difficult to unequivocally agree on.

8.7. GREEN ECONOMY AND SUSTAINABLE DEVELOPMENT

The phrases GE and sustainable development are sometimes used equally, with the goal of preserving environmental resources for future generations in mind. Furthermore, both GG and sustainable development are concerned with minimizing social inequality. Despite a shared fundamental goal, both approaches target various aspects of human wellbeing.

Sustainable development is also a much larger notion than GG, which focuses on the economy-environment relationship. Sustainable development encompasses all types of investments and technology developments that are economically meaningful.

This comprises efforts aimed at increasing both natural and human capital. GG, on the other hand, emphasizes achieving economic development only via investments and technologies that result in improved environmental quality. Sustainable development seeks to strike a balance between economic growth and environmental damage.

It necessitates the implementation of a far larger set of policies with the goal of making considerable improvements in the quality of life of all living creatures on our planet, not just humans. In addition to policies that promote entrepreneurship and job creation, sustainable development objectives include giving high-quality education and health care, as well as enhancing the living standards of all species.

The objectives are designed to minimize inequality and promote a high standard of living for everybody. According to UNEP (2011), the GE focuses on social inclusion, with the goal of reducing poverty through economic growth and green job possibilities. As a result, "GG must be regarded as a way to achieve sustainable development rather than as a replacement for it."

8.8. GREEN GROWTH AND SUSTAINABLE DEVELOPMENT

To begin with, sustainable development is a topic that exploded into scientific discussions across a wide range of disciplines in the late 1980s as a result of the publication of the report "Our Common Future" in 1987. The paper assessed humanity's triumphs and failings in the twentieth century, citing sustainable development as a viable approach to improve the current situation.

The standard and commonly stated definition of sustainable development is development "that satisfies the demands of the present without jeopardizing future generations' ability to satisfy their own needs." The notion acquired significant traction during the Rio de Janeiro Earth Summit (1992), which developed a model program for pursuing sustainable development known as "Agenda 21."

Immediately following the Earth Summit, the concept of sustainable development became widely embraced by governments, and it had a considerable influence on the priority treatment of environmental goals in many nations. Since the Brundtland Commission established the initial definition of sustainable development, a number of efforts at alternate definitions of this term have been made.

Some critics argue that the word "sustainable development" is an oxymoron since it is inconsistent and mutually incompatible. Furthermore, it is hypothesized that if someone can redefine and use the term "sustainable development" for their own purposes, it becomes insignificant in practice or, worst, could be used to conceal activities that are destructive to society and the environment from a broader perspective, or just to pretend "going green."

The worldwide trend toward sustainable development slowed dramatically with the turn of the millennium. Practical actions done by governments in this regard were insufficient to avert global environmental changes. Sustainable development has become simply one of many responsibilities of governments. A need for a "new approach" evolved in this scenario, although informally.

GG developed and was proposed in 2005 as a potential means of creating a new, low-emission model of sustainable development for rapidly rising Asian countries. GG advocates underline that it is not a replacement for sustainable development, but rather a means of achieving it.

GG, like sustainable development, seeks to demonstrate that environmental conservation does not have to come at the price of human welfare. GG, on the other hand, directly addresses the problem of economic growth, in contrast to sustainable development.

Sustainable development overlooked topics such as general compatibility between growth and environmental preservation, as well as a reevaluation of the basic economic goal, namely "progress." GG not only emphasizes such compatibility but also contends that environmental conservation may really help to improve growth ratios.

It is commonly stated that sustainable development is a very wide phrase that encompasses various, usually mis-defined aims. This resulted in the term's meaning being questioned or perhaps giving rise to more conservative or extreme interpretations by diverse groups of interest.

GG, on the other hand, appears to be a more focused idea that may attract a smaller set of supporters (and may even be criticized by "green" opponents), but its meaning is extremely obvious. GG is genuinely novel in this regard.

It should surely be seen as a "child" of sustainable development, but in fact, it is a response to the shortcomings of sustainable development, with a special emphasis on climate changes and economic growth, both of which have lately dominated in the public discourse.

As according to Zervas (2012), there are several distinctions between the concepts of GG and sustainable development. To begin with, sustainable development encompasses a broader set of objectives. Green development "loses" the social component in favor of focusing only on environmental and economic concerns.

Second, as the name implies, GG focuses on the category of growth rather than the growth itself, which is a larger phrase. GG is simply economic growth that makes use of the environment and can have a negative influence on the environment. Furthermore, as one of the remedies recommended in response to the current economic crisis, green development is accompanied by additional economic or social initiatives.

The author agrees with S. Konstanczak that completely questioning the legitimacy of the notion of sustainable development makes absolutely no sense. Sustainable development is a logical path for the advancement of our civilization.

As a result of such thinking, the concept of a new global order has emerged, which contends that civilization must not be eradicated, but rather its growth should indeed be redirected toward the so-called "green" culture. GG was acknowledged as an essential component of sustainable development during the G20 Summit in Seoul in November 2010.

8.9. GREEN GROWTH–GREEN ECONOMY–SUSTAINABLE DEVELOPMENT MODEL (GG-GE-SD MODEL)

Even though both GG and GE can be viewed as indicators or subcategories of sustainable development or even its direct results, it is evident that these concepts must be distinguished in many circumstances. The author believes that the concurrent operation of three "green" notions is not contradictory.

On the contrary, they can be shown to have complementary and synergistic associations. The perspective that sustainability, and hence sustainable development, is the ultimate objective we should strive for is the beginning point for analyzing the relationships among these three notions.

The basic premise of the concept of a GE or GG is not to replace the concept of sustainable development, but the conviction that attaining sustainable development should be built on an appropriately oriented economy is developing. The creation of a GE based on the assumptions of the GG strategy must become an important part of economic policy on the path to sustainable development.

Mutual feedback must be considered while considering the concepts of GE, GG, and sustainable development. Previous techniques focused on competing interactions, omitting the reciprocal functioning of the ideas under consideration. The suggested relationship model will do this: Green Growth (GG) – Green Economy (GE) – Sustainable Development (SD) (Figure 8.6).

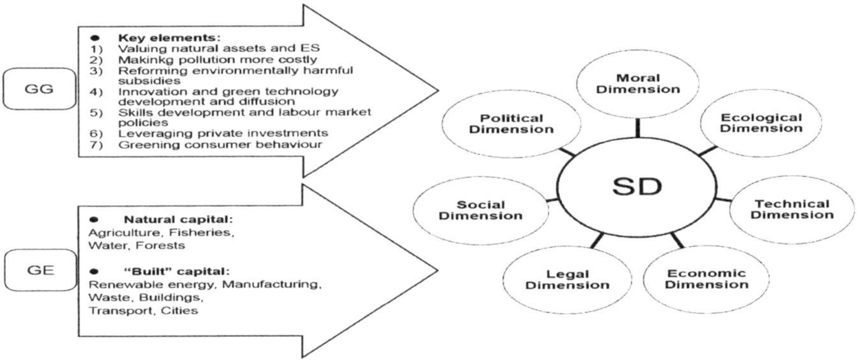

Figure 8.6. Green growth (GG) – green economy (GE) – sustainable development (SD).

Source: Image by Wikimedia commons.

Sustainable development has consistently remained the ultimate, primary goal of operations carried out in accordance with this paradigm. So far, no other equally excellent answer for the development of current and future generations has been suggested; so, we should focus on "what we can do to succeed" rather than "why we cannot succeed."

The author argues that the assumptions of GG and a GE provide potential answers in this regard. As a starting point, the proposed model for attaining sustainable development implies a well-developed green growth strategy (GG). It should be underlined once more that GG should not be confused with sustainable development.

On the contrary, it should represent a practical and adaptable method to achieve precise, demonstrable success in two major areas: economic and environmental, while fully acknowledging the social ramifications of greening respective countries' growth. GG may solve economic and environmental concerns while also creating new sources of growth:

- Strengthening the effective use of resources and natural assets: increasing effectiveness, minimizing waste and energy consumption, and assuring the most efficient use of available resources.
- Introducing innovations that might be promoted by laws and general terms and circumstances allowing for the application of novel solutions to environmental concerns.

- Providing new markets by increasing demand for green technology, commodities, and services; creating new job possibilities
- Strengthening investor trust by increasing the predictability and stability of the government's operations with significant environmental protection concerns.

More sustainable macroeconomic circumstances, lower fluctuation in resource pricing, and budget consolidation, for example, by examining the structure and efficacy of public expenditure and rising income as a result of pollution assessment. GG plans should pay special attention to a variety of social issues, including equity, which can directly result from national and international solutions.

Effective plans should address the seven major factors contained in the model that will condition the attainment of sustainable development. The second component is the GE. The idea here is to identify all spots that should "become green." On the one hand, the GE encompasses natural capital-based industries such as agriculture, fishery, forest management, and water management.

These sectors have a considerable impact on the economy not only because they offer the foundation for manufacturing, but also because the rural population's living circumstances are directly dictated by such resources. The GE, on the other hand, refers to sectors based on so-called "human-made capital," which are traditionally referred to as "brown" sectors of the economy.

Sectors such as transportation, energy, and manufacturing offer significant potential for energy and resource savings. Such savings can also help to boost economic development as well as a growth in employment Effective resource use is a multifaceted topic since it can relate to energy and material effectiveness as well as improved waste management.

The ten areas described must be regarded as critical areas in the economic transformation process. The "greening" of the economy can have long-term and good consequences such as greater wealth, improved economic output, dignified work, and reduced poverty.

GE and GG will enable an overall increase in welfare in the economic dimension; in the social dimension, they will translate into an improvement in life quality; and in the environmental dimension, they will contribute to reducing environmental pressures and improving the effectiveness with which natural capital is utilized.

A well-developed GG strategy, along with a complete "greening" of the economy, will assist it in permanently entering the pathway of sustainable development.

8.10. STIMULATING THE GREEN ECONOMY TRANSITION

8.10.1. The Green Economy Transition Is Already Underway

The UNCSD Rio+20 Conference seeks to promote the GE idea in order to accelerate global progress toward sustainable development. However, it is critical to acknowledge that the transition to a GE is already beginning.

It originated primarily in reaction to the Rio Earth Summit's enhanced public awareness and improved political resolve on sustainable development in 1992. The task for Rio+20 is to generate momentum for the transition to a GE, which is now occurring.

Market indicators indicate that the shift to a GE is progressing. The number of businesses having ISO 14001 environmental management certification increased from less than 40,000 in 2000 to more than 200,000 in 2009, accounting for more than 40% of all registered enterprises are in third world nations.

Significantly, 'green' refers to more than just the environment. It also has to do with social duty. A rising number of businesses are incorporating social issues into their daily operations and relationships with stakeholders. Over 2,000 firms in over 90 countries today practice Corporate Social Responsibility (CSR), up from almost none at the time of the Rio Summit in 1992.

A GE also promotes ethical commerce by utilizing Fair Trading manufacturing chains, which ensure that small developing-country producers obtain better trade conditions and prices. Fair Trade goods sales are increasing all around the world.

In 2008, customers globally spent $5 billion on Fairtrade certified items, nearly doubling the number from the previous year and directly helping over 7 million people in 58 developing nations—farmers, laborer, and their families In a GE, Fair Trade principles may be expected to be adopted more broadly, and relevant products to draw higher demand.

Motivation toward a green economic transformation is seen in a variety of sectors, including energy, agriculture, forestry, and services, among others, in both developed and developing countries. Global growth in renewable energy sources contributing to global primary energy supply currently outpaces growth in fossil fuel-based energy sources.

Since 1990, yearly growth rates in solar photovoltaic (PV), wind, and biofuel supply capacity have averaged 42, 25, and 15%, respectively, compared to only 1.3% for oil. $211 billion was invested in renewable energy supply in 2010, more than five times the amount invested in 2004, with more than half of this investment going to underdeveloped nations.

8.10.2. National Actions to Accelerate Green Growth

It will not be easy to make the shift to a development-led and inclusive GE. Effective frameworks to promote the long-term growth of the GE would necessitate national and international changes. National policies and actions are necessary to stimulate and mature GE marketplaces, while institutional frameworks are required at the international level to enable poor nations reap attractive advantages from participating in a global transformation.

Because of the wide, cross-cutting character of the GE transition, encouraging, and supporting it will need a diverse set of national policies and initiatives, as well as strong institutions to implement, monitor, and enforce them.

The best blend of national policies will be determined by a country's institutional framework, degree of development, resource endowments, and distinct social needs as well as environmental factors. Authorities may push the change using a variety of tools, including regulation, market-based instruments, investment initiatives, and communication campaigns.

All of these factors may be included into a national GE policy framework. Gradually phasing in and tightening regulation to adjust production and consumption patterns can cause structural changes in industry and commerce over time without generating economic disruptions. Regulations are also required to create new markets for GE activity.

Regulations requiring mandated recovery of glass, metal, plastics, and electronic equipment, for example, are required to incentivize enterprises to populate specific recycling industries. Government policy frameworks frequently employ complementing regulatory and market-based mechanisms to reposition enterprises and consumers throughout transitions (Figure 8.7).

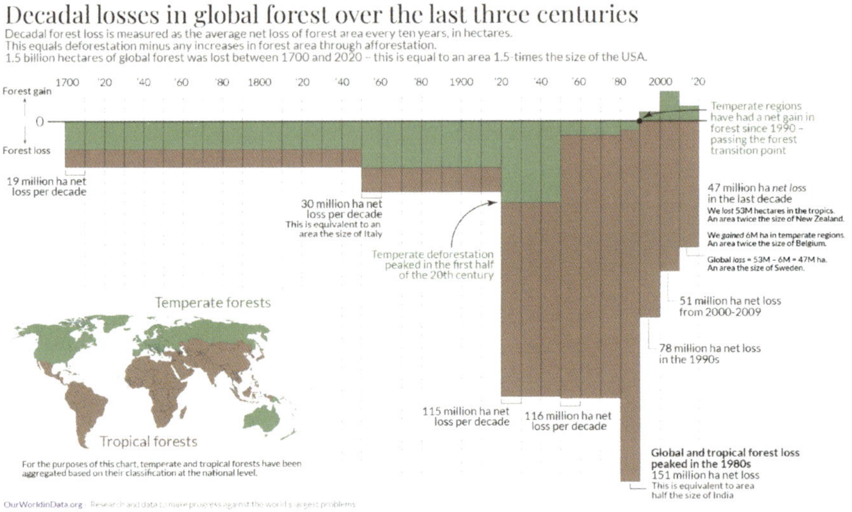

Figure 8.7. Long-term-forest-loss.

Source: Image by Wikimedia commons.

In the electricity sector, for example, feed-in tariff laws can be combined with market-based incentives to encourage people and businesses to invest in renewable energy systems and become independent power producers. Regulation can also be used to impose phased performance and technological criteria in order to force fresh private investment in green technologies over time.

8.10.3. International Actions to Support Green Growth in Developing Countries

A smooth transition necessitates tackling enormous problems confronting many poor nations, which lack the necessary financial, technological, and human resources to structurally alter their economies along a new green trajectory. International cooperation in the form of capacity building, technology transfer, and financial aid will be critical in closing these gaps.

As a result, there is a need for international cooperation and collaboration in research and development (R&D), as well as for putting green innovations into the public domain and instituting governmental incentives for green technology transfer in both developed and developing nations.

Greater policy consistency, as well as financial and technical collaboration, will consequently be required as nations go through the GE transition period. Capacity-building programs also are required to assist developing nations in identifying, creating, and implementing strategies to boost growth in green sectors activity.

Programs should help poor nations develop their green products and services industries so that they may engage in global GE commerce and capitalize on its potential.

Deliberate policies and improved institutions are required to create an enabling environment at the domestic level, which, when combined with increased green market openness, can promote increased investment and the transfer of skills and technologies required to build green supply capacities for domestic and export markets. UNCTAD is actively working on practical analytical tools to help with this.

Access to new, extra, and innovative sources of finance to help their transition to a GE is a sine qua non prerequisite for many developing nations.

Green technology transfer, climate change mitigation and adaptation, biodiversity conservation, desertification mitigation, export capacity development in green sectors, capacity-building on international standards (e.g., GE related SPS, TBT, and private standards), and assistance in mainstreaming GE policies into national economic, employment, and trade policies are some of the GE domains in which developing countries require financial assistance.

Even with global economic downturn continuing, industrialized economies' treasuries are under considerable strain. As a result, new GE financing cannot rely primarily on government grants and development aid. It should also include private investment spurred by the government.

The creation of a suitable domestic environment consistent with the country's own green economic and broader sustainable development objectives is a critical priority for developing nations interested in attracting private investment in green projects and industries.

However, given large disparities in institutional development, resource endowment, and human capital, many poor nations will have little or no ability to attract private investments in green projects and industries. These nations should be the principal recipients of new and increased state financial assistance.

8.11. POLICIES AND MEASURES FOR PROMOTING GREEN ECONOMY AND SUSTAINABLE DEVELOPMENT

To achieve a multi-dimensional conclusion, the three dimensions of sustainable development (environmental, economic, and social) should be included into the GE idea. The following are some policies and actions that may be implemented to foster a more ecologically sound economy in the context of long-term growth.

8.11.1. Recognizing the Economic and Social Value of Environmental Resources

It is critical for policymakers and the general public to recognize the economic and social value of the environment, and that trying to conserve resources such like clean air, water, forests, and mangroves, among others, have positive externalities that are valuable for meeting basic and human needs in addition to their intrinsic environmental value. Conservation should consequently be encouraged, as should expenditures in natural resource restoration. Recent studies have compared the advantages of conserving or sustainable use of natural resources with the benefits of maximizing short-term profits at the expense of the environment, such as revenues (Figure 8.8).

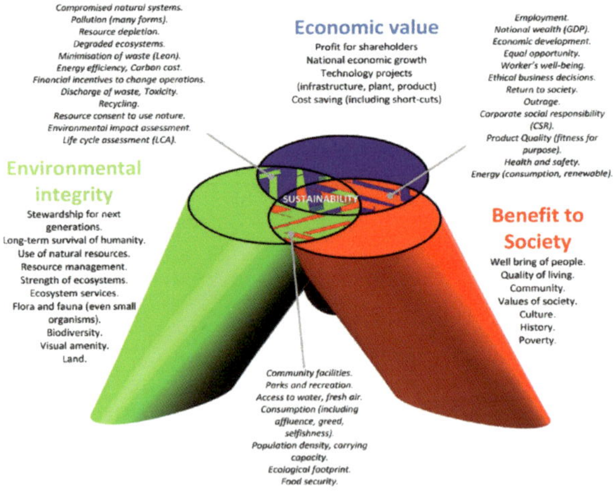

Figure 8.8. The three pillars model expects sustainability to be achieved by finding a holistic solution to three separate dimensions of value: environmental integrity, economic value, and benefit to society.

Source: Image by Wikimedia commons.

Many case studies measuring the economic worth of mangrove swamps, forests, and other ecosystems have been included in recent papers on the economics of biodiversity natural resources, arguing that protecting them frequently yields greater value than turning them to commercial aquaculture and other uses.

8.11.2. Conserving Resources and Restoring Damaged Environments and Eco-Systems

Although there are advantages to conserving natural resources, the opportunity cost of not "exploiting" or depleting the resources should also be considered. The short- and long-term usefulness of using Nature, as well as the short- and long-term usefulness of conserving Nature (or making sustainable use of resources), should be recognized and reconciled, and international assistance should be made accessible to underdeveloped countries to offset the potential costs.

The Yasuni Initiative of Ecuador is an intriguing proposal from a poor country for sharing the opportunity costs of conserving natural resources, in which the country is ready to forego the advantages of oil profits in order to conserve a huge tract of biodiversity-rich forest. The authorities would keep the crude oil field in Yasuni National Park underground indefinitely under the proposed strategy.

The worldwide community would contribute half of the cash generated by extracting the oil, while the government would bear up to half of the opportunity cost of maintaining the oil in the ground. The money of the fund will be invested in renewable energy projects, and the fund's interest will be used to protect forests, assist small farmers in reforesting, and promote energy efficiency and social development.

It is also vital to invest in rehabilitating damaged ecosystems (such as forests, slopes, and water catchment regions, as well as mangroves). The ecosystems have suffered severe damage, and restoration would mitigate the negative consequences and allow for the resumption of environmental functioning.

However, many underdeveloped nations lack the financial means to conduct ecological restoration on the scale required, necessitating international assistance.

8.11.3. Enabling Prices to Better Reflect Their Environmental Value, While Ensuring Access to Basic Goods and Services

A fundamental problem in sustainable development (and so in any GE program) is reconciling the two concepts of enabling pricing to better reflect environmental values while maintaining public (particularly poor) access to basic utilities and livelihood possibilities. As a result, both the environmental and social dimensions must be considered.

The lower pricing of natural resource-based items such as water and wood encourage over-exploitation of natural resources and accompanying waste. This underpricing might be the result of prices not being able to integrate or fully incorporate the cost of unpleasant side effects during manufacture, or it could be the result of subsidies or other causes.

The state plays a critical role in addressing the inadequacy of market pricing to represent true environmental values. In general, pricing should better represent environmental values, including the costs of negative consequences. Environmental levies, as well as pricing policies for public services, should be employed.

Nevertheless, this should have been done in a way which does not damage the poor or ordinary people, particularly when the items or services in question are necessities. Thus, if water is usually underpriced, a system of transparent pricing responsive to maintaining accessibility for the poor might be established through a revaluation of the price of water given by the state.

The first block of water for households in a quantity necessary for family use may be charged at an affordable price point, with higher rates at subsequent blocks; water supplied to hotels and industries may be charged at higher rates; and community water in poor areas may be provided free in developing countries. Overall, the cost of water should further accurately reflect its ecological worth.

Subsidies for ecologically hazardous activities or goods have also been widely lobbied for elimination or decrease. However, this should be done with the understanding that it should not interfere with the poor's cheap access to basics such as energy or food, or negatively impact their livelihoods.

Subsidies to the fishing industry, for example, have contributed to overfishing and the fast depletion of fish populations. Negotiations are underway at the WTO to rein down fisheries subsidies. Many poor nations, however, have pushed for exclusions or more lenient treatment for subsidies granted for their fishing sector, which is characterized by small scale and artisanal fisherfolk.

In another example, if fossil fuel subsidies are decreased or removed (as recommended in the G20 process), this should also be done in a way that does not jeopardize the poor's access to energy. But from the other hand, incentives (subsidies, credit, tax breaks, and so on) should be offered to companies and consumers in order to encourage good manufacturing processes and goods (renewable energy, sustainable agriculture, no-emissions cars).

Subsidy and other rewards are especially crucial for emerging countries since numerous new sectors and habits must be developed. Such subsidies must, of course, be adequately structured and administered in order to achieve long-term development objectives.

8.12. CONCLUSION

The promotion of a GE was a key theme at the Rio+20 Conference held in June 2012 to mark the 20th anniversary of the Rio Summit. A number of non-government organizations and partnerships have also developed in recent years which aim to promote the GE as a concept and undertake research, analysis, and outreach.

In June 2009, in the lead up to the UN Climate Change Conference in Copenhagen, the UN released an interagency statement supporting the GE as a transformation to address multiple crises. This led to a great deal of international attention on the GE and related concepts and the publication of numerous reports and other literature aiming to further define and demystify the concept.

There is no internationally agreed definition of GE and at least eight separate definitions were identified. The concept of a GE supports—and does not replace—sustainable development. One of the key reports was the flagship GE Report released by UNEP in November 2011 under its GE Initiative.

Importantly, the report also provides a working definition of 'GE' which has since been cited in numerous other publications. This report adopts the definition provided by UNEP in its 2011 GE Report. Apart from the title of the report, there is no further reference to a GE and it appears that the term was used as an afterthought by the authors.

UNEP defines a GE as one that results in "improved human wellbeing and social equity, while significantly reducing environmental risks and ecological scarcities." In 1991 and 1994 the authors released sequels to the first report entitled Blueprint, Greening the world economy and Blueprint, Measuring Sustainable Development.

REFERENCES

1. (n.d). *Introduction to the Green Economy Approach*, 2–19. [e-Book] Available at: https://www.un-page.org/files/public/module_1_introduction_to_the_green_economy_approach.pdf (accessed on 21 June 2022).
2. Bina, O., (2013). The green economy and sustainable development: An uneasy balance? *Environment and Planning C: Government and Policy, 31*(6), 1023–1047. [online] Available at: https://econpapers.repec.org/article/saeenvirc/v_3a31_3ay_3a2013_3ai_3a6_3ap_3a1023-1047.htm (accessed on 21 June 2022).
3. Georgeson, L., Maslin, M., & Poessinouw, M., (2017). The global green economy: A review of concepts, definitions, measurement methodologies and their interactions. *Geo: Geography and Environment, 4*(1), e00036. [online] Available at: https://rgs-ibg.onlinelibrary.wiley.com/doi/10.1002/geo2.36 (accessed on 21 June 2022).
4. Lavrinenko, O., Ignatjeva, S., Ohotina, A., Rybalkin, O., & Lazdans, D., (2019). The role of green economy in sustainable development (case study: The EU states). *Entrepreneurship and Sustainability Issues, 6*(3), 1113–1126. [online] Available at: https://www.researchgate.net/publication/331802913_The_Role_of_Green_Economy_in_Sustainable_Development_Case_Study_The_EU_States (accessed on 21 June 2022).
5. Second Preparatory Committee Meeting for United Nations Conference on Sustainable Development, (n.d). *The Transition to a Green Economy: Benefits, Challenges and Risks from a Sustainable Development Perspective*. [e-Book] Division for Sustainable Development, UN-DESA. Available at: https://plagiarism.repec.org/trica-papuc/trica-papuc2.pdf (accessed on 21 June 2022).

INDEX

K

L

M

N

O

P

R

S

T

U

W